Black Hills Ghost Towns

BLACK HILLS GHOST TOWNS

Watson Parker and Hugh K. Lambert

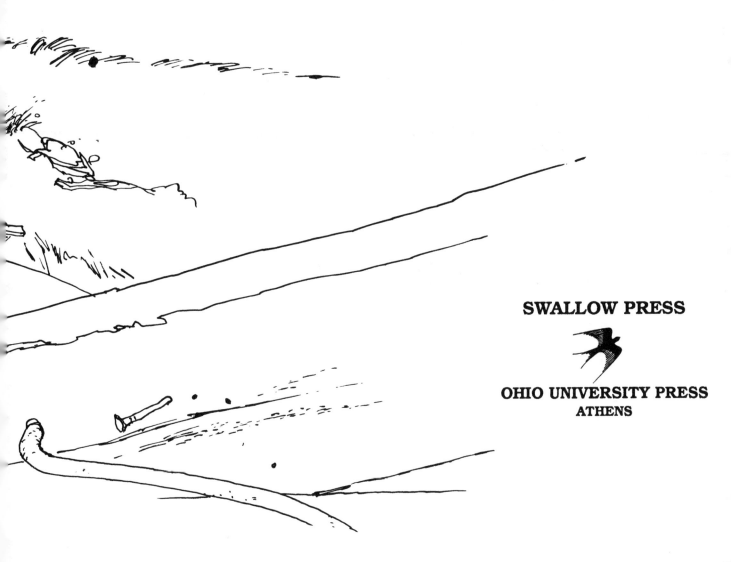

SWALLOW PRESS

OHIO UNIVERSITY PRESS
ATHENS

First Swallow Press / Ohio University Press edition printed 1980
10 09 08 07   10 9 8 7

Swallow Press / Ohio University Press Books are printed
 on acid-free paper ∞

Library of Congress Catalog Card Number 73-1501
ISBN:0-8040-0638-5 (pbk.)

Contents

"How doth the city sit solitary

PREFACE

This book is presented to the reader with the hope that its listing of some six hundred towns—some thriving, but most of them defunct—in and around the Black Hills of South Dakota will prove of interest and use to tourist, adventurer, scholar, and historian, all of whom may have had some difficulty in locating some of the older and forgotten communities in the Hills.

The listings include as many named localities, other than single-family ranches, as could be discovered through diligent research in newspapers, histories, and maps. Each is described by county, quarter section, section, and township, with a question mark following any part of the location that appears to be unreliable. Population figures are from the 1970 census; where no population is officially listed but inhabitants are in evidence, their presence has generally been mentioned in the text. The area covered is, in general, the Black Hills, the Bear Lodge Mountains, the plains in between, and the foothills and timbered land around them. Now and then a spot is mentioned, like Sarpy's Post on Rapid Creek, which is well out of the Hills but so intimately connected with their history that its omission would have left a noticeable gap. Mines are listed only if they seem to have been centers of population or are important in Black Hills history. Caves, too, have been disregarded, except for those of historical importance. Railroads have been called by their current names, or, if abandoned, by the name most commonly used for them; the diligent buff can trace their paths by the trail of sidings, water stops, wood stops, and depots which they left in the Hills.

Anyone who writes history owes a debt beyond repaying to those libraries and collections that provided the materials that he used. Among those collections which were the greatest help to us were the Phillips Collection at the University of Oklahoma, the Jennewein Western Collection at Dakota

hat was full of people!"

Lamentations, 1:1

Wesleyan University, the Library of the South Dakota School of Mines and Technology, the Rapid City Free Public Library, the Adams Memorial Museum at Deadwood, the Deadwood Public Library, the Homestake Library at Lead, the Society of Minnelusa Pioneers at Rapid City, the South Dakota State Historical Society at Pierre, and the collection of Troy L. Parker of Hill City. We thank them, every one.

Among those many friends whose generous assistance and wide knowledge made the field work for this book a constant pleasure are the late Prof. J. Leonard Jennewein of Dakota Wesleyan University, Dr. and Mrs. Roland E. Schmidt of the University of Oregon, and Mr. and Mrs. Troy L. Parker of Hill City. Special mention must be given to Professor Carl Albert Grimm of the South Dakota School of Mines and Technology, for without his assistance much that is new and rare in this book would never have been discovered. For more than thirty years he has been a guide to the byways, back roads, caves, canyons, mines, and mysteries of the Hills, a spirited companion, valued mentor, and invaluable friend. To Mrs. Grimm, also, we owe a vast debt of gratitude and affection for innumerable satisfying lunches and for hot dinners when exhausted explorers staggered home long after sundown. We would also like to thank our wives, whose patience and forbearance have allowed us to find these towns down dangerous roads on which they would not accompany us, though they have always welcomed us home again no matter how late or unexpected our return.

The division of responsibility between us has been, with a good deal of give and take, about as follows. Watson Parker dealt with the historical aspects of finding towns in old newspapers, on old maps, and in musty books of history; and he has written the descriptions of each of them. Hugh

Lambert has in many cases located the towns on the ground, corrected their location on the maps, drawn the maps accompanying this book, selected the pictures (which we both took—Lambert's are the good ones), and laid out the book in the form in which you see it.

It is inevitable that in a work of this kind many errors will appear, and we would be the first to admit that some of them are our fault entirely, the product of our own mistakes. Others, however, are due to the nature of local history, which passes from eager lip to receptive ear in an often garbled fashion, and is further distorted when at last a written record is finally made. Spellings subtly alter (witness the current sign *Cutty's Ark* now marking the location of the *Cutty Sark* mine), towns change location, county lines shift and are resurveyed, names given to one spot move on down the road to appear as some place else. Sometimes sources of information are downright unreliable and are nearly, but not quite, unusable; we have had to use them as best we could or do without any information at all on some of the Black Hills' most interesting localities. If you differ with us let us know, so we can correct our errors and tell you how we came to make them.

WATSON PARKER
Oshkosh, Wisconsin

HUGH K. LAMBERT
Northbrook, Illinois

7

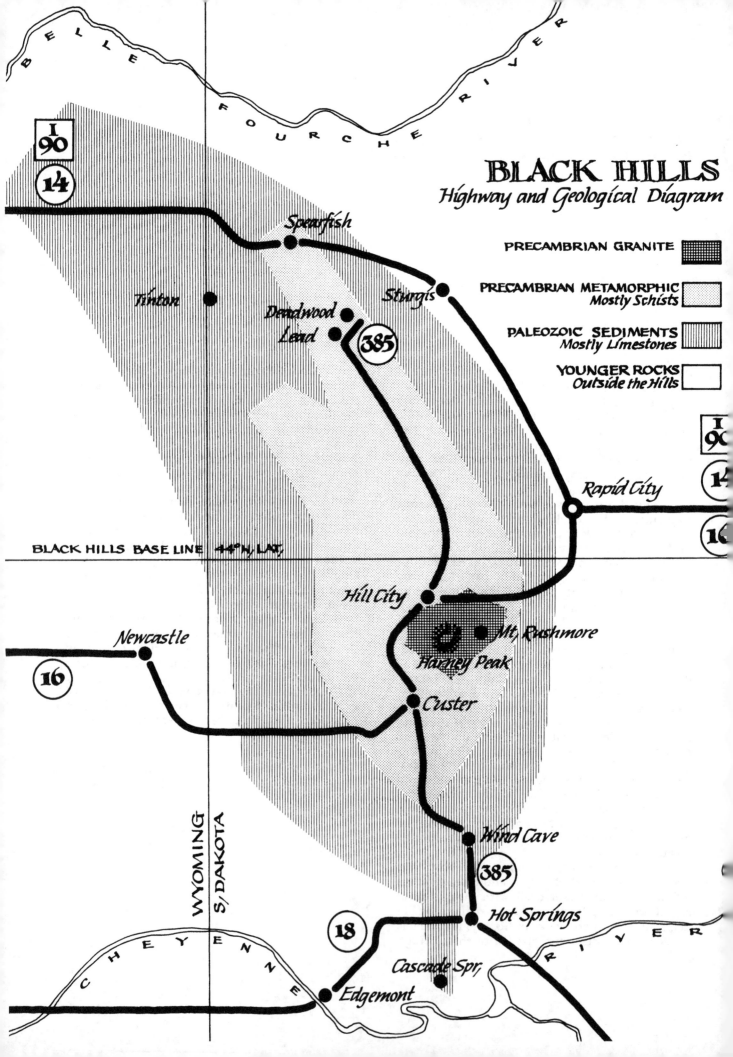

BELLE FOURCHE RIVER

I 90
14

BLACK HILLS
Highway and Geological Diagram

PRECAMBRIAN GRANITE

PRECAMBRIAN METAMORPHIC
Mostly Schists

PALEOZOIC SEDIMENTS
Mostly Limestones

YOUNGER ROCKS
Outside the Hills

Spearfish

Tinton

Sturgis

Deadwood
Lead

385

I 90
14

Rapid City

16

BLACK HILLS BASE LINE 44°N. LAT.

Hill City

Newcastle

16

Mt. Rushmore

Harney Peak

Custer

WYOMING
S. DAKOTA

Wind Cave

385

Hot Springs

18

CHEYENNE RIVER

Cascade Spr.

Edgemont

Out of the sea of grass that waves from the Missouri to the Rockies rise the dark, mysterious mountains known to the Sioux as the *Paha Sapa*, the Black Hills of Dakota. Thrust up by countless eons of geologic action, Harney Peak, in the central granite uplift, towers more than seven thousand feet above sea level, and many of the peaks and ridges of the high limestone country in the western Hills soar to similar elevations. Countless ages of erosion have riven the granite mountains into crags and pinnacles and carved the limestone plateaus into deep and jagged gulches. The forces which thrust up the Hills also filled them with precious minerals and clothed them with a mantle of green pines which seen from the plains fades to a dusky purple and gives the Hills their name. To these mountains in 1874 came invading miners to dig their shafts and drive their tunnels and build their towns which now lie vacant and deserted among the hills and pines.

HOW THE TOWNS BEGAN

The Walsh Ranch east of Custer is a splendid example of the sturdy architecture employed by those pioneers who came to stay and built their farm houses accordingly.

Although gold mining of many kinds undoubtedly gave rise to most of the towns in the Black Hills, it was not the only reason why towns sprang up in the wilderness to flourish, prosper, and decline. In an area as varied as the Black Hills it was inevitable that towns should be born for many reasons, reasons as rich and as various as the mountains and meadows, rocks and forests of the Hills themselves.

After the Indians, who left no named communities behind them in the Black Hills, came the fur traders and mountain men, hairy, greasy, tough as nails, and full of life and lies. These men knew of the miraculous echo that took eight hours to rebound from the sheer west wall of Harney Peak, so that all a weary traveler had to do to assure that he would wake up early was to bawl out "Git up, you S.O.B.!" before he went to bed at night. They knew of the infernal creek on the side of Harney Peak (tho' of course the Peak had not been named in the 1830s when they visited the Hills) that ran so fast it boiled before it got down to the valley, and a man could catch a fish in its upper reaches and poach it as he walked downhill to camp. They knew of the miraculous crystal mountain, so transparent that it could only be located by the bodies of the birds and animals that had broken their necks running into its invisible bulk. Boulder Hill, near Rockerville, where the mica schist glistens and glitters in the afternoon sun, may well be the mountain that started such a legend.

No one can know where the traders and trappers stayed when they passed through the Hills or wintered in their sheltered valleys. Old Jedediah Smith went up French Creek from the east in 1823, and was there assaulted by a ferocious grizzly bear that nearly chewed his scalp from the top of his head. When his comrades finally killed the bear, Smith invented the phrase "Well, don't just stand there, *do* something" and took the lead himself in sewing back on the skin that the bear had gnawed. As they came out of the Hills, Smith's companion Jim Clyman noticed a stump of petrified wood that stood so high he could not reach the top of it from his horse's back. Perhaps this is the very stump that now graces the public park in Edgemont. The trappers knew of the petrified woods in the Hills—even Edgar Allen Poe wrote of them—and told tales of how petrified birds sat on petrified tree limbs and sang songs so old that even Adam had forgotten them.

This may well be Jim Clyman's petrified stump, so tall that a man on horseback could not reach the top of it. It is in the Edgemont public park beside the railroad tracks.

There was a fur trading post near Cache Butte, to the southeast of the Hills, and another, Tom Sarpy's post at the mouth of Rapid Creek. (Sarpy's post blew up in 1832, showering the entire West River country with beaver traps.) Some say that dates going clear back to the 1830s can be found on beams in some of the cellers around St. Onge. During the late 1860s, a chap named Nick Janis took over Camp Warren, near present-day Newcastle, and ran it as a trading post until he relinquished it to Professor Walter P. Jenny in 1875. The trappers and traders may have left only a few names on the land, but the stories they told—tales of beaver, beauty, and winter comfort in the sheltered gulches—let the world know that the Black Hills awaited the white man when railroads and transportation brought them nearer to civilization.

The army posts of various kinds that sprang up in and around the Hills gave rise not only to respectable towns that grew up where once the soldiers camped, but to towns of a more vigorous nature which grew up just far enough away to escape military supervision and close enough to cater to the baser passions of the soldiers. Scoop-town, near Fort Meade, prospered by "scooping in" the military payroll after each monthly payday. Lt. G. K. Warren built Camp Warren just south of present-day Newcastle when he explored the Hills in the 1850s. Professor Jenney, making a geological exploration of the Hills in 1875, took over the camp and named it Camp Jenney, by which it is still known to this day. Camp Bradley, at the foot of Inyan Kara mountain, briefly housed troops during the Sioux War of 1876, as did Camp Collier, in Red Canyon, and Camps Ruhlen and Sturgis—the latter two forerunners of Fort Meade.

Two or three spots were called "Camp Crook" in honor of General George Crook, who first expelled the miners from the Hills in 1875. His first Camp Crook later became Pactola; his second was just south of Crook City during the Sioux War of 1876. During the summer of 1874, following a couple of weeks on the heels of Custer, the Reverend Samuel Hinman entered the Hills in search of a location for an Indian agency. He established a camp on French Creek. The next year Captain John Mix, fighting winter storms to expell the invading Gordon Party from their stockade south of Custer, found Hinman's camp, and from it hunted down the Gordon group; so he named the spot Camp Success in commemoration. The Gordon Stockade itself was named Camp Harney, and a Union Stockade was built in Custer to protect the troops and miners from the Indians, and to provide a safe refuge for Captain Jack Crawford's "Custer Minute Men," who never got so far from town that they could not get back again in a minute.

Transportation gave rise to a very large number of small towns. At first the stage stations, spaced from five to ten miles apart to provide a change of horses for the rapidly moving coaches, lined the trails into the Hills. Each stage station was a small but determined fort along the pathway to the new Eldorado. Often, during times of Indian troubles, the stage stations were manned by several company employees. Most stations had their corrals, barns, and houses, some with bars and eating facilities. Not every station served regular meals to passengers, but each was equipped to do so in case the stage was held up or delayed by trouble or bad weather. These stops, each with its name, remained on the map no matter how far from them later stage routes shifted. Some of the stations grew, temporarily or permanently, into considerably larger communities; others, of course, declined into farms or ranches, or faded away entirely.

Traces of these old stage stations can be found all through the Hills. Even the quarter-mile posts that once led the drivers through the winter snows from Cheyenne up Red Canyon on into Custer can still be seen along the trail as you pass Red Canyon Station, Spring-on-the-Hill, Spring-on-the-Right, Pleasant Valley, and Four Mile; and the ruts of the coaches and freight wagons can still be followed where they lead up over limestone outcroppings. Spring-on-the-Hill's buildings are gone, but a cold celler remains; and the spring itself, starting out of the rock at the top of a hill, is now as it was in '76, a welcome sight to weary and thirsty travellers. Some time in 1878 this route was abandoned, due to Indian attacks in Red Canyon.

This stop on the Cheyenne-Deadwood stage route was about a mile northwest of Kiddville and the Penobscot mine.

The corrals at the Spring-on-the-Hill stage station at the head of Red Canyon.

Buffalo Gap was a famous stage station and later a cattle town, on the stage route leading up the eastern side of the Hills from Sidney, Nebraska, to Rapid City, the same route that was later followed by the Chicago & North Western Railroad.

The Harney Peak Hotel in Hill City, a famous old hostelry along the Cheyenne-Deadwood stagecoach trail.

From Custer the stages went north through Hill City, or Hilyo as it was called in the early days, then on to Golden City or Sheridan, Pactola, Rochford, Bulldog Ranch, and Ten Mile, and thence down into Deadwood Gulch with its many mining camps. Later the route swerved westward, away from Hill City, for the population of that town had dwindled in the late 1870s to one man and a dog, so they said; and the stages preferred to go northwestward through Twelve Mile Ranch, Mountain City or Deerfield, Gillette's and Reynold's Ranches, then into Rochford, and on north to Deadwood Gulch.

After the Red Canyon route was abandoned, the stages from Cheyenne went up the west side of the Hills, to the Jenney Stockade, Beaver Station, Canyon Spring, Cold Spring, Cheyenne Crossing, Divide, and Ten Mile—a rough and rugged trail. In the early days the freight wagons had to be lowered down into Deadwood Gulch with ropes and pulleys to hold them back on the steep and rocky slopes.

On the eastern side of the Hills passengers and mail and treasure shipments were served from Sidney, Nebraska. The coaches lumbered northward, across the new Platte River Bridge, past Horsehead Station, Buffalo Gap, Hermosa, or Strater as it was then called, past the dangerous, bandit-infested Black Gap in the slate hills, and into Hay Camp or Rapid City, then up past Stage Barn Canyon, Spring Valley Ranch, Sturgis, and on through Boulder Canyon to the northern mines at Lead and Deadwood.

A ride on the swaying stagecoach was no great treat for the uninitiated. For that matter, it was no great treat for the initiated. The coach, hung on leather thoroughbraces, swung violently in every direction as the horses trotted or galloped over the rutted roads, and many travelers became acutely seasick until they got used to the odd motion. The fare served at the stage station— hard tack or soda biscuits, fried salt pork, coffee thick enough to float a worn-out horseshoe—did not do much to settle any queasy stomachs. Bandits made every trip a nervous one. They were eager to rob a treasure stage; and later, when treasure stages were armored and guarded, just as anxious to pick the pockets of well-to-do travelers. Several spots along the trails were aptly named "The Robbers Roost." Persimmons Bill Chambers and his brother hung out at Cheyenne River Station, near present-day Dudley, and are said to have had a hand in murdering and robbing the Metz family in Red Canyon. Indians, too, were a threat to the ill-prepared or the unwary, although the story that they rolled rocks down on travelers from the cliffs above Red Canyon seems an exaggeration, for any Indian big enough to roll a rock that far could probably have just stood in the middle of the road and let the coach run into him.

The innumerable trails left by the railroads are ideal for hikers: smooth, level, and with only an occasional gap when a bridge is out or a tunnel has fallen in.

Railroads, too, created many new communities. Every whistle stop, platform station, section house, and siding had its name and its ambitions. The Black Hills & Fort Pierre, the Deadwood Central, the Chicago, Burlington & Quincy, the Fremont, Elkhorn & Missouri Valley, the Chicago & North Western, the Wyoming & Missouri River, the Missouri River & Northwestern—all these railways tangled, conjoined, and competed, but served the Black Hills from one end to the other. The Burlington, pushing northward from Nebraska, came into Edgemont, then sent one branch up along the western edge of the Hills toward Dewey, Clifton, Newcastle and points west, and another branch toward the center of the Hills, with an eastward spur toward Hot Springs, passing through Minnekahta, Custer, Hill City, Mystic, and northward to Deadwood, where there were many spurs and branches to serve the northern mines.

The Chicago & North Western also came up from Nebraska, reaching Buffalo Gap, Fairburn, Hermosa, Rapid City, Piedmont, and Whitewood. It was joined to the Burlington at Mystic by the "Crouch Line," as the Missouri River & Northwestern was generally called, which ran up Rapid Canyon from Rapid City past connections to Warren Lamb lumbering roads. It also joined the Burlington farther north, by means of the Fremont, Elkhorn & Missouri Valley lines leading from Piedmont to Englewood.

Around Deadwood itself the Deadwood Central and several other standard and narrow-gauge lines served the mines, hauling the ore to centrally located smelters and cyaniding plants, and hauling in lime, timbers, powder, and steel.

Spurs connected many promising communities with the main lines. One ran northward from Newcastle to tie Cambria's anthracite mines into the rail network. Another, already mentioned, connected Hot Springs with the Burlington, and also with the North Western. One ran eastward from Hill City to Keystone and was surveyed on to Spokane to tap the varied mines of that region. The little "1880 Train" still makes many runs a day, for tourists, from Hill City to Keystone and back again through incredibly lovely Black Hills scenery. A line ran from Trojan to the side of Spearfish Canyon, hesitated a moment, then made its way down that precipitous gorge, arriving at the bottom at Elmore, then pushing northward down the bottom of the Canyon to Spearfish itself. A spur pushed westward from Belle Fourche to the shallow coal fields at Aladdin. The Deadwood Central ran a line into Galena, to serve the silver mines, and for years the little Natalie, a narrow-gauge engine, hauled ore cars on the competing Branch Mint line.

Logging and lumbering railroads, some as big as standard-gauge, penetrated deep into the mountains and valleys. The Warren Lamb Lumber Company operated out of Rapid City and ran lines from McGee's Siding clear to Sheridan Lake; another Warren Lamb line went from Fairburn, on the North Western, into what is now Custer State Park, going westward as far as Center

The ruins of a trestle at McGee Siding. Dozens of bridges carried the Crouch Line, "The crookedest railroad in the country," around the curves and over the creek in Rapid Canyon as it wound its way westward from Rapid City to Mystic.

Fairburn boomed when the Warren Lamb Lumber Company used it as its base of logging operations in what is now Custer State Park, but nowadays the business district is nearly deserted.

Lake, and hauling their logs over 30% inclines near Coolidge Inn. The Homestake used the many lines of the Fremont, Elkhorn & Missouri Valley to haul timber from as far south as Este and Merritt; they brought in lime for their boilers from the Calcite lime kilns near Piedmont. The McLaughlin Tie and Timber Company ran a standard-gauge line westward clear across the Wyoming border to harvest bug-infested pines from the area around Moskee.

Each stop on every railroad had a name and was listed on the schedule, and you could buy a ticket, and if you lived there you told your friends that you lived at Addie or Baltimore or Besant Flats or Jolly Dump or Brennan Siding. The railroads were the arteries that pumped the life of commerce and prosperity into the Hills in the early days, and they left their names upon the land, even when at last the rails were taken up, the spikes gathered, and the ties torn up for fire wood. The railroad grades are still there, some of them marked by the South Dakota Historical Society, providing smooth and level pathways to a past that measured its days by toots on a Shay or Heisler engine's whistle.

With or without railroad connections, logging operations brought in many boisterous but temporary towns, where the loggers lived briefly in boarding houses or with their families in

The logging railroads used narrow-gauge geared engines like this three-cylinder Shay to negotiate sharp curves and 12% grades.

tar-paper shacks. Pine Camp, beside the Burlington's Hill City-Keystone Spur, prospered by taking logs out of the wild country between Mount Rushmore and Harney Peak. Fairburn, as previously mentioned, was the central point for the Warren Lamb Company's State Park enterprises and housed the shops and facilities that kept that operation going. The Warren Lamb Company also tried to run a flume down Slate Creek, to bring logs toward Rapid City, but, as has often been the case in the Hills, insufficient water made the flume a failure. Otis, where the State Game Lodge now stands, was once a sawmill, and the Game Lodge itself now rests on the foundations that once supported the mill. Moskee, the Homestake logging camp at the western end of the McLaughlin's timber operations, hauled its logs and timbers to Spearfish mills and on into Lead by truck; in fact, all rail logging operations ceased by the end of the 1920s, as large trucks made road hauling practicable and bulldozers made it possible to load where the logs were felled. Nowadays a good deal of Black Hills timber is harvested for posts, poles, and pulpwood; the giant ponderosa pines have almost all been cut and it will be some years yet before the Forest Service's care and thinning can replace them. A few areas of virgin pine still exist in Custer State Park where you can still see the magnificent trees that once made Black Hills lumber famous.

Many towns were never much more than a post office, often consisting of little more than a few pigeon holes arranged in a discarded dynamite box in some local farmer's kitchen. Manhattan, Maverick, and Maitland in Fall River County; Moon, in the Limestone Country that

The ponderosa pine of the Black Hills has given rise to innumerable one-horse sawmilling operations, but few of them are as well laid out or as substantially built as the Mountain Company's plant near Berne Siding.

Old railroad ties still show that an embankment, now used as a dam for a stockpond, was once a part of the Black Hills & Fort Pierre Railroad at Apex.

Box Elder School in the central Hills.

blossoms red and blue and yellow with the summer flowers; Elk Mountain, somewhere east of Newcastle—those were such places, names in the post office directory, names that still decorate the maps but have now vanished from the land itself. Almost anyone with political influence could get a postmastership if his candidate for congress got elected, and those who were ambitious for their community, or simply for a little extra income, often applied, sorted the mail for a few years until their ranch became a named locality, then abandoned the post office business and their hopes forever.

Many communities rose up around the schools that gave them their names. Not that schools were by any means a permanent fixture on the land: house movers made their living shifting one-room school houses to be nearer newly elected school board members. Some schools, like Lauzon, Mayo, and Box Elder, seem to have existed, at least in their present locations, almost in a vacuum, the center of a widely distributed population. The teachers boarded around or lived in or under the school itself. All through the Hills you will find abandoned schools, for South Dakota was insistent that its children have an education, and where two or three were gathered together there a teacher was among them; but as school buses replaced the teachers, the schoolhouses have gradually been deserted and forgotten.

Some Black Hills towns began as resorts, to provide rest and recreation for the residents and to attract visitors from the East. Hot Springs was first known as a warm-spring Indian health resort; then in the 1890s it blossomed into a plush spa with ornate hotels and hospitals. Its attrac-

tions were augmented by South Dakota's liberal divorce laws, and many came to establish residence, divorce a spouse, and soak away their aches and pains. Cascade, hoping that the railroad would pass its way, advertised its Cascade Spring waters and built a fine hotel and business block, creating in the southwestern hills a grandiose development scheme that ultimately collapsed completely. The communities in the Custer State

The business block in Cascade, with Allen's bank, the general store, the bar, the bowling alley and general place of entertainment still standing by the road that leads to Cascade Falls.

Park area—Sylvan Lake, Legion Lake, Blue Bell Lodge, the State Game Lodge—all sprang up to provide accommodations for travelers and tourists. The Latchstring Inn and Rimrock Lodge in Spearfish Canyon have prospered for over half a century, and Palmer Gulch Lodge, near Hill City, was originally founded by a group of Chicago men as the Black Hills Country Club. The Flying V Ranch, near Cambria, was once that coal mining community's own country club, with hot and cold swimming pools and a miners' museum. Tourists have always been attracted by the beauty and history of the Black Hills, and today tourism is one of the area's major industries. Oddly enough, however, most of the travelers rarely leave the paved roads, and a few hundred yards from the highways the Hills are just the way the gold rushers left them, with gaping mines and abandoned cities awaiting the adventurous.

Many other recreational activities go forward in the Hills. Church camps—Camp Judson, Camp Remington, Placerville, Camp Columbus—attract visitors from the entire state. Boy and Girl Scout camps dot the Hills—Paha Sapa, Old Broadax, Camp Mallo. Summer home groups, leasing cabin sites from the Forest Service, as at Palmer Gulch, Black Fox, Lafferty Gulch, China Gulch, and Sunday Gulch, provide well-organized residential communities for summer visitors. Artificial lakes—and all the lakes in the Black Hills are artificial—have given rise to new recreational communities along their placid borders, and marinas have sprung up where Pactola, Sheridan, and Deerfield once housed boisterous miners, bullwhackers, and logging crews. Deer camps, like Zimbelman's, Sturm's and Roetzel's, house sportsmen in the fall during the Black Hills hunting season. A ski resort is a recent addition to the slopes of Terry Peak, and even the old mining towns of Trojan and Bald Mountain may boom again with winter visitors.

Abandoned miners' homes may once again revive and prosper if Trojan can establish itself as a ski resort on the slopes of Terry Peak amidst the deep snows of the northern hills.

Some towns grew up as suburbs of enterprising towns. Schaeferville is an appendage of Rapid City, as Dudley is of Edgemont. Cornish Town is the southern end of Hill City. Antelope City, high on the hill overlooking Cambria, provided fresh air for residences high above the choking fumes of the coke-burning operations. Deadwood had Ingleside on the edge of the valley, and even little Galena was divided, geographically speaking, into Cariboo and Hardscrabble.

Although gold mining was doubtless the most fruitful source of new towns in the Hills, many other sorts of mines gave rise to a wide variety of communities. Most of the mining towns, though by no means all, lay on the celebrated "mineral belt" which covered a long rectangle from Keystone to Whitewood on the east, and from Terry to Custer on the west, an area roughly coinciding with Ranges 3 and 4 east of the Wyoming border. Within this belt of mineral deposits, or lying close upon its outskirts, lay the mineral wealth of the Black Hills.

The sandstone quarry at Buena Vista, at the mouth of Red Canyon, produced thousands of enormous grindstones which were hauled away on a spur line of the Burlington railroad.

Quarries founded many communities. Odell and Evans Siding near Hot Springs quarried the rich, soft sandstone of the southern Hills, not only for local use but to ship far into neighboring states. Similarly, a quarry near Spearfish provided the building stone for many public buildings there. Gravel, mainly for railroad ballasting, made Marietta, along the Cheyenne River, prosperous for years. Fuller's earth was dug west of Argyle, and probably was responsible for the establishing of that tiny railroad station. Feldspar, for pottery and ceramics and glazes, is mined all over the Hills, although the greatest production seems to center around Keystone, where over sixty minerals were once profitably mined. A grindstone mine at Buena Vista, at the mouth of Red Canyon near Camp Collier, left behind a few unfinished stones that measure more than eight feet in diameter, unmovable relics of quarrying activity.

Lime burning, using the abundant Black Hills limestone, was carried on at Calcite, on the Chicago & North Western Railroad, and at Loring, to the south of Pringle; the lime was used to sweeten the boilers at the Homestake mine at Lead. Gypsum, for plaster and building board, was mined and processed near Piedmont and Blackhawk. Salt was boiled out of the brackish waters of Salt Creek near Newcastle and shipped in wagons eastward to provide chlorine for the early gold reduction mills at Deadwood. It is said that the places where the teamsters paused still attract the deer, who come to lick the salt that once sifted from the wagons. All of these bulky, heavy materials depended upon good transportation for their markets, and as rail lines shifted and changed, production varied or ceased to yield a profit, and the towns around the quarries faded back into the rocks which had given them birth.

Coal was responsible for the Hills' most spectacular ghost town, Cambria, which was reached by a Burlington spur running northward from Newcastle. Here a high-grade anthracite that suited mountain-climbing railroad engines was produced for many years; it yielded an additional bonus, for each ton of it contained a few dollars worth of gold, and it was often worthwhile to pan the ashes for it. Coal was also mined at Aladdin, west of Belle Fourche, and was hauled to town over the little Wyoming & Missouri River Railroad. There was coal around Rapid City, too, although the mines were hardly more than a convenience for the farmers in the vicinity. Oil, a related product, made Newcastle boom following the Second World War. Oil has also been sought in Red Canyon, where some maps still conscientiously indicate the presence of an oil well—and the old cables, now deeply tangled in the grass, can still trip up an intruder.

Silver, usually in carbonate ores, was respon-

The headframe over the deep shaft of the Seabury-Calkins silver mine at Carbonate.

sible for the rise of Galena, Moll, and other towns along Bear Butte Creek. It founded Carbonate, northwest of Lead, a town that consisted of at least three mining areas and had a major smelter. Silver was going to pay for the processing of lead, zinc, and arsenic at the Spokane mine, southwest of Keystone. Copper was found in minor quantities at the Blue Lead and Calumet mines, east of Sheridan, and at Copper Camp high in the Limestone Country. Graphite was dug around Rochford, although never with much success. Bog iron, or ochre, gave rise to Ochre City, and the mining of it to this day provides a permanent blot upon the landscape and pollutes the creeks with a rusty and pervasive scum.

Uranium, first mined near Rochford for use as a coloring material, was found in paying quantities in the southwestern Hills, where it permeates the sandstone formations from Edgemont north to Newcastle. The brightly-colored "calico" stone is a sure guide to its presence, and the mine dumps in Craven Canyon are a rock hunter's delight because of it. After WW II a processing

An old boiler and hundreds of feet of cable mark the site of oil drilling at the mouth of Red Canyon. Scratched into the nearby sandstone cliffs are aboriginal drawings.

Down in the valley by the mill, downstream from the smelter, was an odd house, with inside walls partitioned off with Indianhead muslin and papered over so. (Carbonate)

mill was established at Edgemont to handle the production of this mineral, and the southern Hills enjoyed quite a boom, but have since quieted down considerably as government demands for uranium have tapered off. For a while, however, every man you met in the back country had a Gieger counter slung around his neck, and was intently listening for the tell-tale clicks and sputterings that would lead him to a fortune. Some pitchblende and related minerals are found at the Bob Ingersoll mine near Keystone. For years it was hoped that the pegmatites of Harney Peak would prove to contain radioactive riches, but nobody seems to have found them yet, and about all that remains of the central Hills uranium activity are a lot of shallow holes bulldozed into the ground "to prove up the claim." Abandoned, the claims have, if anything, faded and illegible claim notices tacked to trees.

All in all some six hundred or more towns were once created, named, and settled in the Black Hills. Each one had its reason, sometimes many reasons, for coming into existence, and those that faded did so for a variety of causes.

The names on the land came from many sources, and each reflects something of the men and women who built and named the towns. Cambria was in the Cambrian coal measures. Potato Creek was named by several hungry miners who once shared a single potato among them for their dinner. Keystone was named for a Masonic watch charm. Bulldog I was named for the nearby Bulldog mining claim, and Bulldog II for a couple of bulldogs that the proprietress kept in her yard to keep passing bullwhackers from stealing her property. Tigerville was named for the nearby Lucky Tiger claim, and that, presumably, was named for the famous hair tonic so favored by the barbers of the Victorian Age.

Mystic was supposed to be a "Mistake" noted on a map by a semi-literate railroader, but its proximity to Nahant indicates that both towns were probably named by New Englanders from the Atlantic coast. Moskee means "I don't care (what you name it)" in Pidgin English. Nemo may have been called after the comic-strip character Little Nemo, or for Jules Vern's enigmatic Captain Nemo, or some one may have thought the name a good Omen, spelled backward.

Some names were purely descriptive, like Bugtown, which was named for the infested logs with which the miners built their cabins; or Dark Canyon, so narrow that outstretched arms could touch both of its rocky sides. Point-of-Rocks was the spot where a granite dike nearly touched the Cheyenne-Deadwood stage trail, and the blood-red walls of Red Canyon seemed gloomily prophetic concerning the destiny of the military post at Red Canyon Station. Tinton was named for hoped-for tin. Negro Hill (so spelled in all the local papers) was named for a group of black miners who struck it rich in the placers there. Deadwood Gulch was filled with fallen timber, and Belle Fourche was on the "Belle," or beautiful, fork of the Cheyenne River.

Military heroes and commanders lent their names to many places—the Hills were settled only eleven years after the Civil War, and the Indian Wars were still in progress—so Generals Crook, Sheridan, Warren, and Meade are all commemorated; Camps Bradley, Sturgis, Collier, and Ruhlen were set up and named but soon forgotten. Crook's Tower, Harney Peak, Custer Peak, and Signal Knob all stand as monuments to military men and their activities.

The names of the inhabitants of course were a fertile source of nomenclature. Bakerville, Dewey, Brashville, Brennan, Burke's Siding, and Goiens all commemorate some early dweller in or near their confines. Other names were merely descriptive of the surroundings of the town or of the hopes of its founders. Buena Vista, down in a canyon, was supposed to have a view, but didn't. Cascade had the gushing Cascade Spring and rippling Cascade Falls on either side of it. Edgemont, fittingly enough, was on the southwestern edge of the Hills. Floral, in the Limestone Country, was notable for the flowers which grow in such profusion in the higher Hills. Various "Golden" names like Golden City, Golden Gate, and Golden Slipper derived their glitter from their founders' hopes, while Poorman's Gulch and Poverty Gulch indicated a more realistic attitude.

The ruins of the Golden Reward chlorine process mill at Astoria, southwest of Lead.

In short, the names on the land are an indication of the origins, inclinations, opinions, and ambitions of the settler, and as such they constitute a monument to his hopes as well as to his imagination. Nowadays new communities, mainly for recreation, summer homes, and vacations, are springing up, many of them at places which were once named communities; but the old names in many cases are forgotten, and new names are now given to new towns built up upon old ruins. The same processes took place in the past: towns faded, names grew dim, and then a brightened town again on the same spot, with a new name—over and over again. Little Gregory, north of Rochford, seems to have been known by at least half-a-dozen titles, maybe more, and now that it is owned by a local church, it will probably be renamed yet again. For their size, the Black Hills have more history, more legend, more tradition, and all of it stirred up in less time, than almost any other area.

It is the hope of this book to preserve, while it is still fresh in the memories of the men who best know it, the history of the Black Hills towns, wherever and however they were created. There is hardly a town in the Hills that was not at some time in the past more populous, prosperous, and bustling than it is today, and even those that prosper now still contain, for the eye that seeks to see them, the ghosts of a more flambouyant past. If anyone objects that a town or two that is included is not yet a "ghost town" it can only be said, just wait a while; there were many towns here, long ago, that had ambitions, and now they moulder into the sod and the grass waves over them, and but for the memories of oldtimers and the efforts of historians, they would now be forgotten. If this book preserves for the future something of the joy and the happiness, the pleasure and the adventure which the study of the Black Hills' past has given to its authors, they will feel themselves amply repaid for the efforts which have gone into its preparation.

Not many years ago Galena was crowded with abandoned homes, saloons, and store buildings. The few remaining inhabitants, however, chopped them down for firewood one hard winter, and only a few like this one now remain.

They always built the cemetery on a point of rocky ground. Some say it was to get the departed nearer to heaven, and probably many of them needed all the help they could get. Others say it was to get off the wet valley floor, for no man in his right mind would want to spend eternity in a grave that wasn't properly drained. But mainly they picked out the most ornery patch of ground there was, and that nobody wanted, and made a graveyard out of it. The fences were to keep the cattle from bedding down on the graves. (Harney)

Dewey, which came into existence about the turn of the century, was probably named for Admiral George Dewey who won the Battle of Manila Bay during the Spanish-American War.

FINDING YOUR WAY

When it comes to finding your way, the very best and handiest maps are those put out by the Forest Service and available at most ranger stations throughout the Hills. These show, in varying amounts of detail, the towns, streams, springs, caves, highways, trails, paths, and ranches, and they are bound to be your principal guide to the Hills.

The even more detailed geodetic maps of the U.S. Geological Survey, which show almost every building, contour, and forestration and which come to within a maximum error of forty feet in locating man-made features, are a delight to have with you. They are big, and hence clumsy, and it takes about eighty of them to cover the whole area, but the real explorer will want to have them sooner or later.

A good compass is a must, preferably one that can be used for sighting, adjusted for magnetic declination, and used to take bearings. (The declination in the Hills makes your compass needle point about 14° east of true north; either adjust your compass to compensate for this or remember to allow for it every time you take a reading. Remember also that your car, power lines, even a good jackknife, will seriously deflect your compass needle.) Often a single sighting on a distant mountain will give you enough information to tell whether or not you are somewhere near the town you are looking for. Two bearings, on two mountains, can give you your location with surprising accuracy, but unfortunately most of the towns are down in valleys where you cannot see any mountains at all.

I was out with a friend once who told me that it was easy to find the spot wanted—just locate a contour line it was on and follow that contour until we reached the place. I laughed—until he pulled an aneroid altimeter out of his pocket and did just that. It's a handy thing to have, for obviously if the town you're looking for is at an altitude of 6,500 feet and you're at one of 4,200 you are probably a good way from where you're going.

The town locations given are in ordinary surveyor's terms, from smallest area to largest: Quarter Section, Section, Tier, and Range; thus, SW¼, Section 31, T2N-R5E.

Individual townships are six miles square, and are designated by Tier and Range. The *Tiers* in the Black Hills are numbered north and south of the 44th parallel, or "Black Hills Base Line." The Tiers are numbered T1N, T2N, T3N, etc. as you go north from the Base Line and T1S, T2S, T3S, etc. as you go south, as illustrated in Figure 1. The *Ranges* all begin at the Wyoming border, starting with R1E, R2E, R3E, etc. as you go east. In Wyoming the base meridian is different, ending with an incomplete Range, R6OW, next to the South Dakota border, as shown in Figure 2.

Each township, measuring six miles on a side, contains 36 square miles, and is designated by the Tier and Range that it is in, as T6N-R2E, which is where Spearfish is located. Most modern maps give the Tiers and Ranges along the sides, but on old maps you may have to do a little calculating before you can figure out exactly where you are, even though the lines themselves may be there.

In each township the thirty-six mile-square *Sections* are numbered, beginning at the northeast corner and proceeding consecutively, back and forth. Large-scale modern maps usually place the section number in the middle of each section, but old maps do not, and as the back-and-forth

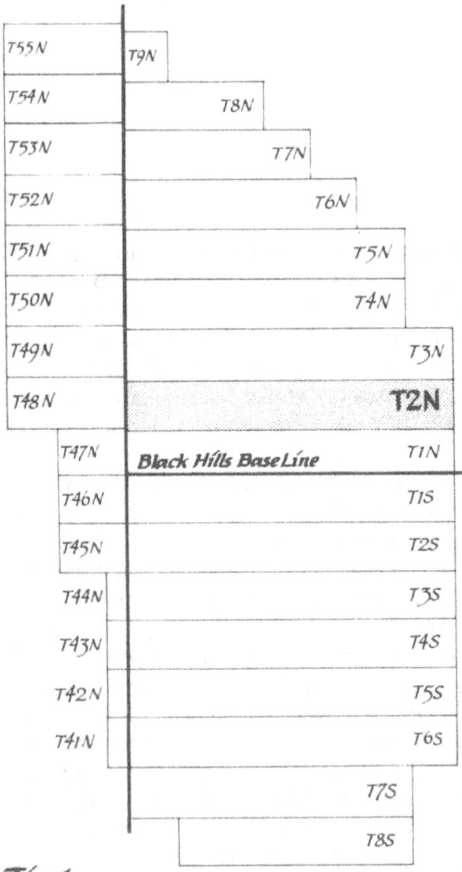

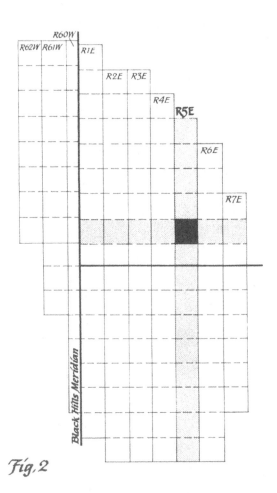

Fig. 1

Tiers are east-west strips 6 miles wide, numbered "North" or "South" beginning at the Black Hills Base Line. Tiers 1 through 9 North (T1N through T9N) go as far north as Belle Fourche, and Tiers 1 through 9 South (T1S through T9S) go as far south as Hot Springs and Angostura Dam.

Fig. 2

Ranges are north-south strips 6 miles wide, numbered, in the Black Hills, from the Black Hills Meridian at the Wyoming border and working eastward, as R1E, R2E, R3E, etc. In Wyoming numbering begins with an incomplete R60W and works westward through R61W, R62W, etc.

numbering, illustrated in Figure 3, tends to be confusing it is wise to make a little chart of section numbers and paste it on the bottom of your compass for easy reference.

Each section is divided into four quarter sections, described as the Northwest quarter (NW¼), Southwest quarter (SW¼), and so on, as shown in Figure 4. That brings the description down to an area of 160 acres, a quarter of a mile on a side, and any town located that close ought to be easy to find. The SW¼, Section 31, T2N-R5E, for example, contains most of Silver City.

You will find as you travel through the Hills that the U.S. Forest Service has done a great deal to help you find your way. Directional signs, Forest Service road numbers, and hard-to-find but extremely accurate little surveying plaques, tacked up on trees with the exact spot marked by nails driven through them, will tell you where you are. The excellent Forest Service maps, too, are kept up to date and can guide you over roads that were built since the detailed USGS maps were made.

Almost anyone in the Hills will be glad to direct you to where you want to go if you ask informed and intelligent questions. Most inhabitants are happy to let you roam over their private land if you first pause to request their permission. Indeed, stopping to ask questions is often the best way to get acquainted with the land and with its history. On the other hand, you should be extremely careful about entering property that is "posted" or that appears to be inhabited. Parts of the Black Hills are still wild and rugged, and almost every family has its gun for hunting purposes, and now and then you may encounter a recluse who feels very strongly about preserving his privacy and seclusion. In the main, however, an intelligent interest in the past is a key that will unlock most gates and unbar most doors, a passport that will guide you safely to the ghost towns of the Hills.

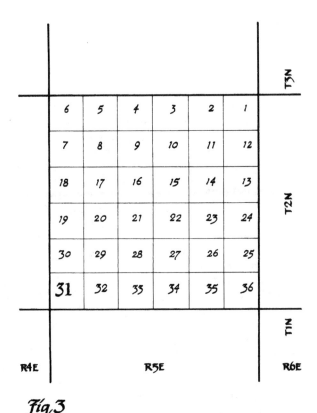

Fig. 3

A *Township* is defined by the intersection of a tier and a range; for example, T2N-R5E measures 6 miles on each side and contains thirty-six *sections* numbered alternately from right to left and left to right.

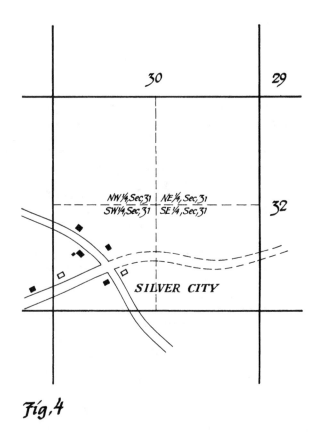

Fig. 4

Each section can be divided into four *quarter-sections,* one in each corner: the NW¼, the NE¼, the SW¼ and the SE¼. The location of Silver City, for example, is noted as follows: SW¼, Section 31, T2N-R5E; it is read as follows: the southwest quarter of Section 31, the second tier north of the Black Hills Base Line, the fifth range east of the Black Hills Meridian.

MINES AND MINING

No activity in the Black Hills has produced more towns, more abandoned hopes, or consequently more ruins than mining; and of the mining towns the early placer towns are doubtless the most abundant and the hardest to locate with any certainty. Placer mining, the extraction of free gold from alluvial gravels, by its very nature tended to take place in streambeds and on gravel banks, where the springtime floods have long ago washed away the ruins that the miners left behind. Nevertheless, the adventurer who knows where to look can often find a few ruins to indicate where glittering placer gold deposits once lured prospectors to the Hills.

The gold in the alluvial deposits was originally contained in the quartz ores which intruded into the country rock of the Black Hills. Here millions of years of rainfall eroded the mountains, freed the gold, and swept it downhill to rest amid the gravel bars. Often the gold sank as far down as it could, coming to rest only when it encountered the impermeable bedrock stratum. At other times, however, the free gold seems to have formed in layers, often mixed with "black sand," that miner's friend and guide, which due to its similarity to gold, often was commingled with it. Such a layer might occur anywhere, from the grassroots to the bedrock, and when found the happy miner could pan it out, often encountering a rich—but transient—bonanza. No matter where the gold might lie in depth, however, it did not lie in solid sheets, but in pockets and concentrations caused by the swirls and eddies of prehistoric streams; and though the miner tried to guess where these might once have run, basing his calculations on the present courses of mountain streams, or, more reliably, on the immutable configuration of the valleys, he could never be sure when he would find a deposit that would repay his toilsome efforts.

Having located a good prospect, the miner might immediately dig into the gravel and commence operations. More frequently he found that the most likely prospect was wet and needed draining, and his first activity might be to construct a trench, often many hundreds of feet long, to drain away the excess water. Most of these prospectors' ditches, some of them real mining efforts and others constructed only to "prove up" the land, have long since been washed out or plowed under, for they invariably lay in wet bottom land, and they can be located only with the guidance of some oldtimer who may remember where they originally were. Sometimes the miners used "China pumps," water-powered devices of a most unreliable nature, to bail the

Goldbug Nelson sorting out the rocks from a panful of gold-bearing gravel.

water out of workings that were only a little damp, or were so located that a ditch could not be easily dug to drain them. Often a dam, to impound the water for a few weeks, would be constructed upstream from prospective workings, and the miners would work frantically to remove the ore before the dam filled and again flooded the diggings. And sometimes the miner put down his hole as fast as he could and hoped to find a pocket before the hole became too wet for him to work it.

Having found a profitable "bar" of gravel, the miner first tested his prospect by panning, an age-old method of mixing water, gravel, mud, and rheumatism in the hope of finding a few specks of gold. Crouched in a bone-chilling stream, the prospector agitated his pan (containing a half-bushel of gravel) in the icy water, washing away the light loam and sticky clay with the water, and removing larger pebbles with a practiced hand. When, at last, all that was left in the pan was a layer of black sand composed of iron oxide and cassiterite, he knew that he had gotten down to where there might be gold, and with a single dextrous swirl he distributed these "fines" in a long arc across the upper edge of his pan. The gold dust, being the heaviest, traveled the farthest, and if present formed a golden tip to the half-moon of sand formed in the pan. These specks of gold, often finer than a pin head, the prospector picked out with a moistened thumb, the end of a match, or a pair of tweezers, to be stored in a glass vial or buckskin poke. Placer gold normally contained a good deal of adulteration, for the gold itself was rarely pure, and the miners, to be sure of getting all the gold dust, generally took along a good bit of black sand with it. If the prospect con-

sistently ran twenty-five cents to the pan the miner could work it profitably with no further equipment, and might do so if the pocket appeared to be a small one. Even gravel worth ten cents a pan, however, if available in large quantities, could be profitably extracted by the use of somewhat more intricate equipment.

The first piece of machinery that the placer miner turned to was his rocker, a device composed of a "riddle," or perforated iron sieve, onto which he shoveled his gravel and mixed it with water. Large pebbles were removed by hand, while the mud, sand, and water flowed downward into the body of the rocker to be mixed and churned by baffles as the miner agitated the machine. Emerging from the baffles, the slurry of mud and gold flowed over riffles, which caught the heavy gold behind them; then the slurry came out of the rocker over an old blanket, piece of carpeting, or a wad of unwashed wool, which had an affinity for fine gold and thus was undoubtedly the origin of ancient legends of the "Golden Fleece." A rocker was useful for washing sticky, clay-like ores and to make the maximum use of limited supplies of water, but if a large amount of gravel was to be washed, the prospectors turned to an even more impressive piece of equipment: the sluicebox and its accompanying earthworks.

A sluicebox required huge amounts of water for its operation, and this was generally obtained by damming the creek upstream to impound a considerable head which could be released at intervals to wash the gold. Sometimes it was profitable to build quite extensive flumes and ditches to the placers, for it was considered to be easier to move water in a ditch than gravel in a wagon. These flumes, often high on the sides of canyons, and toward the distribution ends, have of course survived the floodings in the valleys and can still be followed through the Hills, some of them for

Some of Goldbug Nelson's placer mining equipment was exceedingly complex for the 1930s. Author Watson Parker observes, with youthful interest, the ingenuity of the inventor.

miles, from source to point of application. At Hayward, for example, the flume began far up in Battle Creek canyon and traveled past the town, where Rushmore Cave now is (the cave was discovered when water from the flume leaked away into it), and on to the high ground to the south, a matter of four or five miles.

The sluice itself had a riddle, usually made of perforated board, over which an attending miner could ply a short twelve-tined pitchfork, forking out the pebbles which would have caused eddies and ripples and interfered with the settling of the gold if allowed to tumble on downward. Six sluice boxes, each a trough one foot square and twelve feet long, were a usual string. They had to be carefully leveled and graded so that the gravel would move along through them under the pressure of the water, but not so steep that the gold would refuse to settle down behind the riffles. At the end of each day the riffles were removed and the gravel caught behind them washed—it was nice to know how the day's work had panned out, and besides, it removed temptation from greedy neighbors whose workings might have been less successful than your own. A sluicing operation might easily leave considerable piles of gravel, as at Hayward and Bear Gulch, but generally these have washed away and little remains to mark the site of even major placer operations.

The Hayward flume began far up Battle Creek and used a ditch to carry water to the placers high on the side of the valley below the town.

Folks with more time than judgment still now and then work the rich placers below Hayward with the traditional sluice boxes.

The flume that brought water to the Old Standby mine from far above Rochford. At the point shown here it was supported on a trestle high above the road where it crossed over Rapid Creek to follow the southern edge of the valley down to the mill.

A modern-day piece of placering equipment near Junction City.

27

The windrows of coarse, washed gravel left behind by a dredging operation are unmistakable. These, at Castleton, are full of deep, still pools, ideal for summer swimming.

Dredging operations are much easier to find than placers for they leave huge windrows of sterile rock along the creeks or even in the middle of open meadows. These dredges were simply big gold-washing machines, gigantic rockers, mounted on huge barges floating in their own ponds. As they dug the gravel up and washed it they moved the pond forward along with them and heaped the gravel up behind them. The old Evans dredge workings at Castleton can still be seen, and the ribs of the old barge there are still visible by the side of the road. Other dredge workings are in Pleasant Valley south of Four Mile, and west of Custer near Tin Mountain. Even in the 1970s a dredge was operating in Whitewood Creek north of Deadwood.

Having found a suitable placer prospect, the prospector would "stake out a claim," usually three hundred feet along the valley. As long as he worked it, the other miners would respect it. Each mining district elected its own "recorder," who noted the location and owners of the claims: "number four below discovery," and so on. It was possible to get a more legitimate title, but since the claims were usually worked out in a few months, few of the miners in early days bothered to do so. The hardrock miner, on the other hand, finding a suitable outcropping of what appeared to be paying ore, would stake out a claim three hundred feet wide and fifteen hundred feet long, presumably along the general trend of his vein; this, as long as he worked it sporadically, could be registered and eventually "proved up" and obtained under a patent from the government. It is simply astonishing to see the number of mining claims, both placer and hardrock, that seem to coincide almost exactly with the farming land in the fertile valleys.

These hardrock claims produced what are unquestionably the most impressive and romantic relics left by the Black Hills mining activity. Here the miners dug deep into the rock, trying to follow gold-bearing veins that had outcropped at the surface. Such mines today are always dangerous for the amateur to explore, for the earth is always trying to heal its wounds and close up the shafts and tunnels. The shafts especially are treacherous now: the ground around them has a tendency to break away as you try to peer down into them or the rotted timber collars may collapse beneath your feet.

Many mines, like the Penobscot at Kiddville, were worked by a "glory hole," as the miners pulled the ore out from underneath and left a huge, cratered opening on the surface.

If you come upon a well-preserved hardrock operation, what you will see is a shaft house, where a boiler and hoisting equipment were operated, lowering men into the mine and hauling the ore back up in ore cars of various sorts. This shaft house might be anywhere up to a mile or more from the mill which actually processed the ore, and connected to it only by a long tramway over which the ore cars ran. At the shaft itself would be a big waste dump of "country rock," the barren rock dug out of the mine in order to reach the gold ore. At the other end of the tramway from the shaft would be some sort of a mill, and below the mill the "tailings" which resulted from the ore being ground up and the gold washed out of it. Sometimes, as at Trojan, the tailings can fill a mile of valley up to the brim, and as they erode in the rain they are often carved into fantastic "badlands" formations.

Any miner could make an arrastra from boulders available on the ground. You will never find one in working condition, for when the mine closed down the arrastra was taken up and the gold panned from between the cracks.

You probably will never see one, but the earliest form of gold ore milling used in the Hills was the arrastra, or "raster." This consisted of a circular trough paved with smooth rocks, around which a millstone was dragged, grinding the ore to a powder for further processing. Sometimes this crushed ore was then panned, just as one would pan a placer gold deposit, but more frequently the ground ore was mixed with mercury, which formed an amalgam with the gold. This amalgam, which could be washed out of the tailings, was then distilled, leaving behind the gold, while the mercury itself, caught in a bucket of cold water, could be used again. The miner who had only a small quantity of amalgam to distill often placed it in a hollowed-out potato, which, when baked, absorbed the mercury, leaving behind a pellet of gold. Squeezed, the baked potato would yield the mercury for use another time. Most arrastras were torn up when mining operations were ended, so the gold and amalgam which had settled in the cracks between the stones could be recovered. Some stories say there was an arrastra near Carbonate, but it is gone now.

The Chilean mill was a more elaborate arrastra in which two huge millstones set on edge rolled around on the ore. A sheet metal collar was used at Kiddville to keep the unground pebbles from splashing out before they were ground fine.

The shaft house at Tinton, precipitously perched over the inclined tramway that led down into the mine.

This mercury amalgamation process was the backbone of the early hardrock mines which worked the "free-milling" ore in which the gold was simply contained in a mechanical union. Such mills can be identified by their very foundations, for they always ran crosswise to the slope of the hill on which they stood. Ore was trammed in along the top of the mill and distributed to ore bins, and thence to a number of stamps (forty was the customary size, in batteries of five) which ground the ore into a very fine powder. Mercury was sometimes added to the stamp batteries, but it tended to turn into an ineffective, floury powder, especially in cold weather. In any event, below the stamps were long, sloping copper-covered amalgamation tables coated with mercury, placed so that the slurry of water, ground ore, and gold that issued from the screens of the stamps ran slowly over them. On these tables the amalgamation process was completed. A thoughtful mine manager was always careful to see that he got back from his operation just about as much mercury as he put into it; if he didn't, it meant that somebody in the mill was stealing his amalgam. The process tended to get about half of the gold in the ore; the other half went out with the tailings. The Uncle Sam mine at Roubaix was considered a wonder because its ore was so free-milling and its mills so efficient that it lost only ten percent of its possible yield. You'll find the ruins of dozens of such stamp mills and amalgamation processes in the Hills. The Golden Summit east of Hill City, the Lookout mill at the foot of Bloody Gulch, and the Old Standby south of Rochford are among the most impressive.

Ore which was free-milling and amenable to the mercury process was not common. Often the gold was so fine, or held in so complex a bond with the ore, that simple crushing and amalgamation could not extract it. It was with these "refractory" ores that more complex milling methods came into use.

The earliest of these, the chlorine process, was first used in the Georgia gold fields shortly after their discovery in the 1820s; it called for a good deal of equipment and engineering skill. It was ideally suited for getting the gold out of pyritic ores in which the gold was held in a quasi-chemical bond with the sulfur of the pyrite. The ore was first coarsely crushed, then roasted at carefully controlled temperatures for a considerable period to soften the ore and loosen the gold within it. The roasted ore was then more finely ground and put into a heated lead-lined mill, along with suitable proportions of water, salt, and sulfuric acid. The free chlorine released from the salt combined with the gold to form gold chloride. This chloride pulp was then filtered out and the gold precipitated by the addition of ferrous sulfate. The precipitate, once dried, could

A giant wooden bullwheel connected to a steam engine drove the batteries of stamps housed in their framework of fourteen-inch timbers. (Old Standby mine)

The bullwheel turned a long shaft that extended through the stamp batteries; cams on the shaft lifted and rotated the stamps alternately. (Old Standby mine at Rochford)

The stamps, in batteries of five, ground the ore in a castiron mortar until it was fine enough to flow through a screen (missing here) onto the mercury-coated amalgamation table. (Old Standby mine)

The Whiffley table "classified" or sorted ore by jiggling it over a serrated surface that separated the waste from the values. It moved every whichways, all at once, and had more knobs on it than a Chinese submarine. (Penobscot mine at Kiddville)

be mixed with a flux of soda and borax and smelted, with the gold at last being poured into small ingots.

A chlorine-process mill would have the usual stamps, a very considerable roasting furnace, and the foundations of the lead mills. Even the ruins of such a plant are hard to miss. You can still see the base of the chimney of the one which stood where the School of Mines in Rapid City is now located; and the brick work for the roasting oven at Maitland is still in evidence. This process accounts for the avid interest the Black Hills mining community took in Cambria's salt and coal mines, for salt (sodium chloride) was the principal source of the chlorine used in the process.

The most recent, as well as the most thorough, way of getting gold out of refractory ores is the cyanide process. Cyanide mills and their ruins can generally be identified because they run downhill, rather than across the slope of a hill.

Ore cars carried ore from the mine to the mill and carried "country rock" out of the mine to the ever-growing piles of waste. (Bald Mountain mine at Trojan)

The ore was ground to a powder in a rotating ball or rod mill (you can find the worn rods and balls around most of the abandoned mills) and then mixed with a solution of calcium, potassium, or sodium cyanide which dissolved the gold out of the ore. The resulting solution was then passed through zinc shavings on which the gold precipitated out as a black slime that could be washed off of the zinc, purified, dried, melted, and cast into ingots. The distinctive ruins of such mills are always the huge steel, or more commonly wooden, vats in which the ore was soaked. Near Trojan, for example, there is a whole row of steel vats, abandoned for over sixty years, but their interiors, preserved by the effects of the cyanide, are still bright and free from rust.

The cyanide process was invented in 1887 but did not get started in the Hills until the 1890s. You can see it in full swing at the Homestake in Lead, where the odor of the chemicals pervades the whole town, and the slime colors the creek leading from the mill a steely gray.

Leaching vats from the cyanide process, across the valley from Trojan. An idea of their size can be gained by noting the 55-gallon drums half buried in the sand.

A variation of the cyanide process, introduced in the early 1900s and used in the limestone area northwest of Lead, was based on the supposition that the gold was not distributed evenly through the ore, but lurked, instead, in the cracks and interstices of the rock. Mills set up to treat such ores simply cracked the rock into quarter-inch pebbles, which were then leached out as usual, leaving distinctive gravelly tailings behind.

In every phase of mining operation it was possible for an unwary speculator to be deceived by the ingenuity of a thoughtful swindler. Placers could be "salted" with a dusting of gold and a

31

prospective buyer directed to select his samples from the area thus enriched. Even a few grains of gold dust under an old prospector's fingernails could so fortify a pan of gravel as to make it appear the product of a rich deposit, and a squirt of gold-laden tobacco juice into a sluice or rocker could make a trial run of gravel appear considerably richer than it actually was. Many a man loaded his shotgun with gold dust instead of shot and fired it into the working face of a barren tunnel, so that a prospective buyer could have visual proof of grandiloquent claims. Sometimes the seller would haul in ore from a paying mine and blandly assure a prospective buyer that it was "just like the stuff they're taking out of the Homestake"—and many times it was, exactly. The wise buyer or mining engineer was careful to blast down fresh rock and to make his selection of sample ore without the supervision, or even the presence, of the seller. Even so, a hypodermic syringe full of gold chloride could be surreptitiously inserted into a sample bag, where the injection could do much to augment the values of the sample. Nuggets could be dropped into the stamp mill along with the ore, or old mercury, still partially clogged with gold, spread upon the amalgamation tables; so even a trial run of a few tons of ore could not be accepted as conclusive evidence of the quality of the ore. In the 1870s common medicines for venereal disease often contained gold chloride, and many an unhappy prospector managed to relieve himself of both his ailment and his mine by a wise distribution of his own mineral values.

Many buyers, however, were not even wise enough to take samples or to consult an experienced engineer, relying upon the word of promoters, supported by the seeming activity of their mines as evidence of prospective riches. The Black Hills soon gained a name for ingenious promotional swindles, and to this day stock is sold in enterprises designed more to enrich the promoter than the investors. One enterpriser built his mine and mill beside a railroad track and brought a host of prospective buyers clear out to the Hills from Chicago. As the train approached the workings the engineer blew one long blast on his whistle, the mine started up, the miners bustled vigorously about their tasks, the mill stamped and thumped, and presumed assayers peered thoughtfully at retorts seemingly full of gold. The activity continued all day long; when the train departed, the operations, as far as mining was concerned, closed down, never to reopen. The sale of stock, however, continued for a considerable period. A good many of the ruins which decorate the Black Hills mining scene are more than likely relics not of genuine mining but of mining promotions which had but little hope of successful prosecution though they were of course rewarding to their promoters in many other ways.

Wood-burning boilers to run the hoists, stamps, and air compressors were the sole source of early-day power, and their foundations last forever. (Electro-Chemical Reduction Company at Mystic, on Castle Creek)

A fine screen held the ore in the mortar until the stamps had ground it to a flour-fine slurry which then passed over the amalgamation tables. (Old Standby mine at Rochford)

Mining machinery is hardly ever abandoned; it just moves on to another mine. This ore car at the Old Ironsides, however, is so deep in Squaw Creek Canyon that nobody will ever get it out.

A copper ore hopper on Blue Lead Mountain, southwest of Sheridan Lake. The cable for the aerial tramway that carried the ore to the Calumet smelter can be discerned at the lower right.

The King of the West, near Myersville, sank many shallow shafts in search of gold, but like so many operations of the depression days its promise proved elusive.

THE TOWNS are listed in alphabetical order and include, roughly, those within the timber of the Black Hills from Edgemont in the south to Belle Fourche in the north and from Rapid City in the east to the Bear Lodge Mountains in the west. This includes all or part of the following counties: Butte, Custer, Fall River, Lawrence, Meade, and Pennington in South Dakota, and Crook and Weston in Wyoming.

The towns are generally listed under their most common and familiar names. When a town has been known by more than one name, alternatives are indicated by italics; often additional information on the town, pertaining to it when it bore a different name, is given in these secondary listings. Where two or more towns share the same name they are distinguished by roman numberals (e.g., Summit I, Summit II, Summit III, Summit IV).

SPELLINGS are from maps, newspapers, and current usage in the Hills and are often open to dispute. Addie Camp, for example, has been known as Kennedyville, but appears on the USGS maps as Canadaville.

LOCATIONS are given by quarter-section, section, tier, and range, in that order: see pages **22 and 23** for details. When towns were found only on old maps without cadastral divisions or on maps that appeared to be inaccurate, the dubious part of each town's location is followed by a question mark (?) in parentheses.

DETAIL MAPS of the various towns, often compiled from the spoken word, are sketches rather than scaled drawings and are intended to help you to find and identify the ruins rather than to provide a surveyor's map of the locality.

A MAP LIST of the Hills is given in the Bibliography; it is always wise to make use of the most modern maps when traveling in the Hills, for roads in the area change with astonishing rapidity.

RAILROADS are called either by the names in use today or by the names they used when the towns in question flourished beside their tracks. A discussion of Black Hills railroad lines can be found on page 13.

THE PHOTOGRAPHS were taken within the past fifteen years; most of them are considerably more recent than that. Even so, some of the buildings shown in the illustrations have now vanished forever and only their foundations mark the places where they once stood.

BLACK HILLS TOWNS

"All doors are locked to honest men," this ancient hasp and padlock seem to say, on a shed door in Addie Camp. If you see something that you think is too valuable to be left lying around, let the stealing of it be on someone else's conscience.

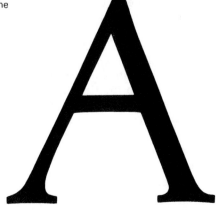

The headframe over the shaft at the Good Luck tungsten mine at Addie Camp.

ADDIE CAMP
Pennington County
NE¼, Section 33, T1S-R5E

Addie Camp served the great Addie mine of the Harney Peak Tin Mining, Milling, and Manufacturing Company, an English firm exploiting the cassiterite deposits around Keystone and Hill City. In December 1892 the Grand Island & Wyoming Central (now the Chicago, Burlington & Quincy) Railroad ran an eastward spur to the Addie to haul ore to the tin mill just east of Hill City. The mine was explored by shafts and drifting to 800 feet, but was never profitable. Addie Camp took on new life when the railroad was extended to Keystone, February 25, 1900. The town had a platform station, saloon, boarding house, sidings, and a commissary car for the railroad workers. In July 1917 the tracks to the Addie itself were taken up, and Addie Camp became a small farming community.

Addie Camp was also known as *Addie Spur*. The USGS maps show it as *Canadaville*, probably a corruption of *Kennedyville*, so called in honor of the proprietor of the saloon. The few scattered houses which remain are on the north side of the CB&Q tracks, 2½ miles east of Hill City on the old Hill City-Keystone gravel road.

Small doors and windows and chinked log walls indicate that this was once a home, rather than, judging by its size and shape, a barn. (Addie Camp)

A spur of the Burlington line led ½ mile down this road to the great Addie tin mine, at Addie Camp.

The "1880 Train" passing by the site of the Addie Camp station platform.

A miner's cabin dug into the hillside at Addie Camp.

The Canaday or Kennedy house once housed the bar and grocery store at Addie Camp.

AJAX

Pennington County
NE Corner of T2S-R8E

On the Chicago & North Western Railroad, about 5 miles north of Hermosa.

ALADDIN

Crook County
Center of Section 28, T54N-R61W

Originally a coal mining community, connected to Belle Fourche by the Wyoming & Missouri Valley Railroad, Aladdin is now little more than post office and gas station by the side of state highway 24.

ALBANY

Lawrence County
SW¼, Section 19, T3N-R4E

Even early maps show only a single house, on Boxelder Creek.

ALKALI

Meade County
SW¼, Section 17, T5N-R6E

Leland Case describes this as "a neighborhood northeast of Sturgis"; the above location is that of the Alkali School, on Alkali Creek.

ALLEN'S CAMP

Pennington County
T1S-R3E(?)

Andreas' *Historical Atlas* mentions that in 1875 or 1876 a Mr. Allen commenced placer mining on Spring Creek at a point soon known as "Allen's Camp." He took out some $2,200 worth of gold dust and apparently was a likeable man, for he was elected recorder of the Slate Creek Mining District and, on his return to Cheyenne, served in the Wyoming legislature. It is not clear whether "Allen's Camp" was a part of the Slate Creek Mining District, but it is possible that it was, since Slate and Spring Creeks come close together around Gillette Prairie, the location given above.

ALLERTON

Lawrence County
E½, Section 30, T4N-R4E

A monument at Brownsville mentions that Allerton was in 1883 the end of the Black Hills & Fort Pierre rails and the scene of the disastrous fire at the Hood & Scott lumber mill boarding house. Allerton was ½ mile east of Brownsville, along Elk Creek.

ALTA

Pennington County
SW¼, Section 26, T2N-R3E

This small settlement, also known as *Altamine*, is very nearly the same as *Myersville*. As early as 1878 it had a population of 20. In 1883 the Alta Lodi Mining Company built a 40-stamp mill, later removed to Lookout, but failed to make a go of it. In 1893 James Cochran built a 16-ton Huntington mill, which he operated during the summers until 1917. Exploratory work continued sporadically until 1936, but it is probable that only in its earliest days could Alta be called anything more than a single mine and its community.

The town lies about 1½ miles southwest of Rochford and is probably best reached from the Rochford-Reynolds Prairie Road or from the Castle Peak lookout.

ALVA

Crook County
SE¼, Section 5, T54N-R63W

Alva, at the northwest end of the Bear Lodge Mountains, is almost completely outside of the Black Hills, but there are so few towns of any description in the Bear Lodge that they all should be mentioned.

AMERICAN CITY

Lawrence County
T6N-R2E(?)

American City reportedly was at the mouth of a long valley leading into Spearfish Canyon, but repeated floods in the area have removed all traces of it.

ANCHOR I, ANCHOR CITY

Lawrence County
Section 28(?), T5N-R3E

Anchor was an early mining town near Deadwood, on Deadwood Creek, above Golden Gate and Central City, and in 1880 it had a population of 291.

ANCHOR II

Lawrence County
Sections 28 & 29, T5N-R2E

Another town by the name of Anchor was in the Ragged Top mining district and doubtless took its name from the Balmoral and Anchor group of mining claims.

Far up the creek from Central City was Anchor City and its mine, now the source of much of Deadwood's water supply.

The old New Reliance mine is falling into complete and entire ruin along the banks of Annie Creek.

ANNIE CREEK
Lawrence County
NE¼, Section 3, T4N-R2E

At the above location, on Annie Creek, is the Annie Creek Mining Company, formerly known as the New Reliance, and still earlier as the Reliance group. The mine buildings, boarding houses, office building, and a two-story home are still standing. The Reliance produced over $600,000 worth of gold up to 1916, and further sampling was done around 1935, but no recent production is reported. The mailing address of the Reliance Mill was *Portland*; 1915 USGS maps seem to show a narrow-gauge railroad leading almost to the mine.

The Reliance Mine is 1½ miles west of Trojan, or 2 miles northeast of Elmore. Roads to the mine are well marked and are passable in good weather, but they have a tendency to wash out in storms.

The old New Reliance boarding house at Annie Creek. The rafters over each bed in the attic were marked to show the number of sheets and blankets that each bed had.

The mouth of the main tunnel at the New Reliance mine on Annie Creek breathes fetid blasts of icy air with every change of the weather, an indication of vast depths below.

39

ANTELOPE CITY

Weston County
NW¼, Section 29, T45N-R61W

Antelope City was the name of the residential section of Cambria, perched high on the hill to the west of town and reached by a 600-step stairway.

ANTHONY'S

Lawrence County
NW¼, Section 24, T4N-R4E

A whistle stop on the Black Hills & Fort Pierre narrow-gauge line from Bucks to Piedmont via Crystal Cave, Anthony's was about 1½ miles from Bucks and an equal distance from Holloway.

APEX

Lawrence County
NE¼, Section 34, T4N-R4E

Apex was a station on the Black Hills & Fort Pierre narrow-gauge railroad from Bucks to Piedmont via Nemo. It was about 11 miles from Englewood.

ARCHMORE

Fall River County

The 1900 Rand McNally atlas lists this as a post office in Fall River County, but the mapmakers may have confused it with Ardmore which is south of the Black Hills on the Nebraska border.

ARGENTINE

Fall River County
SW¼, Section 10, T7S-R1E

Argentine was apparently an earlier name for *Burdock*. The USGS map of the area for 1902 shows it as possibly one house at a crossroad, beside the Burlington & Missouri River Railroad; the current Forest Service map shows the town of Burdock, with one house and a school, in the same location.

ARGYLE

Custer County
NE¼, Section 16, T6S-R4E

Named for an early settler, Argyle now consists of a single shed by the side of the Burlington tracks. Large deposits of fuller's earth and volcanic ash lie about 2½ miles to the west, in Section 12, T6S-R3E, and in earlier times considerable commercial shipments were made from them.

Argyle is easily reached on the gravel road leading southward from Pringle to Minnekahta.

ASTORIA

Lawrence County
SE¼, Section 6, T4N-R3E

Astoria was the home of the great Golden Reward Gold Mining Company, which operated from 1887 to at least 1918. Over $21,000,000 in gold was taken from 440 claims in the Ruby Basin and Bald Mountain mining districts, and additional income came from custom milling and smelting operations. The ore was brought to the mill by a complex tangle of narrow-gauge and standard-gauge railroads. The mill was a pioneer in the use of natural gas for smelting. Its remains can be seen to the west of US 85, about 2½ miles southwest of Lead.

ATLANTIC CITY

Custer County

Atlantic City was the home of the Atlantic mine and its 40-stamp mill, which should have left a considerable amount of spectacular ruins. Atlantic Hill is in the SE¼ of Section 5, T3S-R4E, north of Custer and about 2 miles west of Berne Siding, but where the mine was is a mystery.

AVALON

Lawrence County
SW¼, Section 30, T4N-R4E

An early name for *Brownsville*.

AZTEC

Lawrence County
NE¼, Section 18, T4N-R3E

Aztec was the junction of the narrow-gauge Deadwood Central Railway coming from Terry, with the standard-gauge Burlington line from Englewood down into Spearfish Canyon. It is reported to have been a mine site, although early maps do not seem to show any buildings around it.

Argyle, once a shipping point for fuller's earth, is now only a spot where the road crosses the Burlington tracks on a broad prairie in the southern Hills.

The waiting room of the Chicago, Burlington & Quincy Railroad depot, at Hill City. Coal, which once fired the locomotive boilers, is still the traditional fuel of the railroad man.

B

BAKER TOWN
Crook County
SW¼, Section 27, T54NR61W

Baker Town was contiguous on its west with Barrett Town, and Barrett Town adjoined Aladdin, all three within ¾ mile of each other, working the coal seams of Coal Land Ridge. The mines were connected to Belle Fourche, 16 miles to the east, by the Wyoming & Missouri River Railroad, which ran coal trains and a drover's caboose for passengers — and, when business was slack, a little gasoline-powered open passenger car. The ruins of the last operating coal mine in the vicinity are technically at Baker Town, but they are so close to Aladdin that it makes little difference.

BAKERVILLE
Custer County
W½, Section 29, T4S-R6E

The USGS map of the area for 1901 shows just two houses here, on the South Fork of Lame Johnny Creek. In 1887 it had a post office and in 1900 a population of 27 as well.

All that is left of Bakerville, on the South Fork of Lame Johnny Creek in Custer State Park.

BALD MOUNTAIN
Lawrence County
NE Corner of T4N-R2E

References to Bald Mountain probably referred to either the Bald Mountain mining district or to the area in the center of it now known as *Trojan*.

BALMORAL
Lawrence County
SW¼, Section 28, T5N-R2E

Balmoral was one of several settlements which sprang up in the Ragged Top mining district to work the shallow deposits of silicified gold ore which were discovered there in 1897. The USGS map for 1900 shows Balmoral with a solidly built-up business district around a crossroad, with a half-dozen houses scattered around. Other towns in the area were Preston, Dacy, the upper part of Victoria, and *Cyanide*, which last seems to have been a later name, at least on the USGS map for 1915, for Balmoral. The area is now known as *Preston*, and a Forest Service sign has been posted to that effect, but a careful comparison of maps seems to show that Preston was actually about ½ mile northeast of the sign. Several houses and sheds remain, as well as the well-preserved Ragged Top school.

Balmoral and its neighboring towns can be easily reached from Trojan by traveling 2 miles west over the old Burlington right of way to Spearfish Canyon, then turning northward for about 1½ miles on the most-used dirt road available.

BALTIMORE
Lawrence County
W½, Section 1, T4N-R2E(?)

The Baltimore *mine* was in the above location, and was reached by a narrow-gauge spur line in the Ruby Basin area. Baltimore may be sometimes confused with Balmoral, but was likely only a mine rather than a settlement.

BARE BUTTE
Meade County
Common Corner of Sections 17, 18, 19, & 20, T6N-R7E

An early name for *Bear Butte*. Captain Raynolds, exploring the area in the 1850s, took meticulous care to note that it was pronounced *Bewt*, to avoid giving offense to the delicate-minded.

BARRETT TOWN
Crook County
SE¼, Section 28(?), T54N-R61W

Barrett Town was a small mining community adjacent to Aladdin on the Wyoming & Missouri River Railroad, working the shallow coal measures of Coal Land Ridge 16 miles west of Belle Fourche. The town, which was contiguous with Aladdin on the west and Baker Town on the east, contained many houses and the Olsen Store and Hauser Hotel.

BATTLE CREEK, BATTLE RIVER
Pennington County
Section 31, T2S-R8E

An early name for *Hermosa*, although the original townsite was not exactly where Hermosa is now.

BEAR BUTTE

Lawrence County
NE¼, Section 3, T4N-R4E

In addition to being the name of the mountain near Sturgis, Bear Butte was the name for a mining town on Bear Butte Creek, approximately where *Galena* is now or perhaps a bit farther east down the creek. The present Bear Butte school and church are at the crossroads at the common corner of Sections 17, 18, 19, & 20, T6N-R7E, but this of course is not the site of the earlier mining town.

BEAR GULCH I

Lawrence County
NE¼, Section 19, T5N-R1E

One of the earliest of the placer gold camps in the Nigger Hill mining district, Bear Gulch is ½ mile northeast of Tinton and is easily reached by a 5-mile drive eastward from Spearfish Canyon on the Iron Creek road.

In 1880 the town was estimated to have a population of 1,000, but the tax list showed a valuation of only $447, probably declared by the one honest man in the area. By 1887, however, the population had shrunk to 200, employed in tin mines, quartz mills, tin smelter, and two sawmills, with a valuation of $575,000 and a post office. By 1900 the population was down to 100, and the decline has been steady ever since, until now it may not be possible to find Bear Gulch at all.

The grave of Martin Waterman: died August 16th, 1877, buried in Bear Gulch cemetery.

A conveyor for loading placer gravel, at Bear Gulch.

Bear Gulch is strung out a considerable distance along the creek, and this miner's cabin is just about at the downstream end.

BEAR GULCH II

Pennington County
NE¼, Section 4, T1N-R5E

A stop on the Rapid Canyon line, between Silver City and Pactola, and now submerged beneath the waters of Pactola Lake. It seems to have also been known as *Elkhorn*.

BEAR LODGE MINING CAMP

Crook County

As the name implies, this was a mining camp in the Bear Lodge Mountains of Wyoming, although the mine is also described as being "halfway between Sundance and Beulah."

43

BEAR ROCK
Custer County
NE¼, Section 27, T3S-R4E

Bear Rock, about a mile west of Custer on US 16, was an early placer camp. A cave in the rock was the Black Hills' first post office, mail being left there for the miners to sort over and distribute among themselves.

BEARSVILLE
Crook County
SE¼, Section 33, T50N-R61W

Bearsville was an earlier name, or a nickname, for *Moskee*. The community had 20 houses.

BEAVER CITY
Lawrence County
T4N-R4E(?)

This was evidently a placer camp, laid out in January 1878, in the Germania district, ½ mile above Quartz City, which in turn was on a supposed junction of Hay and Elk Creeks.

BEAVER CREEK STAGE STATION
Fall River County(?)

Brown and Willard's *Black Hills Trails*, quoting the Sidney, Nebraska *Telegraph* of May 20, 1876, lists Beaver Creek as a stage stop 22 miles, presumably southeast, from Custer, on the Deadwood-Sidney line. It was not the same, by any means, as the Beaver Station on Stockade Beaver Creek at the western edge of the Hills.

A *station* on a stage line normally meant a place where horses were changed, but a *stage station* a place where the passengers could find rest and refreshment. Of course, the facilities offered varied with the routes of the stages and the abilities of the station tenders, so many a stop that once offered food continued to be referred to as a stage station long after its hospitable functions had ceased.

BEAVER CREEK CAMP
Pennington County
Center of E½, Section 28, T1N-R1E

One of the many hunters' camps in the Limestone Country, 2 or 3 miles east of the Wyoming border.

BEAVER SIDING
Meade County
NW¼, Section 6, T4N-R6E(?)

Beaver Siding, in 1896, was on the Fremont, Elkhorn & Missouri Valley Railroad (now the Chicago & North Western), between Tilford and Sturgis. It certainly was very close to, if not identical with, *Meyers Siding*. The location given above is the place where the railroad tracks cross Beaver Gulch.

BEECHER ROCK
Custer County
NW¼, Section 24, T4S-R4E

When the Black Hills were settled in 1876, newspapers were filled, week after week, with horrific details of the adultery trial of the famous New England minister and reformer, the Reverend Henry Ward Beecher. Although later acquitted, Beecher apparently was commemorated by naming these huge pinnacles in his honor. An early map refers to "Beecher's Pillar."

BELLE FOURCHE
Lawrence County
Sections 10, 11, & 14, T8N-R2E

This is a cattle town at the north end of the Hills, actually out on the prairie, but its justly celebrated "Black Hills Roundup," held during the Fourth of July holidays each year, certainly entitles it to a place among Black Hills towns.

BENCHMARK
Lawrence County
NE¼, Section 13, T3N-R4E

At the confluence of Hay and Boxelder Creeks, Benchmark had a depot, later used as a section house until torn down in 1930, and was served by the Black Hills & Fort Pierre narrow-gauge railroad as it ran from Englewood to Piedmont via Nemo. A summer cabin and a few ruins remain and can be easily seen 4½ miles northwest of Nemo on the gravel road leading to Roubaix.

An old ranch at Benchmark.

BENGAL TIGER MINE
Pennington County
NE¼, Section 13, T1S-R4E

This small but famous mine was noted for its tiger-striped ore, in which rusty quartz made orange stripes on glistening mica schist. It is often assumed that the mine gave its name to Tigerville, but as the two are several miles apart it is hard to see how this could be so.

BERNARDSVILLE
Lawrence County

In 1877 Bernardsville was a small mining community in Bear Gulch, to the west of Spearfish Canyon. At that time it claimed to have a population of some 1,500 miners. The town, which has totally disappeared, was named for Joseph Bernard.

Bear Gulch runs northward from the Tinton area for 10 miles or more about ½ mile east of the Wyoming line.

Benchmark, named for a geodetic survey point, was on the Black Hills & Fort Pierre Railroad.

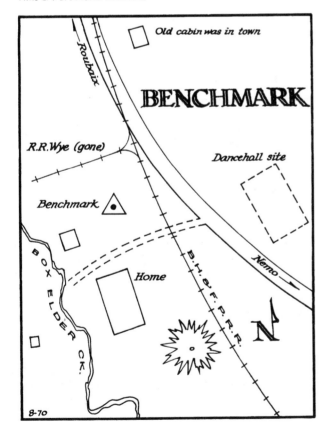

BERNE
Custer County
E½, Section 4, T3S-R4E

Berne is a siding on the Burlington, serving the Crazy Horse Monument and, recently, a wood pulp chipping plant. About a mile to the east is the Old Mike mine, in the NW¼, Section 2, T3S-R4E, which has been a famous producer of mica since the 1880s, contributing well over a million pounds of this rare mineral during World War II.

A couple of miles east of Berne Siding, high on the rocky cliffs, is the Old Mike mine which has produced mica for 90 years.

BESANT, BESANT FLATS, BESANT PARK
Lawrence County
Sections 27 & 28, T3N-R2E

A McLaughlin Company logging and wood-cutting camp, Besant was reached by a long standard-gauge spur running westward from Nahant, through Besant, and on to within a few miles of Moskee. It had two houses in 1916, and they seem to be there still.

BETHLEHEM CAVE
Meade County
SW¼, Section 22, T4N-R5E

This is the current name for *Crystal Cave*. The name was changed when a religious order took over the cave.

BEULAH
Crook County
NE¼, Section 31, T53N-R60W

Noted in its early days for its sawmills, Beulah later became famous for Moe Annenberg's celebrated summer home, "Ranch A," which was later operated as a summer resort and is now a fish hatchery.

A tremendous flume, often supported high on trestles, brought water from a dam near Pactola down Rapid Valley to a power-generating plant at Big Bend.

BIG BEND
Pennington County
Section 8, T1N-R6E

A small but active residential community on SD 40, the Rimrock Highway, Big Bend is 8 miles west of Rapid City. It once had a large electric generation station powered by water carried by a still-visible flume from near Pactola.

BIG BOTTOM
Meade County
Section 9, T7N-R5E

Well out of the Hills to the north, Big Bottom was founded in 1878 by Thomas D. Pryor, who built a two-story frame house and store and opened a dance hall and saloon that became notorious in the area. In 1880 a post office was established, and later a school was built. The railroad, however, bypassed Big Bottom, the store and saloon were closed in 1887, and now all that remains is the basement of the Pryor house.

BIG HORN LODE
Lawrence County
Adjacent to Lead

This town was listed in the Lawrence County deed book, with Lot Number One adjacent to Lead.

BIG SPRINGS RANCHE
Lawrence County

Collins' *Directory* describes it briefly as "midway between Rapid and Crook Cities—A. M. Morse, proprietor—saloon and hotel." If the town continued in existence it probably turned into either Tilford or Piedmont.

BION
Lawrence County
T4N-R4E

Bion was a mine stop on the narrow-gauge Deadwood Central Railway, somewhere between Galena Junction and Galena. The Bion mine was in the SW¼, Section 9, T4N-R4E, and operated around 1901 but does not seem to have been a producer.

BISMUTH
Custer County
NW¼, Section 27, T2S-R6E

Bismuth was a settlement of half a dozen houses north of Iron Creek. The USGS map for 1901 shows it about 1½ miles northwest of Spokane. It is on Iron Creek to the north of the present Iron Mountain Road, US 16A, about 5 miles southeast of Mount Rushmore; some ruins and a new, artificial lake mark the spot. The town once supported a store and a baseball team, but it is now part of a tourist campground.

Although a new community of summer camps and cabins is now growing up here, this old house is all that is left of the Bismuth of long ago.

BLACK FOX
Lawrence County
NW¼, Section 14, T2N-R2E

The Black Fox area today includes a public campground and a Forest Service summer home group.

BLACK GAP
Pennington County
NE¼, Section 8, T1S-R8E

Black Gap is a pass over the low, black, slaty hills, about a mile north of Spring Creek on SD 79; it was famous in early days for various robberies committed in the vicinity.

BLACKHAWK
Meade County
SE¼, Section 6, T2N-R7E

Blackhawk is a thriving little community with a population of 200, just north of Rapid City, on the Chicago & North Western Railroad tracks and US Interstate 90.

BLACK HILLS COUNTRY CLUB
Pennington County
NW¼, Section 4, T2S-R5E

The Black Hills Country Club was set up in 1925 by a group of Chicago men who built a golf course, several summer homes, and some rental cabins along Palmer Creek. The golf course was maintained until 1932, at which time Troy Parker, one of the founders, took over the operation and ran it as *Palmer Gulch Lodge.*

BLACK HILLS LIME COMPANY
Custer County
W½, Section 23, T5S-R4E

A steady lime producer southwest of Pringle, the Black Hills Lime Company sells most of its lime to the Homestake mine for water softening.

BLACK HILLS ORDNANCE DEPOT
Fall River County
T10S-R2E

See *Igloo.*

BLACK HILLS PLAYHOUSE
Custer County
NE¼, Section 8, T3S-R6E

This University of South Dakota drama department's playhouse was originally housed near Legion Lake in a wood-and-canvas structure reminiscent of the early days of the Gem in Deadwood. It soon moved to an abandoned Civilian Conservation Corps camp about ½ mile northwest of Center Lake; the department converted the end of one of the barracks into a stage and presented everything from Ibsen to *The Importance of Being Earnest* to summer audiences. More recently a splendid wooden auditorium was built to house their activities, but you can still identify those who used to attend in the early days: they bring blankets with them, just for old time's sake. A notable production, given weekly during the summers, is *The Legend of Devil's Gulch*, a drama laid in gold rush Deadwood.

BLACKTAIL
Lawrence County
N½, Section 28, T5N-R3E

An early mining camp between Central City and Gayville, just about where Blacktail Gulch joins Bobtail Gulch.

Part of the Homestake mine's milling operations at Blacktail, near Central City and Deadwood.

BLUE BELL LODGE
Custer County
E½, Section 11, T4S-R5E

Named for the Bell Telephone Company, rather than the flower, this resort was built in the 1920s by a Mr. Eisentraut, and now has a gas station, store, and several summer homes in its vicinity.

BLUEVALE
Pennington County
T2N-R6E

Cram's Unrivaled Atlas of the World shows Bluevale northwest of Rapid City, but it is hard to determine where in relation to anything else. Population in 1890 was just 18.

BOBTAIL GULCH
Lawrence County
SW¼, Section 28, T5N-R3E

This was the gulch along which *Terraville* grew up; early maps show it nearly solidly packed with mills and houses.

BOUGHTON
Lawrence County
T4N-R3E(?)

An old map shows Boughton as southwest of Deadwood, on the east side of the Fort Pierre Railroad, and southwest of Pennington.

BOULDER, BOULDER PARK
Lawrence County
Section 14, T5N-R4E

Although shown on some early maps, Boulder showed no population in the 1890 census. It would be about 4½ miles southwest of Sturgis.

BOX ELDER
Pennington County
Between Sections 19 & 20, T2N-R9E

Box Elder, on the Chicago & North Western Railroad, was for many years merely a store and post office a few miles east of Rapid City. With the building of the Ellsworth Air Force Base to the north of the town, the community has become larger and more prosperous.

The town of Box Elder and some places in the Hills incorporating that name are spelled with two words, whereas the spelling of Boxelder Creek and its branches collapses Boxelder into one word.

BOYD
Weston County
SW¼, Section 6, T47N-R60W

On the maps Boyd seems to be not so much a town as a scattered group of farms, well supplied with roads, but off in the western foothills.

BRAINERD INDIAN TRAINING SCHOOL
Fall River County
NE¼, Section 19, T8S-R5E

This is a flourishing establishment, with nine or ten buildings, on a branch of Cascade Creek that leads northward toward Payne and Lindsley Canyons, to the northwest of the ghost town of Cascade.

BRASHVILLE
Lawrence County

John Brasch was installed as postmaster of Brashville, so spelled, on February 2, 1881, but the post office was discontinued in June of the following year.

BRENNAN
Pennington County
SE¼, Section 35, T1N-R8E

Brennan was named for John R. Brennan, an early settler, an Indian Agent, and one of the founders of Rapid City. Brennan does not seem to have ever been more than a house or two. About 1940 it was renamed *Warbonnet*; it has also been known as *Siding Eleven*. It is about 7 miles southeast of Rapid City, on the Chicago & North Western Railroad.

BRIDGEPORT
Custer County
T3S-R7E(?)

A map of 1891 shows Bridgeport to the east and south of Custer, more than likely along the Chicago & North Western Railroad, but that is the only knowledge of it which has so far come to light, save that the same atlas which contained the map also indicated a post office—but no population.

BROUGHTON
Lawrence County
NW Corner, T4N-R3E

Broughton was about 6 miles south of Lead, on the railroad from Central City to Brownsville. In 1891 it had a population of 151. Eusebe C. Volin was its first postmaster, in 1880, but the post office was discontinued in October of 1882. Broughton is probably the same as *Boughton*, but since there were notable men of both names in the Hills it is hard to be sure.

BROWNSVILLE
Lawrence County
SW¼, Section 30, T4N-R4E

Brownsville was an early Homestake lumber camp, run to supply timbers for the mine, lumber for the buildings, and fuel for the boilers. It was named for David Brown, the contractor who for many years supplied much of the logging equipment and supervision. As early as 1880 some 400 men were employed at Brownsville, and this number probably increased when the narrow-gauge Black Hills & Fort Pierre Railroad came in. In 1883 a disastrous fire destroyed the Hood & Scott sawmill half a mile northeast of town and killed eleven of the men employed in it.

Today, Brownsville is a gas station, store, and tavern on the west side of US 385, about 6½ miles south of Pluma. Other names of the town were *Avalon* and, more recently, *Esther's Place* and *Anderson's Place*.

A cabin in Brownsville, with US Highway 385 in the background. You do not have to go far from the beaten paths to find the relics of the past.

Deserted home at Brownsville.

BUCHHOLZ
Lawrence County
SE¼, Section 11, T2N-R3E

Although Buchholz was probably only a ranch, an 1883 map showed it as a town on the South Fork of Rapid Creek, about 7 miles west of Rochford, about where Black Fox Camp Ground is now.

BUCKHORN
Weston County
SW¼, Section 8, T48N-R60W

The current Forest Service map shows a single house, in a loop of US 85, about where that highway crosses Cold Springs Creek. The early USGS maps show nothing. In 1880, however, Buckhorn had a post office, served by a semi-weekly buckboard coming eastward from Raw Hide Buttes.

BUCKINGHAM
Custer County
NE¼, Section 25, T2S-R8E

See *Fort Buckingham.*

BUCKS
Lawrence County
NW¼, Section 27, T4N-R4E

Bucks was an important junction on the Black Hills & Fort Pierre Railroad, though it does not appear to have had much population or many houses. In 1882 this line was built by the Homestake as far as Bucks, mainly for fuel and lumber, and in 1890 it was extended 22 miles eastward to connect with the newly arrived Fremont, Elkhorn & Missouri Valley Railroad at Piedmont. In 1898 the Black Hills & Fort Pierre extended southward from Bucks to Este, with a spur to the wood camp at Merritt. When the northern branch of the line washed out in 1907, this southern branch was extended from Este through Stagebarn Canyon to Piedmont, where it insured a good connection for hauling lime and heavy equipment into Lead.

The old railroad grade may now be passable to a jeep, since it was often used as a road when the tracks were taken up; ways were found, somehow, around any missing bridges or filled in cuts.

An excellent account of railroading in this area is found in Mildred Fielder's "Railroads of the Black Hills," *South Dakota Historical Collections,* Volume XXX (1960), pages 35-316; much of this is incorporated into her 1964 book of the same title.

At Bucks, the Fremont, Elkhorn & Missouri Valley Railroad divided as it came from Englewood, the northern branch going to Piedmont and the southern to Merritt. This embankment was the foundation of a trestle that carried the line across Elk Creek.

Potential grindstones piled up at the Buena Vista sandstone quarry at the mouth of Red Canyon north of Edgemont.

BUENA VISTA
Fall River County
SW¼, Section 17, T8S-R3E

A comparison of various references indicates that Buena Vista was probably the location of the Edgemont Quarry, which produced sandstone for buildings in Edgemont and Cascade and produced several thousand high-quality grindstones. In 1902 there were half-a-dozen buildings, reached by half-a-mile of railroad spur leading northwest from a point on the Burlington about 3 miles from Edgemont.

Buena Vista is now clearly marked on current Forest Service maps as being in Stone Quarry Canyon, on a dirt road, 3½ miles northeast of Edgemont.

BUENA VISTE
Lawrence County

An early town located on the north side of the old toll road between Deadwood and Central City.

BUFFALO GAP
Custer County
Sections 29 & 32, T6S-R7E

Buffalo Gap, named for the nearby gap through which Beaver Creek flows and through which the buffalo moved into the Hills, has always been a cattle town. In its early days it had, according to one report, 48 saloons—and other places of entertainment on a scale to match. In nearby Calico Canyon is a natural bridge and the quarry which produced the celebrated calico sandstone of variegated and brilliant colors. Present population of Buffalo Gap is 155.

An interesting account of early days in the area is Baron E. de Mandat-Grancey's *La Breche aux Buffles*, which tells of this Frenchman's experiences in the 1880s on a nearby horse ranch. (Another book by the baron, *Dans les Montagnes Rocheuses*, has been translated into English as *Cow-Boys and Colonels*, but it does not deal as specifically with this area.)

A hotel by the Chicago & North Western tracks in Buffalo Gap.

A small, tidy, abandoned store in Buffalo Gap.

There never was a wilder cattle town than Buffalo Gap in its early days. This was one of the hotels.

BUGTOWN

Custer County
SE¼, Section 12, T3S-R3E

Bugtown was an early mining camp northwest of Custer and was so named because the logs of which the miners' cabins were built were heavily infested with bugs. It was deserted by the 1880s, but in its memory the gulch in which it was situated is still called Bugtown Gulch. The foot of the gulch is about 4 miles west of US 16, on the gravel road leading toward Zimbleman Deer Camp.

BULLDOG, BULLDOG RANCH I

Lawrence County
NW¼, Section 21, T3N-R3E

The Bulldog Ranch, run by a Mrs. Bulldog, was a famous old stage station on the Custer-Deadwood line. It has figured in Black Hills history as a ranch, inn, bootlegger's depot, and place of entertainment generally. All that remains now is a large, respectable white house and several outbuildings west of the Burlington tracks, 6½ miles north of Rochford.

BULLDOG RANCH II

Meade County
T5N-R6E(?)

There seem to have been at least two Bulldog Ranches: the one north of Rochford and Nahant named for the Bulldogs (human) and another about 8 miles from the foothills east of Sturgis named for the bulldogs (canine). At the latter location a lady weighing in at one eighth of a ton maintained two bulldogs to keep passing freighters from stealing her chickens. The ranch had achieved a good deal of notoriety—type unspecified—during the early days of the gold rush, says Dr. Nelson Armstrong in his *Nuggets of Experience* (1906), and retained its title even after the notorious activity diminished. It is remotely possible that the present-day community of Bear Butte, at the corner of Sections 17-18-19-20, T6N-R7E on South Dakota highway 34, might be the old ranch, but that would put the good Dr. Armstrong a bit north of the direct trail he was following toward Fort Meade, Scooptown, and Sturgis.

BULL SPRINGS

Custer County
Section 34, T2S-R2E

P. S. Rydberg's *Flora of the Black Hills* mentions this spot, either as a town or possibly as one of the places at which he camped; or it may have been a transient groggery of some sort, now long abandoned and forgotten.

BURDOCK

Fall River County
SW¼, Section 10, T7S-R1E

Burdock, the current name of *Argentine*, is at the western edge of the Hills, on the CB&Q. At its peak it had a school, post office, three or four dwellings, and a combination store and gas station. One gets the impression that maybe the young folks held out there as long as grandma in her little cabin looking toward the mountains lived, but when she died, they folded up the store and headed for civilization.

A tiny cabin, with its porch facing eastward toward the hills and pines.

The Bulldog Ranch, between Rochford and Lead, was a famous place of refreshment and entertainment on the stage route from Custer to Deadwood. It should not be confused with a ranch of the same name and reputation east of Sturgis.

A school, a couple of houses, and a combination gas station, store, and grocery building are all that there ever was to Burdock, and even these stand empty nowadays.

BURKE'S SIDING

Fall River County
Section 15, T7S-R6E

This siding on the Chicago & North Western, about 5 miles due east of Hot Springs, served the Burke Quarry. Large quantities of Dakota sandstone were shipped. Among the buildings built of Burke stone were the Omaha Public Library; the Fort Dodge, Iowa Public Library; The First National Bank in Lead; the railroad station and Franklin Hotel in Deadwood; and public buildings in Sheridan, Wyoming and Lincoln, Nebraska. In 1903 and 1904 alone this quarry shipped 1,100 carloads of sawed stone. Discovered in 1893 by Henry Bering, who also owned the Evans Quarry, it operated until the Second World War.

BURLINGTON JUNCTION

Pennington County
SE¼, Section 34, T2N-R4E

One mile north of Mystic, this was the junction of the Black Hills & Western from Rapid City and the Chicago, Burlington & Quincy from Edgemont to Deadwood. It was also known as *Canyon Junction*. There does not seem to have been much of a settlement at the junction itself. The Black Hills & Western tracks were taken out in 1947.

When the big wind blows on the plains to the west of the Black Hills, folks say it comes all the way from the North Pole with only a barbed wire fence to hold it back — and, as at Burdock, that fence has a hole in it.

The Burdock store, against a backdrop of Black Hills and clouds, gives some idea of the vastness and emptiness that faced the pioneers when they tried to make the Great Plains blossom like the rose.

BURNT RANCH

Pennington County
SW¼, Section 4, T1S-R6E

The old mining area of Burnt Ranch is about 2 miles east of Sheridan Lake on old SD 40. This was the spot, described in detail in Lee Case's *Guidebook to the Black Hills,* where a miner, Norman McCully, was murdered by a deserting soldier who stole his $3,000 poke of gold. Sent to prison and put to work in the prison sawmill, he was chided by one of the other prisoners about the murder; the irate murderer shoved his fellow prisoner into a buzz-saw and "parted his hair clear down to his belly-button." The soldier was immediately hanged from the rafters.

BUTTE HALL

Butte County
SE¼, Section 15, T8N-R5E

In 1913 Butte Hall consisted of two houses on a dim road a mile or so south of the Belle Fourche River, some 5 miles east of Newell.

Old bones bleach beside a cabin in Clifton.

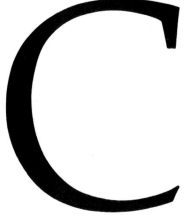

CALCITE
Meade County
SW¼, Section 30, T4N-R6E

Calcite, also known as the *Quarry*, was near the east end of the Black Hills & Fort Pierre Railroad, about 4 miles northwest of Piedmont. It was the site of the Homestake Limestone Quarry which from 1904 to 1931 produced some 70,000 tons of lime to neutralize Homestake ores for cyanidation and to soften water for the Homestake boilers. It was this supply of lime for the mills at Lead which led to the BH&FtP being extended eastward from Bucks to Calcite and on to Piedmont, in 1890, and to its being rebuilt, after washing out in 1907, from Este via Stagebarn Canyon.

In 1933 a Veterans' CCC camp was established near the remains of the old lime plant, but this, too, has long since been dismantled. All that remains of Calcite is a series of stone and concrete mill foundations, a marker commemorating the CCC camp, a huge pile of Birely's soft drink bottles, and the trace of the old spur which led to the mill, kilns, and quarry.

Grinding mill and kiln foundations of the Homestake Mining Company's lime operation at Calcite.

CAMBRIA
Weston County
Section 29, T46N-R61W

Cambria was a coal mining town, built to supply high-grade anthracite to the western lines of the Chicago, Burlington & Quincy. The deposits were discovered in Coal Creek Canyon in 1887 by Frank Mondell, and a spur railroad was built northward to them from Newcastle.

The building of the town and operation of the mines were handled by the railroad contractors Kilpatrick Brothers & Collins, who drilled a 2,345-foot well, built a reservoir, then constructed more than 150 miners' homes both in the valley and on its western edge. They also built two churches, a school, a lodge hall for the Odd Fellows and Knights of Pythias, a three-story hotel, a miners' recreation hall, a bank, a courthouse, and company offices. Their big commissary store attracted shoppers from all over the Hills, while their opera house once put on a sold-out performance of *Faust*.

On December 4, 1889 they were ready for business. Half a dozen mines worked on both sides of the valley, hauling coal over long trestles to bins over the tracks in its center. Seventy-four beehive ovens burned waste coal into coke for the smelters of the northern Hills—and the coke itself ran up to $5.60 a ton in gold.

Cambria, with the principal coal mine in the background. When the mines were in operation, the entire valley was filled with railroad lines, some on the ground and some overhead on trestles, to haul away the coal.

A miner's cabin up against the east side of the canyon, in Cambria. When Parker visited the town in the early 1930s, the pots still stood on the stoves and the dishes and silverware were still on some of the miners' tables.

A miner's cabin, with the steeple of a Cambria church near it in the foreground.

A false-fronted store in downtown Cambria. The false fronts made a building more impressive and provided a ready-made signboard for advertising the business underneath.

The company brought in contract labor from Greece, Macedonia, Sicily, and Slovenia, paying the miners' passages over and outfitting them when they arrived. By 1904 the mine employed 550 men, and the town had a population of about 1,400. Many are still there, beneath ornate tombstones in the cemetery northeast of town. Some, especially children, died of disease; some were killed in the mines; but others, including one Giacchino, a saloon keeper, and his driver Pete Nora, were killed in bootlegging brawls, for the company attempted to prohibit the importation of any liquor stronger than beer.

Stables for the mules that worked in the Cambria mines.

The scale house, where the carloads of anthracite were weighed on their way to the coke ovens or to the Burlington engines.

By 1928 the coal vein had pinched down to less than three feet and the company announced that if new deposits didn't appear the mine would have to be closed. The miners didn't believe it, and when on the final day they heard the noon whistle blow the traditional disaster warning—a series of short blasts—a kind of panic seemed to come over the town. Without bothering to pack, miners rushed off to get first chance at any jobs available nearby. Others left for a vacation, sure that the mine would soon reopen. By evening even clerks and storekeepers had left. The town was so instantly deserted that the sprinkler on the courthouse lawn was left running and is said to have run until the reservoir went dry. The mine never opened again, and as late as the 1930s cards still lay on the green-topped tables in the poolhall, and account books lay open on the desks in the bank, while frayed washing flapped on clotheslines behind the little houses and pots stood on the stoves inside. After a while the Burlington took up its tracks, but the town was not thoroughly dismantled until World War II.

Nearby the company had built an ornate stone museum and an officers' recreation hall which had both a cold fresh-water swimming pool and a hot salt-water one. Now known as the Flying V Ranch, on US 85, it has been used as a resort for years.

Salt had been produced in the area for a long time, mainly for chlorination of the northern Hills gold ores. As early as 1878 James LeGraves had a 6x60 salt pan working on Salt Creek. The places where his wagons stopped on their way to Deadwood—Canyon Springs, Bulldog, Brownsville—became famous as salt licks for the deer. The salt was impure, however, and his efforts were abandoned along with the chlorination process. In 1907 the Cambria Salt Company was organized but after three or four years it too failed.

There are many houses still left in Cambria. The mine superintendent's home, a false-front or two, the stable for the mine mules, several mine buildings, vaults of bank and offices, a steeple from a church, garages, and cold cellars are still there. The 600 steps still lead up to the western rim of the valley where the school and residential section were. If you climb up and look back into the valley, the trees will show you the pattern of streets and houses, and the buildings that are left will indicate something of what was there before. If you listen you can hear the echoes of a past that never dies.

Looking northward toward the town of Cambria, with the beehive ovens that produced gold-bearing coke visible on the left, above the banks of Cambria Creek.

The Commissary, dating back to the 1870s, is the oldest building at Fort Meade.

CAMPS

The large number and variety of Black Hills Camps—military, logging, mining, railroad, deer hunters', CCC, church, and Scout, to name a few —make it impossible to list them all or to do more than mention a few of permanent or historical interest.

CAMP BRADLEY
Crook County

Camp Bradley was Professor Walter P. Jenney's fourth base camp when he explored the Black Hills; it was located about August 21, 1875, and from it his subordinate, Lt. Coale, explored the Bear Lodge Mountains. It was on Inyan Kara Creek, "near the base of Inyan Kara" mountain, but as the creek goes around the mountain in a huge semicircle this does not narrow down the camp's location very much. It is conceivable that Camp Bradley might be roughly the same as the town of Inyan Kara.

CAMP COLLIER
Fall River County
Section 20, T8S-R3E

Another name for *Red Canyon Station.*

CAMP COLLINS
Lawrence County
Sections 23, 24, 25, & 26, T3S-R4E

Camp Collins appears to be the name given to the Army post established at Custer during the summer of 1875, under the command of Captain Edwin Pollock. It is, therefore, another name for *Custer* itself, and not a mistaken spelling for Camp Collier far to the south in Red Canyon.

CAMP COLUMBUS
Pennington County
NW¼, Section 17, T2N-R6E

A Catholic summer camp on Boxelder Creek, named for the Knights of Columbus.

CAMP CROOK I
Pennington County
NW¼, Section 2, T1N-R5E

An early name of *Pactola.*

CAMP CROOK II
Lawrence County
NE¼, Section 33, T6N-R4E

An early name for *Crook* or *Crook City.*

CAMP CUSTER
Custer County
NW¼, Section 12, T3S-R3E

This was a Civilian Conservation Corps camp just east of Zimbleman Deer Camp; the original sign, many foundations, a pond, and two summer homes south of the road remain.

CAMP D
Crook County
SE¼, Section 14, T49N-R61W

Another name for *Commissary D*, end of the McLaughlin Tie & Timber Company's logging railroad near Moskee.

CAMP ESTE
Lawrence County
NE¼, Section 3, T2N-R5E

A Boy Scout Camp two miles south of Nemo. Earlier, it had been the Este Civilian Conservation Corps camp, and before that the Este Lumber Camp on the site of the famous Forest Service "Case One," the earliest attempt at federally managed forest utilization.

CAMP FIFTEEN
Pennington County
Center of Section 2, T1S-R5E

A Warren-Lamb Lumber Company logging camp, at the end of the Spring Creek narrow-gauge line. It was above Sheridan, near *Wheel Inn.*

CAMP GALENA
Custer County
SW¼, Section 22, T3S-R6E

A Warren-Lamb Lumber Company logging camp, later a summer resort.

CAMP GORMAN
Pennington County
S½, Section 31, T2N-R5E

Camp Gorman was an early name for *Silver City.*

CAMP HARNEY
Custer County
SW¼, Section 21, T3S-R5E

Camp Harney was the military camp on the site of the *Gordon Stockade.* It was here that Captain Edwin Pollock, in the fall of 1875, assumed command of the troops sent into the Hills to keep the miners out. His efforts were so forceful and so successful that the miners called him "the devil in disguise," and he became so unpopular that he later refused to serve in the Hills for fear old acquaintances would shoot him. Camp Harney is not the same as Harney or Harney Camp.

CAMP HASSELRODT

A Civilian Conservation Corps camp established May 20, 1933.

CAMP HORSE CREEK

Probably better known by the more euphonious title *Horse Creek Camp*; a Civilian Conservation Corps camp established May 20, 1933.

CAMP IVANHOE

Custer County
SW¼, Section 18, T3S-R6E

A less common name for *Ivanhoe*, which was also known as *Yamboya*.

CAMP JENNEY

Weston County
NW¼, Section 7, T44N-R60W

This is the original but less widely used name of the *Jenney Stockade*.

CAMP JENNINGS

Fall River County
Section 20, T8S-R3E

Mrs. Jim Bell, who owned *Camp Collier*, or *Red Canyon Station*, insisted that the name of the fort was Camp Jennings, and that this was *not* a confusion with Camp Jenny near Newcastle, but no other source mentions this name.

CAMP JUDSON

Pennington County
SE¼, Section 1, T2S-R5E

On the site of *Pine Camp*, Camp Judson is a Baptist summer camp 2 miles west of Keystone on the old Hill City-Keystone gravel road.

The Baptists's summer Camp Judson now occupies the site of Chris Overgard's sawmill at Pine Camp.

CAMP McMASTERS

Custer County
T3S-R6E

This seems to have been very near the Game Lodge but has since vanished from the maps.

CAMP NARROWS

Custer County
In Custer State Park

A CCC camp, presumably in the narrows on French Creek.

CAMP ONE

Pennington County
NE¼, Section 13, T1N-R6E

This camp, south of the Crouch Line leading up Rapid Canyon from Rapid City, was set up by the Warren-Lamb Lumber Company as the base of operations for its logging into Spring Creek. As the little engines used could negotiate a 12% grade, it is sometimes hard to tell the road beds from ordinary wagon roads, but old ties and the few cuts remaining will usually point out the difference.

CAMP PAHA SAPA

Lawrence County
SW¼, Section 21, T3N-R5E

A Boy Scout Camp west of Nemo.

CAMP PROSPECT

Pennington County
SE¼, Section 34, T2N-R4E

Camp Prospect, or *Prospect Camp*, was one of the earliest placer camps in the Hills and was located at the confluence of Castle and Rapid Creeks, a mile or so below Mystic, in the area also known as *Burlington* or *Canyon Junction*. Nearby is the Volin Tunnel, dug in the late 1870s to drain about a mile of Rapid Creek so the placer deposits in the creek bed could be worked for gold.

CAMP RED CANYON

Fall River County
Section 20, T8S-R3E

R. A. Murray, in his article "The Camp at the Mouth of Red Canyon" in the *Periodical* of the Council on Abandoned Military Posts (January 1967), says that the official name of *Camp Collier* was as given in his title.

CAMP REMINGTON

Custer County
On southern end of line between
Section 36, T2S-R5E and Section 31, T2S-R6E

Camp Remington is now an Episcopal Church summer camp on Iron Creek, about a mile north of SD 87, the Needles Highway. An extremely unreliable road leads from Camp Remington to the Iron Mountain Road eastward or to Horsethief Lake on the northwest.

CAMP REYNOLDS
Meade County
Near Common Corner of
Sections 3, 4, 8 & 9, T6N-R8E

The 1876 War Department *Map of the Yellowstone and Missouri Rivers* shows a label "Camp Reynolds," but no exact spot is given. Presumably this was Captain W. F. Raynolds's camp when he passed by in 1859. The camp is mistakenly on the map as "Reynolds," but the captain spelled his name with an "a."

CAMP RUHLEN
Meade County
SE¼, Section 12, T5N-R5E

An early name for *Fort Meade*. The Ruhlen family is still active in the Army, presently represented by at least one general and a lieutenant-colonel.

CAMP SUCCESS
Custer County
Between Sections 3 & 10, T4S-R6E

Camp Success, so named because of the "success" of the expedition, was the base camp on French Creek from which Captain John Mix and troops of the 2nd Cavalry removed the Gordon Party from the stockade 8 miles away, on April 10, 1875. It had earlier been used as a base camp by the expedition of the Reverend S. D. Hinman, who had been sent to the Hills with a military escort during August of 1874 to find a site for an Indian agency. Hinman and the far more famous Custer expedition missed meeting by about two weeks. Hinman's report on the Black Hills was pessimistic: "high, bleak and cold, traversed by fearful storms in winter and spring, and in summertime almost truly said by the Indians to be inhabited by the thunder gods, ever angry and jealous."

CAMP STURGIS
Meade County

Camp Sturgis was on Spring Creek a little to the north of Bear Butte; it was established as a temporary army post in August 1876 and named for Lt. J. G. "Jack" Sturgis who was killed at the Little Big Horn. It is not the same as the town of Sturgis.

CAMP TEN
Custer County
Center of Section 15(?), T3S-R6E

Camp Ten was part of the Warren-Lamb Lumber Company's logging operations in what is now Custer State Park. The company, using Fairburn as a base of operations, ran a narrow-gauge railroad to the site occupied today by Coolidge Inn. One branch of the line continued up Squaw Creek (now Grace Coolidge Creek) to the present-day Center Lake and Black Hills Playhouse area and the other went up over the divide into Bear Gulch, where it branched several times to reach the various cutting areas. The ruins of the engine house and the ashpit can still be seen beside the right-of-way in lower Bear Gulch. The cars and engines were hauled over the divide by a compensated hoist that cleverly augmented a winch at the top by using the weight of descending cars on the other side. The incline coming up out of the logging area in Bear Gulch was 34%; going down into Squaw Creek valley it was 26%. The roadbed is now heavily overgrown with jackpine but can still be followed easily by a determined hiker.

CAMP TERRY
Meade County

This was Professor Walter P. Jenney's third base camp, set up in mid-August 1875, on the south fork of Bear Creek, in the general vicinity of Bear Butte.

CAMP TUTTLE
Pennington County
Section 3 or 4(?), T1N-R1E

Camp Tuttle was a spot where Professor Walter P. Jenney's expedition paused to prospect in 1875. He described it as being in Spring Creek valley, 1,400 feet east of the 104th meridian; however, the Creek now called Spring Creek does not seem to run so far west, so the description given above is pretty much guesswork.

CAMP WARREN

Camp Warren was said to be north of Rapid City on the Deadwood Stage route, north of the standard parallel, and south of Boxelder Creek— a description which simply does not make sense.

CAMP ZIMBLEMAN
Custer County
NE¼, Section 11, T3S-R3E

See *Zimbleman Deer Camp*.

Officers' quarters at Fort Meade, first known as Camp Ruhlen when it was established in 1878 to guard the northern Hills.

An abandoned farm house at Addie Camp, seen through a bunch of shrubbery and a towering gate post.

CANADAVILLE
Pennington County
NE¼, Section 33, T1S-R5E

This is the name by which *Addie Camp* appears on the USGS maps. It was a corruption of *Kennedyville,* Kennedy being a corruption of Canaday, the name of the keeper of the Addie Camp saloon.

CANYON CITY
Pennington County
SW¼, Section 35, T2N-R4E

Canyon City is two miles east of Mystic on Rapid Creek, along the abandoned roadbed of the old Black Hills & Western. In early placer mining days it was a booming camp with a population of about 400, but all that remains today is a smokestack and an abandoned summer cabin or two. In the area is the Volin Tunnel, dug to divert Rapid Creek from placer deposits thought to lie in its bed but since filled in by the Fish and Game Department. The Canyon City area can be reached from the north by a trail that leads down Kelly Gulch from the Gimlet Creek road.

Fording Rapid Creek at Canyon City.

Ruins of a mine or mill, on the north side of Rapid Creek at Canyon City.

61

CANYON JUNCTION
Pennington County
SE¼, Section 34, T2N-R4E

Another name for *Burlington Junction*, near Mystic.

CANYON LAKE
Pennington County
SW¼, Section 9, T1N-R7E

A stop on the Black Hills & Western, near Rapid City.

CANYON SPRINGS
Weston County
Section 3 or 4, T48N-R60W

Canyon Springs was a stagecoach relay station, with a log barn and attached tender's quarters, about 20 miles north of the Jenney Stockade and somewhere east of Four Corners. On September 28, 1878 a gang of five or six overpowered the tender, William Miner, and ambushed the stage with its load of some $100,000 of Homestake gold. Their first shots mortally wounded a guard, Gail Hill, but before he died he and his two companions had killed two of the robbers and so severely wounded a third that he died while escaping. A second guard, Scott Davis, brought help after the battle, but the robbers got away, and only two bars of the gold, one dropped, and the other found on display in Atlantic, Iowa, were ever recovered. The location of the rest of the gold has been a subject of lively discussion ever since.

CAPTAIN JACK'S DRY DIGGINS
Pennington County
Sections 13 & 14, T1S-R6E

This was the first name for *Rockerville*, named originally, obviously enough, for one Captain Jack, possibly Captain Jack Crawford, the Poet Scout. The placers here were thick and gummy with clay and lacked sufficient water to be worked. It was this need to economize on water which led the miners to work these deposits with rockers, and to re-use the water once the mud had settled out of it; this in time led to the name Rockerville.

This log house in Rockerville may date back to the days when the town was called Captain Jack's Dry Diggings and the miners used rockers to conserve their meager water supply.

CARBONATE
Lawrence County
SW¼, Section 10, T5N-R2E

Carbonate began around 1881 when James Ridpath moved into the area and set out the apple orchards which are still there. When he staked out his silver mine, the West Virginia, the town began to amount to something. Originally it was called *West Virginia*, after the mine, later *Virginia*, then, in reference to its carbonate ores, *Carbonate Camp*, and finally Carbonate. In its boom days the area was reputed to have several thousand inhabitants. There were stores, a big hotel, boarding houses feeding a hundred men at a sitting, a bank, a post office, and several places of low entertainment, including several saloons and gambling halls and Fannie Hill's and Lottie Belmont's establishments. A sober element, however, was not lacking, for Estelline Bennett writes of having gone over to Carbonate Camp to go to church.

The most celebrated of the Carbonate mines was the Iron Hill, which was worked as late as the 1930s. A single house and the headframe are all that remain of it, but between 1885 and 1891 the Iron Hill produced $667,000 worth of silver, gold, and lead. When the dump was reworked around 1901 an additional 18,511 ounces of silver and 91 tons of lead were recovered. The underground workings of the Iron Hill can still be entered through a 1,300-foot drainage tunnel driven southwest from the 300-foot level to a branch of Squaw Creek.

The Seabury-Calkins, or "Seabury-Coffin," was next to the Iron Hill in fame and location. It got its nickname from the fact that its miners had dug into Iron Hill ore and been driven out with curses and made to board up their tunnel. Later, however, a disastrous fire in the Iron Hill made it necessary for the miners to avoid their coffins by escaping through the Seabury-Calkins shaft.

The Pocahontas mine was said to have ore in it running $900 to the ton; that would be 50-60 pounds of silver in a chunk of ore about the size of a tea table. The miners' primitive arrastra, however, could not get out anything like that amount of silver, and it is likely that the $900-to-the-ton assay was merely the result of judicious selection of samples rather than representative of the real quality of the ore. But there were mineral values in the area. In 1886 Dave Thompson was able to hack a bar of pure silver out of a deposit on the 165-foot level of the Union Hill. The Spanish R dug out $50,000 before it closed in 1904. The Richmond Hill, Segregated Iron Hill, and Adelphi were all producers. The Black Nell, discovered by Billy Nugent, took its fame not from its wealth but from the fact that everybody knew it was named for the dusky proprietress of a Deadwood place of entertainment.

Although these cabins, running westward from Strawberry Brown's log cabin, are usually supposed to have been "Carbonate," the main town was to the northeast, where all that remains is a sloping, open meadow surrounded by foundations.

Details of the machinery and stairways in the Cleopatra mill near Carbonate.

Curious perforated boards, apparently used in reclaiming values from the tailings of the smelter at Carbonate.

The Cleopatra mill extends from the top to the bottom of the valley of Squaw Creek (now Coolidge Creek), west of Carbonate.

Mortise and tenon construction held together a mill for processing the carbonate silver ores, downstream from the smelter at Carbonate.

In 1885 the Iron Hill struck galena ores—lead sulphide with a good mixture of silver—and began to make money. In 1887 a smelter was built in Rubicon Gulch to the east of Carbonate. The slag, rounded from the crucibles, is still there. Farther down the gulch are ruins of further recovery attempts and the wreck of an old boarding house.

By 1891 the town was about played out. Silver prices had declined. The fumes from the smelter, which used a pyrite flux that was rich in arsenic, killed all the cats in town, and probably predisposed the people to respiratory diseases. At any rate an epidemic of diptheria struck in 1889, and as late as 1910 the signs "Keep out—Black Diptheria!" could be seen on abandoned houses. In 1900 the Hugginson Hotel was torn down to supply timbers for the nearby Cleopatra mill. Some attempts to work the tailings were made about 1910, and the Iron Hill was looked into in the 1930s. In 1939 old Raspberry Brown, the last inhabitant, died.

An excellent account of Carbonate is "Carbonate Camp," by Mildred Fielder, *South Dakota Historical Collections*, Volume XXVIII (1956), pages 99-178.

The best way to reach Carbonate in an ordinary car is to start at Maitland and go west for about 4 miles. For the adventurous, a fire trail leads northward from Trojan, and gets to Carbonate in 5 miles. A third way, possible only in a jeep, is to come up out of Spearfish Canyon from Maurice. The houses in Carbonate are widely scattered, and you will have to hunt for them. The Iron Hill mine was on the highest point, and about ¼ mile north of it are three concentrations of ruins—one on top of the hill, another a little south and downhill from it. The main town, however, encircled an open meadow to the north, and only its foundations now remain.

The house with the Indianhead muslin walls, below the smelter, at Carbonate.

Cloth, instead of wallboard, formed the interior walls of a house downstream from the Carbonate smelter. Some of the pieces of cloth still bear the "Indianhead" trademark.

The mill downstream from the smelter at Carbonate.

CARIBOO
Lawrence County
SE¼, Section 4, T4N-R4E

Cariboo was the name for that part of *Galena* extending from Mrs. Borsch's garden to the mouth of Butcher Gulch, says the *Wi-Iyohi* (November 1950). The area was also known as *Griggs*.

CARTER CITY
Lawrence County

Also known as *North Galena*, Carter City is mentioned in the Lawrence County deed records.

CARTERSVILLE
Lawrence County
Section 4, T4N-R3E

Cartersville, in 1879, had twenty cabins and a restaurant, and was near the Caledonia, Carter, and Lincoln mines on Elk Creek. The Caledonia was later absorbed into the Homestake operations, which would indicate that Cartersville, also known as *Lincoln*, was somewhere near the Homestake, the location of which is given above.

CARTERVILLE
Lawrence County
Section 3, T2N-R3E

The general area of Carterville, 2 miles northwest of Rochford along the Burlington tracks was also known variously as *Elkhorn (I)*, *Gregory*, and *Montana City*. The name Carterville apparently came from a Carter mine (not listed in the *Black Hills Mineral Atlas*) in that region, but obviously not the same as the Carter mine at Cartersville far to the north near the Homestake mine at Lead. Many names, some of them duplicates of the names of other communities in the Hills, have been applied to the Gregory area and are a fertile source of confusion in the Black Hills nomenclature.

CARTHAGE
Lawrence County
Section 6 or 7, T4N-R3E

Carthage, in the Ruby Basin District, was a mile or two north of Aztec, and was served by a spur of the Deadwood Central Railroad. The entire area in Ruby Basin was full of mines and railroads, in an almost unfathomable tangle. Carthage seems to have been the southernmost point of the Whitewood Junction branch of the DCRR, reached from a spur leading straight south from Carthage Junction.

CARWYE

Meade County
SE¼, Section 18, T3N-R6E

Carwye was a railroad and lumbering town
on the Black Hills & Fort Pierre. It is said to have
been so named because it was at the end of the
line, and a "Y" was installed to turn the trains
around. *South Dakota Place Names* mentions that
it had several stores, saloons, and boarding houses,
as well as the homes of the lumber and railroad
workers. It was near the head of Stage Barn Canyon.

CASCADE, CASCADE SPRINGS

Fall River County
W½, Section 20, T8S-R5E

Cascade was founded in 1888 as a resort town
to take advantage of the warm mineral springs
in the area. An ornate, four-story, hundred-room
hotel was built, and 36 city blocks laid out and
partially developed. It was hoped that the Burlington & Missouri River Railroad would go through
town on its way to Hot Springs, but efforts of
some speculators to hold up the railroad for high
prices made it seek another route, and Cascade
gradually declined. By 1900 it had only a post
office and 25 people, distributed over 16 houses.

Today the hotel is nearly gone. A business
block of three houses, one of ornate sandstone,
one of brick, and one, the old bowling alley, of
fancy wood, still stands. A couple of houses, the
old livery barn and stable, and the home of Mr.
Allen, the banker, are scattered over a wide area,
watched over by a single modern farm. A pavillion
east of town marks Cascade Spring itself, which
gushes out 2,000 gallons of warm water a minute.
The stream, which never freezes, is lined with
watercress all year 'round. Two miles downstream
is the pretty Cascade Falls, about 10' high and 40'
wide, covered with water plants.

Cascade, or Cascade Springs, as it is sometimes
called, is in Alabaugh Canyon, about 8 miles
south of Hot Springs on SD 87. The remaining
business block is to the south of the highway, the
other buildings north of it.

Robert Casey in *The Black Hills*, pages 286-290,
tells Cascade's story in an entertaining manner.

The W. Allen Bank and the Fargo Store at Cascade; to the right
is the Cascade Club and bowling alley, and across the street was
the hotel.

Banker Allen's Victorian gothic house, half-a-mile up Alabaugh
Canyon from the highway.

The warm, mineral Cascade Spring that is the source of Cascade
Creek. The site is marked by a pavilion and picnic ground. Even
in the dead of winter, watercress flourishes in the warm waters
of the creek.

Rear of the Fargo Store in Cascade.

The door of the W. Allen Bank at Cascade.

Front view of the Cascade Club, a famous place of entertainment and conviviality.

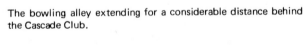

The bowling alley extending for a considerable distance behind the Cascade Club.

CASTLETON
Pennington County
NE¼, Section 8, T1N-R4E

As early as 1876 Castleton had a population of about 200 miners, who were engaged in digging a bedrock flume to work the placer gold deposits of Castle Creek, supporting themselves by farming and ranching while they worked. The completed flume did not have enough fall to carry away the tailings properly, and by 1880 most of the 40 or 50 miners' cabins were abandoned. In the late 1880s Castleton became a railroad construction center, supported by the large gangs of men who dug the two tunnels nearby or laid track on the Burlington line going northward to Deadwood. It was again abandoned, and in the 1890s one Denny O'Brien was able to homestead on the whole area.

From 1911 to 1914 a large dredge, financed by the Evans family of Denver, worked up and down the creek. Although gold recovery was good the irregular bedrock made it impossible to get the gold out of the best pockets. The dredge was eventually abandoned and in 1915 was shipped to John Day in Oregon. It had been worked by electricity, generated in a power plant nearby. All that now remains of the whole operation are the ribs of the barge, sunk in the mud beside the road at the south end of the tailings.

In spite of three booms Castleton never flourished. As late as 1920 some of the old buildings, marked with signs proclaiming them to be the saloon, grocery store, and jewelry shop could be seen, but today only a farm and a few summer homes mark the spot.

Castleton is about 10 miles northwest of Hill City, on the Hill City-Rochford gravel road. The old dredge pools have long been known as good swimming and fishing spots.

An old cabin at Castleton.

Ribs of the barge that carried the Evans Dredge at Castleton.

Central City, west of Deadwood.

CASTLEVILLE

A. J. Lewis was appointed postmaster of Castleville on March 27, 1877, and the post office was discontinued on September 24, 1879. Other than that no information about the town has come to light.

CATHOLICON SPRINGS
Fall River County
SE¼, Section 24, T7S-R6E

On the Chicago & North Western Railroad, to the east of Hot Springs.

CENTENNIAL CITY
Lawrence County
Section 4(?), T5N-R4E

Centennial City was about 2½ miles up the creek from Crook City and in 1876 had a grocery, restaurant, and three or four miner's cabins. The location cited above seems reasonable but is not exact.

CENTENNIAL PARK
Lawrence County
Sections 17, 18, 19, & 20, T6N-R3E(?)

In 1900 Centennial Park had a population of 52, served by a post office. It appears to have centered around a benchmark in Centennial Prairie, and only the early maps show it as a town.

CENTRAL CITY
Lawrence County
NW¼, Section 28, T5N-R3E

Central City began as an early mining camp and has flourished ever since. Its present population, mainly residential, is 188.

It was near Central City that the well-known and much-discussed quarrel between Cephas Tuttle and Henry Keets took place. Tuttle owned the Aurora mine and Keets the Comstock. Both sank shafts, and soon Keets' men tunneled into Aurora ore. Tuttle ordered them out, threatening to blow up the whole works if they remained on his property. All got out except a man named Norris. Tuttle carried out his threat; the blast caved in a good deal of tunnel and permanently deafened Norris. Coming to the surface afterward, Tuttle was caught in an exchange of shots between the Comstock and Aurora men and killed. Nobody was ever hanged for the crime, though several men were pushed as candidates for that honor.

The Keets mine was also the site of an early sit-down strike, when miners holed up, threatening to stay put until they received their pay. Cavalry from Fort Meade was called out with cannon, but wily old sheriff Seth Bullock avoided violence by dropping some burning sulfur (or maybe asafetida) down an airshaft and smoking the miners out.

A warehouse with sturdy walls and iron shutters, presumably for the storage, among other things, of dynamite and gunpowder. The walls would not lessen an explosion, but they might keep stray bullets from setting one off.

69

CHANNING
Lawrence County
SE¼, Section 8, T3N-R5E(?)

Channing seems to have been a settlement strung out along a road some 3 miles northwest of Nemo. It was not on the Black Hills & Fort Pierre Railroad; because only one map seems to show it, the probability is that it never amounted to much.

CHEYENNE CROSSING
Lawrence County
NW¼, Section 22, T4N-R2E

Originally *Spearfish Crossing*, this is now a store and gas station at the head of Spearfish Canyon, where US 85 and SD 89 meet.

CHEYENNE FALLS
Fall River County
NW¼, Section 3, T9S-R6E

The falls themselves are in SW¼, Section 20, T8S-R6E, but the post office, which was there in 1900, was on the line between the two townships and never did have much of a population.

CHEYENNE RIVER RANCH
Fall River County
SE¼, Section 36, T8S-R2E

The Cheyenne River Station, just north of the Cheyenne River on the Cheyenne-Deadwood stage trail, was built in 1876 by J. W. Dear, and housed a telegraph office and accommodations for travellers. Persimmon Bill Chambers and his brother, a couple of horsethieves, seem to have made this their headquarters. The Station appears to have been near the present suburb of *Dudley* on the opposite side of the river from Edgemont.

THE CHICKEN RANCH
Lawrence County
Midway up the section line between Sections 17 & 18, T4N-R4E

The Chicken Ranch, or *Chicken Ranch Store*, is on the other side of Strawberry Hill from Pluma. There is a good deal of loose talk about what sort of "chicken" may have given rise to the name.

CHILSON
Fall River County
NE¼, Section 26, T8S-R3E

Chilson was a railroad section house on the Chicago, Burlington, & Quincy Railroad, about 5 miles northeast of Edgemont. All that remains now is an old cold cellar, a capped well, and one clothesline post.

CHINA GULCH
Pennington County
SW¼, Section 20, T1S-R5E

China Gulch is a Forest Service summer home group, just north of US 16, about 1½ miles east of Hill City. In the past it was government policy to encourage the use of the National Forest by individual summer home owners, grouped together for administration, roads, and water. The increasing demand for picnic and camping areas has now limited such sites, and many summer home groups are being closed out when their agreements with the Forest Service expire.

CHINATOWN
Lawrence County
Part of Deadwood

The Deadwood Chinatown is reputed to have been the largest, in proportion to the town it was in, of any in the country. The Chinese had their own fire engine company, their Lodge of Chinese Masons, and innumerable shops and clubs. According to Estelline Bennett, you could smell the incense or the opium a block away.

CINDELL SPUR
Lawrence County
SE¼, Section 18, T3N-R5E

Another name for *Novak.*

CITY CREEK
Lawrence County
Part of Deadwood, SE¼, Section 22, T5N-R3E

City Creek was a settlement which was absorbed into Deadwood as that city expanded.

Author Parker with a railroader's kerosene lamp, at Chilson.

A ranch south of Clifton. Its location gives some idea of the barren loneliness and general desolation that pervades the western rim of the Black Hills.

CIVILIAN CONSERVATION CORPS CAMPS

These camps, established in the early 1930s for forestry improvement and general construction work on government projects, were finally abandoned about the time of World War II. Sometimes their names were "Camp So-and-So" and sometimes "So-and-So Camp," so look under both headings.

CLARA BELLE CAMP
Pennington County
NW¼, Section 24, T2S-R4E

Frank Hebert in his *40 Years Prospecting and Mining in the Black Hills of South Dakota* mentions Clara Belle Camp, which sprang up in the 1880s around his Clara Belle Mine, about ¼ mile south of St. Elmo Peak. The ruins of this mine, the Golden Arrow, and several cabins and earlier workings can still be seen along the northern edge of Bear Creek, about a mile east of Oreville. The area was also known as *St. Elmo*.

CLEVELAND
Lawrence County
Part of Deadwood

Cleveland was another suburb absorbed in Deadwood's expansion. It seems to have been in the southernmost part of town.

CLIFF HOUSE
Lawrence County
SW¼, Section 36, T6N-R3E

Cliff House has always been a place of entertainment on the road between Deadwood and Spearfish. Early pictures show it nestled down in a valley sheltered by a limestone rim, with Centennial Valley in the distance.

CLIFTON, CLIFTON SIDING
Weston County
NW¼, Section 8, T42N-R60W

Clifton was a cattle-shipping point on the Chicago, Burlington & Quincy Railroad. A section house, water tank, cattle yard, school, and post office served the ranches nearby. Clifton is now collapsed and entirely deserted. A nearby rancher keeps his eye on the few ruined buildings that are left.

The best way to reach Clifton is to drive south from Newcastle on the old part of US 85 for about 16 miles, turning east across the CB&Q tracks at the M W Ranch.

The Clifton school building and its flagpole, now located many miles west of town, out in the sagebrush country.

The foundations of the railroad water tower, a sign noting the name of the siding, and the Burlington tracks stretching northward toward infinity mark the site of Clifton at the western edge of the Hills.

Emma Peterson's cabin in Clifton. In her eighties, the only inhabitant of this barren village, Mrs. Peterson one morning walked out of her cabin, down to the train, and took off to marry a childhood sweetheart. The Newcastle Historical Society has preserved most of what she left behind her.

COLD SPRINGS I
Weston County

The Canyon Springs Robbery is sometimes referred to as the Cold Springs Robbery, but they are two separate places, each one a stage station, even though only about two miles apart. Again, as in the case of Canyon Springs, it is hard to locate the area exactly.

COLD SPRINGS II
Custer County
SE¼, Section 10, T5S-R5E

The Cold Springs cemetery, school, and mine are all along the south edge of Section 10. In the late 1960s there was a movement to preserve the history of the area and to refurbish the school as a historical museum.

The Cold Springs School, beside the cemetery   the same name.

COMMISSARY D
Crook County
SE¼, Section 14, T49N-R61W

This was the last camp, also known as *Camp D* and *Possum Trot*, on the McLaughlin Tie & Timber Company's standard-gauge logging railroad that ran from Nahant nearly to the edge of present-day Moskee. The railroad crossed US 85 just south of the Hardy Work Camp and went down Lost Canyon, then crossed the divide heading northward and came down into the valley that contains the main road to Moskee and Cold Springs. Nothing is left of the community but the old railroad grade can still be seen clearly on the ground, near a couple of watering troughs.

COOLIDGE INN
Custer County
SW¼, Section 22, T3S-R6E

Named for President Calvin Coolidge, whose stay at the nearby State Game Lodge brought national attention to the Hills during the summer of 1927, this spacious building was originally used as a social hall but now houses a variety of tourist facilities. The Warren-Lamb Lumber Company's famous compensated hoist operated nearby, and other narrow-gauge logging lines extended up Grace Coolidge Creek (then called Squaw Creek) as far as Center Lake.

COPPER CAMP
Pennington County
Section 30, T2N-R3E

This was the name locally applied to the community which sprang up at the turn of the century around the workings of the Black Hills Copper Company. The claims held by the company included the Climax, Bee, Solnar, and Copper Reefs No. 1 and No. 2. There were many shallow workings and an 800-foot inclined shaft. Some 800 tons of ore were shipped prior to 1917; in that year 38 tons more, yielding 6.12 percent copper and 2.34 ounces of gold to the ton, were gleaned from the dumps and surface workings.

CORNISH TOWN

Pennington County
SW¼, Section 30, T1S-R5E

The southern end of *Hill City* was called Cornish Town in the 1880s because it was heavily populated by the Cornwall tin miners, the Cousin Jacks, who came over to work the tin deposits owned by the English Harney Peak Tin Mining, Milling, and Manufacturing Company.

CRAZY HORSE

Custer County
NE¼, Section 34, T2S-R4E

Sculptor Korzcak Ziolkowski has been carving a memorial to Chief Crazy Horse, and by extension to all the American Indians, on Thunderhead Mountain since the end of World War II.

CREEK CITY

Lawrence County
SE¼, Section 22, T5N-R3E

A letter from William Gay, an early Deadwood settler, written on March 31, 1876, mentions that the mining camp at the mouth of Whitewood Creek was known as Creek City; it is probably the same community later incorporated into Deadwood and known as *City Creek*.

It is claimed that this shed is the oldest building in Crook City. It may well be, for boards that wide are not easy to find nowadays, but they are just the size the early sawmills cut for the placer mines' sluice boxes.

CROOK CITY I

Lawrence County

This predecessor of the present-day Crook City II was on the tablelands above the valley, and about 2 miles from the present site. Even as early as 1876 it was a ghost town, consisting of a collapsed log cabin, a pile of logs, and a hole in the ground.

Horatio N. Maguire, who mentioned this earlier town in his *American Wonderland*, unfortunately did not say in which direction it was from the newer village, and since there are table lands pretty much all around Crook City II, it is hard to locate its predecessor accurately.

CROOK, CROOK CITY II

Lawrence County
NE¼, Section 33, T6N-R4E

Crook City, named for General George Crook who had camped there in 1875, was one of the first towns in the northern Hills. Founded in 1876, it soon had a population of 2,000-3,000. A reporter passing through noted that it had 250 houses and that every other one of them was a saloon. The liquor, he observed, was a good deal more of a threat to life and limb than the hostile Indians hovering around the neighborhood. The town's newspaper, the *Crook City Tribune*, achieved but a single issue, on June 10, 1876, but otherwise the town flourished, building a church, a school, and other civic buildings. By-passed by the Fremont, Elkhorn & Missouri Valley Railroad, Crook City collapsed, and in the early 1880s was taken over as a homestead by L. W. Valentine and J. L. Denman. By 1900 it had only a post office and a population of 27.

The few remaining homes are about a mile south of Whitewood; local directions will help you find them.

The Crook City Cemetery, high on the slope of the valley to the east of town, contains many monuments dating from the earliest days of the Black Hills pioneers.

CROW CREEK CARBONATE CAMP
Lawrence County
SW¼, Section 10, T5N-R2E

Andreas' *Atlas* mentions this town on Squaw Creek as the home of the Iron Hill Mining Company. Obviously it is the same as *Carbonate Camp.*

CROWN HILL
Lawrence County
SW¼, Section 34, T5N-R2E

Crown Hill was a station on the Grand Island & Wyoming Central (later Chicago, Burlington & Quincy) Railroad, at the top of its line between Trojan and Spearfish Canyon. The grade here was so steep that any cars left on the siding were *chained* down and the chain locked, to keep them from getting away. There do not seem to have been any buildings in the area, though the Crown Hill mine was somewhere nearby.

CRYSTAL CAVE
Meade County
SW¼, Section 22, T4N-R5E

This was a stop on the Black Hills & Fort Pierre Railroad, probably to allow visitors to get off to see the famous cave, which was known from the earliest days. One of its rooms, complete, was knocked out and taken to the World's Columbian Exposition in Chicago in 1893.

The cave is still open, now under the name *Bethlehem Cave.* It is easily reached by going about three miles west from US Interstate 90 at Tilford, along the road which leads through Calcite.

The initials of Lt. Col. George Armstrong Custer, carved on a rock near Custer City, a relic of his expedition to the Hills during the summer of 1874.

The Custer County Courthouse, an official historical site.

This solid and enduring bank in Custer was built of Hot Springs sandstone. The 1881 date, however, was the year the bank was founded, not the year the building was built.

CUSTER
Custer County
Sections 23, 24, 25, & 26, T3S-R4E

Custer, the first town in the Black Hills, is still a lively mining, lumbering, and tourist town. Present population is 1,597. It is at the junction of North-South US 385, and East-West US 16 and 16A.

In 1909 when Troy Parker first visited Custer he put up in the principal hotel, the American House, in the room over the bar. Beneath his bed was a sheet of boiler iron to keep exuberant bullets from coming up through the floor.

Bullwheels, often made on the spot, drove the cam shafts that turned the cams and lifted the stamps that ground the ore. Because they are enormous and of no other use, they generally remain where they were abandoned, like this one at the Custer Peak mine.

CUSTER PEAK COPPER COMPANY
Lawrence County
NE¼, Section 24, T3N-R3E

The greatest activity in this area was from 1900 to 1919; three shafts—250', 90', and 65' in depth—were sunk, but recorded production was minimal. A considerable community, however, came into existence around the mine, for the Nasby post office was moved from Mountain Meadows (II) to a new location at the Custer Peak mine.

Concrete coping around a shallow well at the Cuyahogo mine, an operation that was well laid out, carefully built, and had everything but gold. Piles of the graphite that they did find can still be seen around the entrance to the main shaft.

CUSTER STATE HOSPITAL
Lawrence County
NE¼, Section 14, T4S-R4E

Sanator, the old tuberculosis sanatorium, is now known as Custer State Hospital.

CUYAHOGO MINE
Custer County
NE¼, Section 29, T2S-R6E

The Cuyahogo Mine is another of those mining ventures which seems to have surrounded itself with a large number of ruins. It was an extensive gold prospect before 1904, on Toll Gate Creek south of US 16, the Iron Mountain Road. A sawmill, a boarding house, four dwellings, an assay office, a blacksmith shop, and a powerhouse were built and ore explored by a 700-foot tunnel and several rises which broke the surface. No production has been reported, and the sole product seems to have been a low-grade graphite, a hard, slaty pile of which can be found at the mouth of the tunnel itself. Be sure to explore up and down the valley, for the foundations of the buildings are scattered over a wide area.

The brick and stonework foundations for the steam boilers, like this one at the Cuyahogo mine just west of the Iron Mountain Road, will last forever if left undisturbed.

CYANIDE

Lawrence County
SW¼, Section 28, T5N-R2E

Cyanide was in the Ragged Top district, in the same general area as Balmoral, Preston, and Dacy. There was a school and a post office in Cyanide. Nearby were the Ragged Top holdings of the Spearfish Gold Mining and Reduction Company, as well as its 300-ton cyanide mill, built in 1902, and from which it is possible the town took its name.

The Cyanide area can be reached by going about 2 miles west from Trojan along the old Burlington grade toward Spearfish, then taking a dirt road north for another 1½ miles. There is a spectacular view of Ragged Top Mountain and the ruins of many mining activities.

Wooden hoist barrel, or whim, for pulling ore buckets out of the shallow workings, or hauling mine cars along the many small railroads around Cyanide.

This v-bottomed concrete reservior east of Cyanide stored water for the Deadwood Standard mine across the valley to the south. The mile-long pipeline can still be followed on the ground.

A clamp to tighten the metal hoops on a wooden cyanide vat, at Cyanide. Although steel tanks could be used, there was a general feeling among miners that only wood could long withstand the corrosive effects of so powerful a chemical.

A broken handcart in the grass at Dewey.

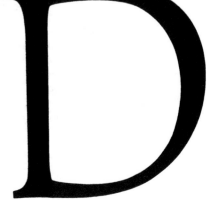

DACY
Lawrence County
NE¼, Section 29, T5N-R2E

The settlement later known as Dacy appears on the 1900 USGS maps as two solid blocks of buildings on either side of a road in the Cyanide area, with eight other buildings scattered around its outskirts. The Dacy mine, which was otherwise known as the Flora E. Group, was nearby and probably gave its name to the town. The mine, owned by the Kilpatrick brothers, sank a 505-foot shaft and attempted to connect with it by a 2000-foot drift coming southward from the bottom of Long Valley. The only production recorded was $20,000 of gold in 1897, and by 1915 the town was reduced to three scattered houses. It can be reached from Trojan, passing through Balmoral, Preston, and Cyanide.

DAKOMING
Weston County
Between Sections 21 & 28, T42N-R60W

Dakoming seems to be only a siding on the Chicago, Burlington & Quincy Railroad, 5 miles northwest of Dewey.

DAKOTA CITY
Pennington County

Peter Rosen lists this as a minor Pennington County post office, but it does not seem to appear on any Black Hills maps.

DANSBY, DANBY
Custer County
NW¼, Section 23, T3S-R3E

Dansby was the location of a custom mill for processing placer gravels hauled in, some of them, in wheelbarrows from the surrounding shallow diggings. The town had a maximum population of 50-75 persons, but as early as 1886 it was pretty well played out and closed down. The foundation of the mill and the site of the dam which furnished it with water, plus a few relics in the shape of decaying wooden bull wheels and so forth, can still be seen.

DARK CANYON
Pennington County
SW¼, Section 13, T1N-R6E

Some maps show Dark Canyon as a stop on the old Black Hills and Western Railroad. It is today a popular summer home area in Rapid Creek Canyon, about 5 miles southwest of Rapid City. There is some dispute over whether the narrow, deep cut of Victoria Creek or the large Rapid Creek Canyon is the true "Dark Canyon."

DEADWOOD
Lawrence County
Sections 22, 23, 26, & 27, T5N-R3E

Deadwood Gulch, so named from the many burned trees the early miners found there, was a booming placer camp in 1876, and has prospered ever since. Its present population is 2,409. The best book on its early times is Estelline Bennett's *Old Deadwood Days*, a fascinating account of her girlhood in the days before the railroad came.

Bow windows provided an excellent view for the folks who lived or did business in the second stories of downtown Deadwood buildings. The signs "China Doll" and "Body Shop" on the businesses beneath are probably just a coincidence. Not long ago, however, a small cafe under one of the thriving upstairs establishments advertised in glowing neon that the wares for sale were "Better than you can get at home!"

Deadwood, viewed from the residential section on the side of the valley northwest of town.

Local folks say that this horse head was symbolic of a livery stable underneath it, but the carving and stonework all seem a bit too ornate for that purpose.

From the hillside residential streets of Deadwood you look up to the houses on the high side of the road and down onto the attics and chimneys on the low side.

The ornate cornice, bow window, and decorative ironwork are typical of the downtown buildings in Deadwood. The whole town burned in 1879, and the ornate Victorian style in which it was rebuilt has set its style ever since.

DEADWOOD STANDARD MINE
Lawrence County
Sections 31 & 32, T5N-R2E

This interesting operation, west of Cyanide and very nearly overlooking Spearfish Canyon, mined the surface ores of the area. Acting on the theory that the gold was contained not in the rock but in the interstices and cracks, the operators merely cracked the ore into quarter-inch granules and ran it through a cyanide process. Either there was not enough gold in the cracks or the process did not get it all, for this method seems not to have been very popular or long-lived.

DEERFIELD
Pennington County
NE¼, Section 26, T1N-R2E

Deerfield originated as a station on the Cheyenne-Deadwood stage line and at that time was called *Mountain*, or *Mountain City*. Good hunting, possibly because the deer gathered to lick the salt spilled from the Cambria salt wagons, resulted in the newer name. When the big Deerfield dam flooded the town's original site (SW¼, Section 30, T1N-R3E) the houses were moved a mile or so northwest, where a gas station, post office, and general store continue to serve the ranchers of the Limestone country and the many fishermen and hunters who enjoy the area.

The old town is under water, but Sawyer's General Store, at the head of Deerfield Lake, still keeps alive the name of Deerfield.

DEER HEAD LODGE
Pennington County
SE¼, Section 28, T2N-R3E

A hunter's camp in or near Pinedale, southwest of Rochford.

DE MORES STAGE STOP
Butte County
E½, Section 10, T8N-R2E

A stop on the Medora-Deadwood Stage Line, which was one of the many enterprises of the flamboyant Marquis de Mores, who hoped to build a cattle empire around Medora in the North Dakota bad lands. If the location given is correct, the stage stop has by now been engulfed by the town of Belle Fourche.

DENIS
Pennington County
SE Corner of T1N-R6E

There are references to Denis in several places, but it is hard to locate accurately. It seems to have been in the very corner of its township, just north of the 44th parallel, 7 miles southwest of Rapid City, just about where the Whispering Pines School is now. In any case, it is not to be confused with the Dennis in Fall River County, between Edgemont and Provo, pretty well out of the Hills.

DENNIS
Fall River County
SE¼, Section 15, T9S-R2E

Dennis, about 7 miles southwest of Edgemont on the CB&Q, appears to be little more than a siding or section house on the way to Provo.

DENVER
Lawrence County
Part of Lead

Mildred Fielder's *The Treasure of Homestake Gold* indicates that the Denver addition to Lead was laid out west of Galena Street by McIntyre and Patterson. The area is just about in the center of the town today.

DEWEY
Custer County
NE¼, Section 18, T6S-R1E

Dewey was originally called *S & G Ranch*, which had been named for its two owners, Sturgis and Goodell. When the railroad came in, the name was changed, for single-word names were easier and quicker for the telegraphers and dispatchers to use.

Today even the Dewey school and post office appear to be closed, and although the town has a population of about 50 it seems to be in something of a decline; the hot summer sun, the icy winter gales, and the distance to any other towns all discourage immigration. Further, in the early days, when cattle from the surrounding ranches went to market by rail, Dewey was a busy shipping and commercial center for the western Hills, but now

The Dewey Post Office, now closed down.

The church at Dewey.

The main street of Dewey, once a thriving cattle shipping town on the Chicago, Burlington & Quincy Railroad.

Dewey, which came into existence about the turn of the century, was probably named for Admiral George Dewey who won the Battle of Manila Bay during the Spanish-American War.

the cattle go to the packers by truck and a few hired hands with machines have replaced the cowboys. The wind blows through the broken windows of half-a-dozen deserted business houses, and even the church is used only on special occasions. The railroad men maintain a storehouse or two by the side of the Burlington tracks, but in a few years Dewey, like Marietta, Argentine, and Owens, all abandoned communities by the side of the tracks, may well be given back to the desert and rangeland that gave it birth.

Several roads lead into Dewey. This is a country where the roadside signs, instead of saying "ten miles to such-and-so town," say "ten miles to Jones' Ranch," and Jones' Ranch may well be the nearest human habitation. Probably the most interesting trail to Dewey is that which wanders southward from US 16, along Tepee Canyon.

Diamond City, east of Rochford, once had a post office and a store and prosperous mines, but now only a single family lives there, and all that is left of the town are the scattered foundations of buildings long since torn down.

DIAMOND CITY
Lawrence County
SE¼, Section 12, T2N-R3E

In 1880 Diamond City had the Enos', or Diamond City, stamp mill, a store, a saloon, a post office presided over by C. W. Yana, and about a dozen homes containing a population of 30 persons. It was about two miles north of Rochford on Silver Creek, and can easily be reached on the Silver Creek road.

Diamond City is a good example of how the information presented in this book was gathered together. It first attracted our attention as an entry in the 1880 census, because Diamond City was, at that time, not included in any organized county, falling, so to speak, between Pennington and Lawrence counties, but not claimed by either. Reference some time later to Andreas' *Atlas of Dakota*, printed in 1884, showed its approximate location, labeled as "Diamond City Stamp Mill." Three newspaper quotations in the *Annals of Early Rapid City*, a manuscript in the Rapid City Public Library, brought to light the name of Enos' Mill, the store and the saloon, and the name of the newly appointed postmaster. At this point, Professor C. A. Grimm of the South Dakota School of Mines & Technology checked over Andreas' map and, comparing it with current maps and his knowledge of the area, was able to give the exact location. In 1968, in conversation with the present property owner, Mr. Richards, we confirmed this location and learned that Richards had torn down the post office the previous year.

DOYLE
Lawrence County
SE¼, Section 25, T4N-R5E

Doyle was a railroad station on the Black Hills & Fort Pierre. It had a post office and was the site of the W. V. Doyle lime plant, which was in operation from about 1895 to 1904. Doyle was in Elk Creek Canyon, about 2½ miles west of US Interstate 90, and should not be confused with Calcite, which was not quite so far up the canyon.

DUBLIN
Lawrence County
Intersection of Sections 25 & 36, T5N-R3E and Sections 30 & 31, T5N-R4E

Dublin does not seem to have been much of a place, for all its widespread location, which can now be found generally in the area of Two Bit and Galena, north of Strawberry Hill.

DUDLEY
Fall River County
NE¼, Section 36, T8S-R2E

Dudley is simply a small suburb of Edgemont, strung out along the highway leading toward Hot Springs. It is roughly in the same location as the old Cheyenne Crossing stage station.

DUMONT
Lawrence County
NE¼, Section 7, T3N-R3E

Dumont, named for Charles Dumont, an early French settler, was founded in 1890 as a lumbering camp and shipping point for cattle. The railroad maintained a section house, and the spur to Hanna branched off from Dumont toward the northwest. The lumbering faded away, the dry years spoiled the cattle industry, and the tracks to Hanna were torn up. All that remains of Dumont is the cattle pen, at the end of a long spur from the Chicago, Burlington & Quincy.

Dumont is about 8 miles south of Lead, on the gravel road to Rochford that branches off of US 85.

Dumont, where the Burlington sent a spur northwestward to carry coal to Hanna, was once a shipping point for cattle, but now the tracks are overgrown, the section house torn down, and the corrals but little used.

The bandstand in the public park in Edgemont, on the Cheyenne River.

E

EAST TERRY
Lawrence County
Center of Section 6, T4N-R3E

Several locations of towns are now known only through their listing in Lawrence County deed books, which places East Terry in the above location, near Bald Mountain and Fantail Creek.

ECKARD
Fall River County
NW¼, Section 17, T12S-R2E

This is to the southeast of the Hills but is included here because those who see it listed in Father Peter Rosen's book about the Black Hills may wonder where it was.

EDGEMONT
Fall River County
NW¼, Section 1, T9S-R2E

Edgemont, on the Cheyenne River, has a population of 1,172 and is a thriving farming and cattle community. Its economy got an additional boost from the nearby Ordnance Depot at Igloo. Early maps show the *T.O.T. Ranch* at about the spot where Edgemont is now, on US 18 about 25 miles southwest of Hot Springs.

Three vacant stores in a row attest to the varying fortunes of Edgemont, in the southwest corner of the Hills. Edgemont has boomed and busted quite a few times; the stores can wait, as in the past, for better days to come.

EIGHTEEN MILE RANCH
Custer County
SE¼, Section 25, T5S-R3E

A string of Ranches, starting with Four Mile, ran southward from Custer on the route of the old Deadwood-Cheyenne Stage trail down Red Canyon. Eighteen Mile was about at the head of Red Canyon, with the other ranches progressively nearer Custer.

ELIZABETHTOWN
Lawrence County
Section 13(?), T5N-R3E

Elizabethtown was one of the mining camps absorbed into Deadwood. It was between Montana City and Fountain City in Whitewood Gulch, and was big enough in 1876 to have its own Fourth of July celebration, with an oration by A. B. Chapline. The 1880 census mentions a population of 316.

ELK CREEK
Lawrence County
NW¼, Section 24, T4N-R4E

Elk Creek, named for the stream it was on, was founded in 1889 when the Homestake extended its Black Hills & Fort Pierre lines to begin new logging operations there. The town shortly had a population of 300-400. Operations soon shifted to Nemo, and as early as 1899 only a dozen houses were left. When this line of the BH&FtP washed out in 1907, it finished the town for good, and it is nearly impossible to find it on present-day maps. Elk Creek seems also to have been known as *Mowatt*.

ELKHORN I
Lawrence County
NE¼, Section 4, T2N-R3E

Andreas' *Atlas* shows an Elkhorn on the stage line from Custer to Deadwood, about where *Gregory* is, but on the west side of Rapid Creek.

ELKHORN II
Pennington County
NE¼, Section 4, T1N-R5E

Elkhorn seems to have been a stop on the Black Hills & Western in Rapid Creek Canyon, between Pactola and Silver City. The location given above is that of *Bear Gulch* which very likely was the same place or very near it. It is now under the waters of Pactola Lake.

Elkhorn (I), across Rapid Creek from Gregory and a mile or so south of Nahant, was never much of a town.

Edgemont, on the Cheyenne at the southern edge of the Hills.

ELKHORN PARK, ELKHORN PRAIRIE
Pennington County

Elkhorn Prairie was Custer's original name for the *Silver City* area, so named because of the high stack of elk horns—several hundred of them—which had been piled on Gillette, or Elkhorn, Prairie at the head of the valley leading into the area.

ELK MOUNTAIN
Custer County
NE¼, Section 16, T4S-R1E

The above is the location of the abandoned Elk Mountain school, but as schools were often moved considerable distances to conform to changes in population or on the school board, the location of the school is not always a reliable guide to the exact location of the town. At least one current atlas mentions Elk Mountain as a community of 12 persons, receiving its mail via Newcastle, Wyoming, but no houses are there now.

ELM CREEK, ELM CREEK SIDING
Fall River County
SE¼, Section 1, T7S-R6E

This siding on the Fremont, Elkhorn & Missouri Valley Railroad was about 7 miles northeast of Hot Springs. It served the Elm Springs Quarry, in Section 2, T7S-R6E, which began operations in 1895 or 1896. The Unkpapa sandstone quarried was easy to dress, but somewhat softer than other local stones, and the quarry was closed after a few years. Both siding and quarry are probably most easily reached from Buffalo Gap, about two miles to the northeast.

ELMORE

Lawrence County
SW¼, Section 9, T4N-R2E

Elmore was named for Mike Elmore, a railroad contractor. It was the spot from which the Chicago, Burlington & Quincy began its narrow-gauge climb up the east side of Spearfish Canyon along Annie Creek. This piece of railroad was one of the most spectacular in the country, and a hike along the old grade will make you wonder how they ever dared take a train over it. The line washed out in 1933 or 1934 and was abandoned. Elmore, on SD 89, is now a group of summer homes, and only the old section house and the railroad sign remain to indicate its past glories. It is about 14 miles south of Spearfish.

Elmore is at the point where the Burlington spur from Trojan and Lead came down into Spearfish Canyon; a hike over the abandoned roadbed reveals the engineering feats involved.

A sand bin beside the Burlington tracks at Englewood. This little town, an important rail junction in the early days, was at the start of a long haul up to Terry and Trojan, or down into Lead and Deadwood, and the locomotives stocked up on sand here, in case the tracks were slippery.

ENGLEWOOD
Lawrence County
NE¼, Section 20, T4N-R3E

Anyone with money to invest in the early days might well have looked at Englewood, a promising rail center and the junction of two lines: the Chicago, Burlington & Quincy to Deadwood and to Spearfish and the Black Hills & Fort Pierre narrow-gauge to Terry and Piedmont. The big engines which brought CB&Q trains into the Hills could not make it down to Deadwood, so a roundhouse was built to service them in Englewood. A generating plant, regaining some of the power used to pump Homestake water over the divide from Hanna, gave the town another industry. However, the diminished use of the railroads, and the coming of diesel power on what was left of them, was the end of Englewood, although a few people live there still.

Englewood was originally known as *Ten Mile Ranch*, a name which was changed when the railroad came in 1891, because railroad telegraphers preferred one-word names. Best way to reach it is to turn south on the Rochford gravel road 5 miles southeast of Lead, then after about a mile, turn northeast for a mile or so more along Whitewood Creek.

EOTHEN
Crook County
SW¼, Section 22, T54N-R62E

A tiny town on the road from Aladdin to Alva; the 1901 USGS Aladdin Quadrangle shows it as having three houses.

ERSKINE
Fall River County
NE¼, Section 7, T7S-R5E

Erskine Siding, on the Chicago, Burlington & Quincy Railroad, is just below the new Cottonwood Spring Dam, about a mile north of US 18, between Hot Springs and Minnekahta. To the east, toward Hot Springs, was a quarry working the soft red sandstones of the area, and to the west of the siding was the National Alabaster Corporation, whose tall concrete plaster kiln still stands beside the railroad tracks.

The kiln of the National Alabaster Company at Erskine, unused since 1911.

ERSKINE CAVE
Meade County
NW¼, Section 32, T3N-R6E

A small but interesting cave 2 or 3 miles from Nemo. It has not been developed, although it has been known locally for many years.

ESTE, ESTES, ESTE JUNCTION
Lawrence County
SE¼, Section 34, T3N-R5E

For many years Este was the end of the southern branch of the Black Hills & Fort Pierre Railroad, but when the northern branch was washed out in 1907, the southern one was extended from Este past Steam Boat Rock and on through Stage Barn Canyon to Piedmont. What is left of the town is on the Nemo road, about 2 miles southeast of that town.

The old Etta tin smelter still stands three stories high, half-a-mile south of Keystone.

The Etta mine worked a glory hole, a huge opening in the top of the hill, into which the ore was thrown, to be trammed out through tunnels at the bottom. The largest crystal in the world, a tremendous log of spodumene, was for years a local curiosity, embedded in the wall of the workings.

ETTA, ETTA CAMP, ETTA MINE
Pennington County
SE¼, Section 8, T2S-R6E

Etta Camp was on the maps long before Keystone, although the two towns are close together. It was originally a tin prospect of the Harney Peak Tin Mining, Milling, and Manufacturing Company, which built a mill and smelter at the mine in 1883. A huge lump of tin, weighing 1,200 pounds and "big as a small boy," was melted out of hand-picked cassiterite from the company's various holdings and shipped to London to promote the sale of company shares. The Harney Peak Company, however, became embroiled in litigation and went broke; the next heard of the Etta mine was when it began making shipments of spodumene, a lithium ore, in 1898. In 1908 a predecessor of the Maywood Chemical Company bought the mine from the receivers of the old Harney Peak Company. It operated until 1959, during which time it was famous for the huge spodumene crystals it produced. As late as 1900, Etta Mine, with a population of 24, was the post office for the Keystone area, at least according to one atlas published at that time.

The foundations of the mill and smelter can still be found; and the Etta mine itself, with its gaping glory hole, is a spectacular, though dangerous, sight. It can be reached on the Glendale road, turning southward from US 16A half-a-mile south of Keystone.

EUREKA
Pennington County

In May, 1877, the Cheyenne *Daily Leader* mentioned rich diggings near Hill City, where the gravel ran $15 to the wagon-load. The towns of Hill City, Young, and Eureka were jubilant.

EVANS PLACE
Lawrence County

This town was not part of the more famous Evans near Hot Springs, but was near Deadwood, on Mineral Lot No. 735.

EVANS SIDING, EVANS QUARRY
Fall River County
NE¼, Section 33, T7S-R6E

The Evans Quarry, owned by Henry Bering, operated from about 1895 to 1942, cutting Dakota sandstone for such buildings as the public library in Sioux City, the Evans Hotel in Hot Springs, and the post office in Custer. The quarry was along Fall River, on the Fremont, Elkhorn & Missouri Valley (later the Chicago & North Western) Railroad, about 4 miles southeast of Hot Springs.

A church at the edge of the Badlands desolation.

F

Fairburn was the point on the Chicago & North Western Railroad where the Warren-Lamb Lumber Company line took off westward for logging operations in the area now known as Custer State Park.

FAIRBURN
Custer County
SW¼, Section 19, T4S-R8E

Fairburn was a railroad town on the Fremont, Elkhorn & Missouri Valley Railroad. It is nearly a ghost town now, though it has a store, a post office, a gas station, and many houses. Southwest of Fairburn, along French Creek, are found the Fairburn agates which have made the town famous for 70 years.

FAIR VIEW
Pennington County
NW¼, Section 28, T2N-R4E(?)

M. le Baron E. de Mandat-Grancey's book *Cow-Boys and Colonels* (London, 1887) has a picture of the town of Fair View showing a sawmill, three or four houses, and an odd structure that looks like the framework for a large stamp mill. The town was on Little Rapid Creek, near where Little Gimlet Creek enters it. Present-day Rapid Creek was called Little Rapid Creek before it combined with Castle Creek; the location given above is the junction of Gimlet Creek with Rapid Creek.

FALLS, THE FALLS
Lawrence County
NE¼, Section 36, T5N-R1E

The Falls was an early name for *Savoy* because it was at this point that the waters of Little Spearfish Creek fell into Spearfish Creek. The flow has since been diverted through flumes into the Homestake Mining Company power plants and the once-famous falls now flow only during the spring floods.

FALSE BOTTOM
Lawrence County

This neighborhood between Whitewood and Spearfish took its name from the "False Bottom" gold rush, in which the rumor was spread that miners, digging in the area, had only hit a "false bottom" and that actually gold was there, in plenty, farther down. Newspapers in those days of bustles made a good deal of play, Leland Case says, with mentions of "False Bottom girls" attending various social functions.

False Bottom Creek wanders in a northeasterly direction from one corner of T6N-R3E to the other, then runs northwest through St. Onge toward Belle Fourche.

FANTAIL JUNCTION
Lawrence County
Center of W½, Section 5, T4N-R3E

Fantail Junction was the point where the Deadwood Central Railroad line, coming southwest from Kirk and Whitetail Junction, divided to send spurs to Baltimore and Welcome.

A stile helped the students across barriers to learning at the Farrall, Wyoming school.

FARRAL
Crook County
SW¼, Section 13, T53N-R62W

A small community in the foothills of the Bear Lodge Mountains.

FIELD CITY
Weston County
SW¼, Section 35, T45N-R61W

Field City was the original name given to *Tubb Town* when it was laid out by F. R. Curran. The arrival of Mr. Tubbs, a grocer, soon gave the community the name of "Mr. Tubb's Town," and later, Tubb Town.

Tubb Town, or Field City, was first a place of refreshment along Salt Creek, and later became the site of considerable oil drilling activity, the remains of which still mark the spot.

FISH AND HUNTER CAMP
Lawrence County
SE¼, Section 28, T6N-R2E

This should not be confused with Fish & Hunter Siding a good many miles to the south. This camp was in Spearfish Canyon, on the west side of the Burlington tracks, about 3 miles south of Spearfish. In 1915 it had half-a-dozen houses.

FISH AND HUNTER SIDING
Pennington County
SE¼, Section 20, T1N-R4E

This siding appears in the same place under two other names, *Fisher and Hunter Siding* and *Pitt's Siding*, but Fish and Hunter, for the big Deadwood mercantile outfit, is probably the best one. In 1916 it was a cluster of four houses west of the Chicago, Burlington & Quincy tracks, about half-a-mile northwest of Slate Creek. It is about 8 miles northwest of Hill City, on the tar-and-gravel road to Mystic and Rochford.

FLATIRON I
Lawrence County
E½, Section 9, T4N-R3E

There is not much left at Flatiron, except the material from which a thoughtful mind can reconstruct a very considerable past. The USGS map for 1915 shows it as a bustling mining town on the Chicago, Burlington & Quincy, about 2 miles south of Lead. A railroad spur leads into town and another railroad begins and ends in the town itself. Some 30 buildings are shown, including a school, some large mills, and a post office. Would you like to hear the story?

Flatiron was the home of the fabulous Wasp No. 2 gold mine which was discovered in the 1890s. Early operation of its beds of shallow ore was not economical until a new general manager, John Gray, came on the job. Under his direction a system of blasting, successively deepening and enlarging the shot-holes, was introduced, and charges of 1000 pounds of powder were often used to loosen and break up 5,000-6,000 tons of ore at a time. The ore was moved from the open pit (and a very considerable pit it is) over the company's own standard-gauge railroad and conveyed through the mill by gravity flow. The company made money on ore yielding only $1.60 a ton and was considered an outstanding example of what good management could do. To the north the Little Blue also prospered, both as a source of ore and as a source of flux for smelting.

The town prospered. A steep spur railroad line was built from the Burlington up to the mill, and fully loaded freight cars were hauled up by a winch. Even the tailings were put to good use, for the Burlington built a special spur to get to them and shipped thousands of carloads of sand away to be used as fill and ballast. In 1927 a violent flood covered the spur, the train, the engine, and the engineer with many feet of sand. The old tracks are just now being dug up, as Lead and Deadwood use the tailings for sanding slippery streets.

Eventually the mines played out. All that is left now are foundations. The office and boarding house of the Little Blue, to the north, can be located by the remains of a safe and big cookstove. The foundations for another boarding house, one farm house, and a huge well can be found at the south end of the pit. The piers for the mill equipment are still in place.

You can reach Flatiron from either Kirk or Englewood. It is a place that lends itself to imagination as much as any ghost town in the Hills. If you listen hard you can hear the clatter of the drills, the call of the powderman, and the dull boom of the blasts that still echo over the silent pits of the Wasp and the Little Blue.

These foundations, towering over the railroad right-of-way, once supported the cyanide mill of the Wasp #2, an operation that blasted out its shallow ores by the hundreds of tons and ran them through the mill by gravity flow so successfully that the mine made a profit on ore yielding $1.60 in gold to the ton.

These tailings from the Wasp #2 mine cover one side of the valley, and over the years have eroded into badlands. For years the Burlington railroad used them for sand and ballast, until a heavy rain caused them to slump, covering the tracks and the train as well. The city of Deadwood is even now still digging out the pieces as they mine the tailings for street-sanding sand.

The mines at Flatiron were based upon large deposits of low-grade ore that would take a long time to work out, and the buildings were built on solid foundations. Judging by the size of the stove in the foreground, this may have been the boarding house that served the miners in the Little Blue.

A single house remains in Flatiron, and in the late afternoon the sunset light shines through its vacant windows.

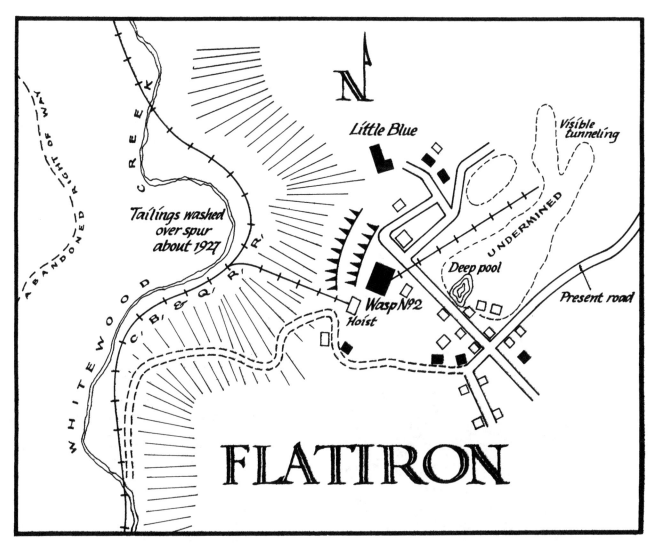

Nearly 80% of the town of Flatiron has fallen into the mines below. Heavy arrows indicate the path of the 1927 landslide.

The office safe of the Little Blue, just north of the Wasp # 2 at Flatiron, with Wat Parker endeavoring to open it.

FLATIRON II
Lawrence County
NW Corner, T7N-R3E

Rand McNally's *Commercial Atlas* for 1921 shows a town of Flatiron near the Chicago & North Western tracks between St. Onge and Red Water.

FLEUR DE LIS
Custer County
SW¼, Section 7, T4S-R6E

The Fleur de Lis was a Percheron horse ranch, founded in the late 1880s by the Baron E. de Mandat-Grancey. The baron had visited the Hills a few years before and so enjoyed his visit that he decided to settle here. The tale of his adventures and ultimate failure is amusingly told in his *La Breche aux Buffles*. Nothing but ruins now remain.

FLORA
Custer County

Flora was a tin mining community which grew up in the 1890s in the tin-producing area north and west of Custer. Its location was apparently somewhere within a mile or two of the Tenderfoot mine but is otherwise obscure. It was *not* a part of the Flora mine to the southeast of Custer but lay to the north of that city, and probably even north of Tenderfoot itself.

FLORAL
Pennington County
SE¼, Section 17, T2N-R3E

Another name for *Florence*.

Dovecotes in the gable of the old log barn on the Sasse Ranch at Florence. Beneath them can be seen the shadowy outline of a shed that once stood up against the barn which was the Rapid Creek Stage Station.

FLORENCE
Pennington County
SE¼, Section 17, T2N-R3E

The little Rochford newspaper, *Black Hills Central*, published for about six months by H. N. Maguire, on December 15, 1878 mentioned that "Florence is a thriving little town on the north fork of Rapid Creek, two miles west of Rochford." Mines in the vicinity were the Livingston, Booz (Boaz?), Jim Fisk, Aurora, and Denmark. The town seems to have been on the site of the present-day Sasse Ranch where a huge and ancient log barn apparently marks the site of the old *Rapid Creek Stage Station*. The community was also known as *Floral*.

A museum built to commemorate the nearby Cambria Fuel Company now forms part of the facilities of the Flying V Ranch, north of Newcastle on US 85.

FLYING V RANCH
Weston County
NW¼, Section 21, T46N-R61W

The Flying V Ranch buildings were originally built as a clubhouse and museum for the nearby coal town of Cambria. Much of the work was done by the miners, and many mine timbers were used in its construction. A hot salt-water pool and a cold one of fresh water were special attractions. The ranch has passed through many hands, with varying success, since Cambria's glory days.

FOLSOM
Custer County
NW¼, Section 1, T3S-R10E

Folsom is far east of Hermosa, at the eastern end of Custer County, but as news of this town is carried in the Custer newspapers it is included here for the sake of completeness. It was once a considerable gold mining town.

FOREST CITY
Crook County
Near Section 19, T5N-R1E

Forest City was an early placer mining town in the Tinton area. It appears to have been nearly on the Wyoming border—northwest of Bear Gulch, due south of Nigger Hill—in T5N-R1E.

FOREST HILL
Lawrence County
Part of Deadwood

Forest Hill was the residential section of Deadwood in its early days. Deadwood, it seems, never was actually a town until long after it began, but was composed of a conglomeration of gulches, camps, and placers, the central one of which, Deadwood Gulch, ultimately absorbed all the rest.

FORKS, THE FORKS
Crook County
SW¼, Section 20, T54N-R60W

Forks is a small community between Belle Fourche and the Bear Lodge Mountains, on South Dakota-Wyoming highway 24.

A neighbor told us that this was once the hotel, or perhaps it was just a stage station at The Forks.

FORT BUCKINGHAM
Custer County
NE¼, Section 25, T2S-R8E

From the ruins, one can visualize the "fort" as a rambling, low structure, consisting of two walls in an L shape with some sort of shelter in the angle between them; the walls are now crumbled nearly to the ground, and only a few remains of the shelter can be seen. Local legend says that the structure was built in 1890 when the Ghost Dance following was at its peak; the whites in and around Hermosa feared a Sioux uprising and felt they needed this added protection.

The fort, which closely resembles every other rock-topped knoll in the vicinity, is about half-a-mile east of the radio tower which is 2-3 miles northeast of Hermosa.

The entrance to the cellar which sheltered the women and children in the center of Fort Buckingham, a private defense against the Indians built by the settlers in the Hermosa area at the time of the Ghost Dance uprising of the 1890s.

The Gordon Stockade, south of Custer, was built in 1874, rebuilt during the 1920s, and rebuilt again in the 1930s. The loopholes were unfortunately placed so low that they would protect Indians shooting in as well as pioneers shooting out, but otherwise it was deemed a safe and substantial fortification.

FORT DEFIANCE
Custer County
SW¼, Section 21, T3S-R5E

Fort Defiance was one of the many names given to what is commonly known as the *Gordon Stockade*. It was so named because the early miners, from behind its sturdy, long walls, defied both Indians and U.S. soldiers. Military authorities have noted, however, that the loopholes in the walls were at shoulder height and would have provided as much protection to an Indian shooting *in* as they would to a miner shooting *out*, so it is just as well that the little fort never had to withstand a siege.

FORT LOOKOUT
Pennington County
SW¼, Section 1, T1N-R3E

The original name, according to some sources, of *Lookout*. It is sometimes confused with a much earlier and livelier Fort Lookout in the plains.

FORT MEADE
Meade County
SE¼, Section 12, T5N-R5E

Fort Meade, originally called *Camp Ruhlen*, was later named for General George C. Meade. It was founded in 1878 and was for many years the home of Custer's 7th Cavalry. In 1892 when Colonel C. H. Carlton assumed command of the 8th Cavalry at Fort Meade he issued instructions that the Star Spangled Banner be played at all military functions and ordered all persons within hearing to remove their hats when it was played. This led later to an order from Secretary of War Daniel E. Lamont requiring the Star Spangled Banner to be played at every army post each evening at retreat.

The Fort is currently used as a Veterans Administration Hospital, with a permanent population of 250. Parts of the old post have been preserved and now serve as a public museum commemorating the guardians of the pioneers.

95

FORT MEADE HYDRAULIC MINING COMPANY
Pennington County
Section 15, T1N-R6E(?)

Why an 1883 map should show this particular mining operation as a town rather than as a mine is not clear. It was on the north side of Rapid Creek, about 7 miles downstream from Pactola, which would put it near the location given, perhaps near Dark Canyon, or perhaps farther up the creek where it broadens out enough to provide room for the operations.

FOUNTAIN CITY
Lawrence County
Part of Deadwood

Fountain City was another of the outlying placers absorbed into Deadwood. It lay between Elizabethtown and Deadwood.

FOUR CORNERS
Weston County
SW¼, Section 1, T47N-R61W

Three or four houses, clustered about the junction of US 85 and Wyoming 585 on Canyon Springs Prairie. Early maps show no settlement here at all.

FOUR MILE
Custer County
NW¼, Section 5, T4S-R4E

Ranches Four, Nine, Twelve, and Eighteen Mile, all measured by their distance southwest from Custer, were stations on the stage line as it came up along the lovely and fertile Pleasant Valley. In 1898 and in 1933 there were dredging operations in the area, and it has been an active mineral district for many years, producing a variety of valuable products.

Four Mile is 4 miles west of Custer on US 16 and currently contains a fence post treating plant, store, school, and several dwellings. A trip southward along the trace of the old stage trail is well worth the trouble.

FOUR R RANCH
Pennington County
NW¼, Section 5, T1S-R7E

The 4-R Guest Ranch was started in the early 1930s by a family of four, the family name beginning with R; hence the title. It was later altered to 2-C when the ranch changed hands. Situated at the top of a high bluff northeast of a bend of Spring Creek and reached by a rough and precipitous road leading southward from old SD 40, the ranch was never a success. It is about 7 or 8 miles southwest of Rapid City. The main log building, barn, and guest house are in good shape.

FRENCH CREEK
Pennington County
SW¼, Section 19, T4S-R8E

Fuller's *Pocket Map* mentions French Creek as an early name for *Fairburn*, presumably so named because of the town's location on French Creek itself.

FRENCHTOWN
Pennington County
NE¼, Section 10(?), T2S-R6E

The *Black Hills Pioneer* on December 30, 1876 mentioned this town as being in the Harney District in the general area of Battle Creek. That would put it about where *Harney* is now. The Last Chance District, it was noted, was down the creek from Frenchtown.

FRUITDALE
Butte County
Center of Section 12, T8N-R3E

Fruitdale is about 8 miles east of Belle Fourche; it is a small but prosperous farming community utilizing the irrigation water provided by the Belle Fourche Reservoir.

Fruitdale grew up to profit by the irrigation waters from the Belle Fourche dam, and at one time was served by a spur of the Chicago & North Western coming east from Belle Fourche. This spacious building may have been a hotel or boarding house.

Few Black Hills characters were more colorful, and none was more ingenious, than Robert "Goldbug" Nelson, whose inventive genius found an outlet in the working of his little placer claim.

Galena, a silver mining town that lost its luster.

An old assay office in Galena, a famous silver-mining town that got its name from the galena (lead sulphide) in which the silver was found.

GALENA
Lawrence County
NE¼, Section 9, T4N-R4E

Although named for a vein of galena, or lead ore, found in its vicinity, Galena was a silver mining town and is surrounded by an incredible number of claims, prospects, and mines, some of which still are worked on occasion. In its early days the town was served by a branch of the narrow-gauge Deadwood Central, which came in in 1902, running as far as Galena Junction over the tracks of the Black Hills & Fort Pierre, then striking out the last 7 miles on its own. Another narrow-gauge line was run by Jim Hardin, owner of the Branch Mint mine; it went through Galena from the Branch Mint mill westward for about 3 miles to the Gilt Edge Maid and other mines. Although the line was abandoned in 1912, it was not until 1953 that its little locomotive, the

"Natalie," was removed from her private shed at the lower end of Galena.

Other great mines were the Golden Crest, which has been recently un-watered, the Oro Hondo, and three named Emma, after an agile young woman who worked in Reuther's boarding house. The glory hole at the Gilt Edge Maid is well worth a visit as the square-set timbering is exposed, and you can see how this intricate method of holding up the roof and sides of the mine was used.

Galena proper was the town down to Mrs. Borsch's garden, *Cariboo* extended from thence to the mouth of Butcher Gulch, and beyond that to the lower end of town was *Hardscrabble*.

Galena still has some population and a great many of the old buildings. It is best reached by turning east at the top of Strawberry Hill, about 5 miles south of Pluma on US 385, then going northeast over the dirt roads for about 2 miles.

The Galena School, built in 1892, and painted, like most of the remaining houses in town, white with green trim.

The clerestory windows, for both light and ventilation, indicate that this building at the Golden Crest mine was either a blacksmith shop or housed some sort of smelting operations.

GALENA JUNCTION
Lawrence County
SW¼, Section 19, T4N-R4E

Galena Junction, located just about where the Tomahawk Golf Club on US 385 is now, was the place where the Deadwood Central Railroad branched off the Black Hills & Fort Pierre tracks to head toward Galena and, we believe, to head the other direction toward Englewood. It is likely that the old railroad right-of-ways can be followed on foot and perhaps even in an automobile if it isn't too low-slung.

The State Game Lodge, 1927 summer home of President Calvin Coolidge, was built on the foundations of the Otis sawmill.

GAME LODGE
Custer County
NE¼, Section 27, T3S-R6E

Game Lodge is the more commonly used name for the *State Game Lodge* in Custer State Park.

GAP CITY
Lawrence County
NW¼, Section 28, T5N-R3E

The name "Gap" City for a town in the Deadwood-Central City-Golden Gate area is probably a misprint or other error for *Gay City*, or *Gayville*.

GARDEN CITY
Lawrence County
SE¼, Section 18, T5N-R3E

An earlier name for *Maitland*.

GARDNER'S
Meade County
SE¼, Section 5, T3N-R6E

A stop on the Black Hills & Fort Pierre, between Calcite and Piedmont. It was probably named for "Cap" C. V. Gardner, one of the leading men in the Hills, who established a flour mill at Spearfish, built the first quartz mill in Deadwood, edited the paper at Deadwood, and ran an inn, perhaps near this spot, for the accommodation of travelers between Sturgis and Rapid City.

GATE CITY
Pennington County
T1N-R7E

Rapid City is often referred to as "The Gate City of the Hills" in reference to the easy access from that town to the rest of the area, and this descriptive title has often been shortened to Gate City.

GAY CITY

Lawrence County
NW¼, Section 28, T5N-R3E

An early name for what later became the *Central City* post office.

GAYVILLE

Lawrence County
SW¼, Section 23, T5N-R3E

Gayville, at the confluence of Whitewood and Deadwood Creeks, was one of the early placer camps later absorbed into Deadwood. At its prime it had 250 houses, 30 business establishments, extensive quartz and saw mills, an assay office, and a brewery. One of the few buildings left from these happy days is now the Lawrence County Poor Farm.

The town was named for William and Albert Gay. William later achieved notoriety by killing a boy who delivered a flirtatious letter to his wife. He was sent to reside in the crowbar hotel for three years; he returned unrepentant and was welcomed back with a brass band. A dissident party, which didn't like the way William dressed —thought he would look better in a rope necktie —hoped to put him up on a platform where everybody could see him, but they were in a minority and nothing was done about it.

GERMANIA

Lawrence County
NE¼, Section 2, T3N-R4E

An early map shows Germania on Hay Creek, along a proposed extension of the Black Hills & Fort Pierre Railroad coming southeast from Brownsville. There were a good many little whistlestops and platforms, logging camps, mining camps, ranches, farms, and what-have-you along this line, and it may easily be that one of these, under some other name, is the right place. Reausaw, for example, is in about the spot where the old railroad grade crossed Hay Creek.

GIBRALTER

Meade County

The *Black Hills Pioneer*, on February 17, 1877, speaks of this as a town on Bear Butte Creek, 10 miles from Crook City, at the junction of Martin's and Smith's road and McKey's road, where Messrs. Myers, Mun, Bosworth, and Ireland were constructing a settlement.

GILLETTE STAGE STATION

Pennington County
SW¼, Section 23, T1S-R3E

The spot is marked by an abandoned ranch, many outbuildings beside the road, and a South

Dakota State Historical Society sign. This was apparently a stop on the early— 1876-1878— route from Cheyenne to Deadwood, a path which was quickly abandoned due to the many Indian attacks on the stage as it came northward through Red Canyon from what is now Edgemont.

The house where weary travelers refreshed themselves still marks the site of the Gillette stage station, between Custer and the northern Hills.

GLENDALE

Pennington County
SW¼, Section 15, T2S-R6E

Glendale, in Greyhound Gulch, was the site of the big Glendale Tin Company, which built a 150-ton tin mill there some time before 1892. Nothing is left of the mill, but three deserted buildings are still in its vicinity, while summer homes and farms are on either side of it. There were numerous mines in the area—mainly feldspar, mica, and beryl—and rockhounds will enjoy a visit to it.

Glendale can best be reached from the Harney-Spokane road, turning northwest about 2½ miles north of its junction with US 16A. Or you can go southeast from the Etta mine, if you have a stout car and good nerves.

Glendale, home of the Otho mine, built during the tin boom of the late 1880s.

GO-TO-HELL GULCH
Lawrence County(?)

Father Peter Rosen lists Go-To-Hell Gulch as an early mining camp but does not tell where it is. The probability is that it was in the Deadwood area, as that was where most of the camps were. There is evidence that the gulch later became *Central City.*

GOIENS
Meade County
SE¼, Section 21, T3N-R6E

Goiens was a station on the southern branch of the Black Hills & Fort Pierre, on Stage Barn Creek, about two miles west of the Fremont, Elkhorn & Missouri Valley line. It was 2.33 miles from Carwye, and 1.8 miles from Stage Barn.

GOLD HILL
Lawrence County
SW¼, Section 8, T4N-R3E(?)

The above location is that of the mouth of Reno Creek, because Gold Hill is described as being laid out in 1877 on Whitewood Creek, at the mouth of Reno Creek, about 3 miles above Kirk.

A very old log cabin at Glendale on Iron Creek.

The ore chute at the Ponca mine. It carried the feldspar and other minerals to the hoppers for crushing and sorting; provision was made for covering the chute against the snow so operations could continue in the wintertime.

Gold, Incorporated, seems to have been a small and fairly recent mining operation southwest of Brownsville. The mill and several cabins are still standing, but the road to the community has washed away.

GOLD INCORPORATED
Lawrence County
SE¼, Section 24, T4N-R3E

Strangely enough, no maps show this fairly modern mine and mill, with a well-developed but abandoned community around it, a mile or two west of US 385 on the road to Deadwood.

GOLDEN I
Lawrence County(?)
West side of T5N-R1E

Golden has been mentioned as an early camp in the Tinton-Nigger Hill area, but it does not seem to appear on any maps readily available.

GOLDEN II
Lawrence County

Golden, overlapping or adjoining the town of *Washington,* was, along with the latter place, incorporated into the city of *Lead.*

GOLDEN CITY
Pennington County
SW¼, Section 12, T1S-R5E

An early name for *Sheridan,* a placer camp given the name because it was possible to pan out at least $20 a day.

GOLDEN GATE
Lawrence County
T5N-R3E

Golden Gate was up Deadwood Creek from Central City, between Central City and Anchor City. The area is now sort of a suburb of Deadwood and Lead.

GOLDEN GATE MINE & TIMBER COMPANY
Crook County
SE¼, Section 33, T50N-R61W

An early name for *Moskee.*

GOLDEN SLIPPER
Pennington County
SE¼, Section 22, T1S-R5E

The Golden Slipper mine, which together with the Forrest City was operated by Empire Gold Mines in 1939-1940, was quite a development, having its own powerhouse, many miners' cabins, a big mill, and a boarding house. The Slipper was discovered in 1893 and production has been reported on and off since that time, but the major activity was from 1937 to 1940 when 17,500 tons of ore yielded 1,642 ounces of gold and 266 ounces of silver, which works out to about $3.30 a ton—not an especially attractive prospect. The mine, and what few buildings are left, is north of US 16, about 1½ miles southeast of Three Forks.

GOLDEN SUMMIT
Pennington County
SW¼, Section 33, T1S-R5E

See *Summit IV.*

GOLDENVILLE
Pennington County
SE¼, Section 8, T2S-R5E

Goldenville was the site of the Michigan mine, which is the location given above, on the west side of Palmer Gulch.

The Gordon Stockade, built in the winter of 1874-75, has twice been rebuilt as a monument to its builders. Fortunately for historical accuracy, Captain John Mix, who removed the Gordon Party from the Hills, prepared a detailed plan of the little fort and its accommodations.

GORDON STOCKADE
Custer County
SW¼, Section 21, T3S-R5E

The Gordon Stockade was built in late December 1874 by the Collins-Russell-Gordon party from Sioux City. They were the first large, organized group to penetrate the Hills after the official announcement of "gold!" came from the Custer expedition earlier that year. The stockade was 80' square with 10' high log walls and bastions at each corner; inside were at least six cabins and a well. Around the stockade, the miners laid out *Harney City*, in the hope of founding the first town in the Hills. However, the Gordon party was in the Hills illegally, and in April 1875 Captain John Mix and soldiers of the 2nd Cavalry came and removed the remaining 18 miners to Fort Laramie. The stockade's most famous occupant turned out to be Annie D. Tallent, whose *Black Hills, or the Last Hunting Grounds of the Dakotah* is a justly celebrated history of the area. *Camp Harney, Fort Defiance,* and *Union Stockade* are the other names which have been used for the stockade and surrounding site.

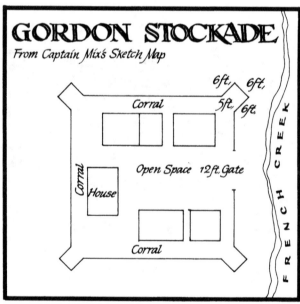

GORDON STOCKADE
From Captain Mix's Sketch Map

The Gordon Stockade, on French Creek 4 miles east of Custer, was built during the winter of 1874-75 by the members of the Collins-Russell-Gordon party, the first white miners to establish themselves in the Black Hills. The stockade was a solidly built structure, with projecting bastions to provide flanking fire to sweep the walls clear of Indian attackers. Captain John Mix, who removed the party, said that if they had resisted him he would have had to go back to Fort Laramie for artillery. Mix's report and diagram show only six cabins in the stockade, but Annie Tallent, a member of the party, listed the messes and their cabins, starting counter-clockwise from the gate, as follows: Logan, Whitney, Lamb, Gordon, Tallent-Cordierro, Witcher-Thomas, and Blackwell-McLaren.

The Grand Junction mine, near Junction City, hauled its gold ore a couple of miles over a little tramway, advertising to prospective investors that economies would be achieved because the road was "all down hill." The practiced eye can still see where the tramway ran through the jackpines that have grown up since operations were abandoned.

The Grand Junction ore was carried on a tramway to this hopper, where it was placed in sliding cars, the weight of the loaded car on the way down serving to haul up the empties on the track beside it. At the bottom of this long slide, the ore apparently was again loaded onto cars and trammed a short distance to the mill. The whole operation appears to have been designed to profit the builders of this complex layout, rather than those who invested their money in it.

Part of the winch that lowered ore cars down the slide to the Grand Junction mill.

GRAND JUNCTION
Custer County
NW¼, Section 29, T2S-R4E

The Grand Junction group of claims was located in 1878 by C. C. Crary, who built a small stamp mill (NW¼, Section 20, T2S-R4E) about a mile from the mine. Subsequent owners built a 40-stamp mill on Spring Creek to the north in 1880, but this shut down after about a year of operation. The name Grand Junction has stuck on the area ever since and is still found in the *Junction* Ranger Station, at the west edge of Section 30. See also *Junction City.*

GRANDVIEW
Pennington County

McGuire's *Coming Empire* shows the town of Grandview about 7 miles northwest of Pactola, just at the south fork of Boxelder Creek, south of the Lawrence County line. There does not seem to be anything there now.

GRASSHOPPER JIM'S PLACE
Meade County
Section 9, T7N-R6E(?)

Leland Case writes that this was a "trading center on Spring Creek, northeast of Bear Butte. Grasshopper Jim was a 'character,' probably an ex-soldier . . . his place was a junkyard, not a real ghost town, yet probably as much of one as some you list."

GREENMONT POST OFFICE
Lawrence County
South side, Section 35, T5N-R2E

This was a post office in the Trojan area, near Portland. It was on the Fremont, Elkhorn & Missouri Valley Railroad and probably was also served by the Black Hills & Missouri River, for the two lines were close together at this point. A person interested in railroading could do far worse than to spend a good deal of his time figuring out the various narrow-gauge lines in and around the Trojan area.

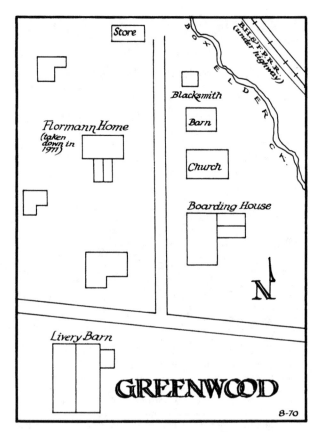

Greenwood, on the Black Hills & Fort Pierre Railroad, from a photograph taken in the 1880s. The town grew up to serve the nearby mines, and faded away with them around 1900.

The Robert Flormann home at Greenwood on Boxelder Creek. Flormann was an active mining promoter and made a fortune from his many efforts, although some of the investors in them did not. In 1912 he fell to his death in his Greenwood mine while attempting to rescue a miner suffocating from a disastrous fire underground.

GREENWOOD
Lawrence County
Center, Section 18, T3N-R5E

Greenwood, which was founded about 1885, was the home of a very considerable mine, and at its prime it had a post office, store, school, livery stable, stage barn, blacksmith shop, and boarding house for the miners. The town survived at least until 1912, when Robert Flormann was buried there, having been killed attempting to rescue one of the miners from the burning mine. In 1971 the last of the houses was torn down, and the last of the grove of trees which gave the town its name was decimated, but many foundations and the mine itself can still be seen.

Father Rosen seemed not to think highly of this mining enterprise:

"Greengood" [counterfeit] would have been a very appropriate appellation. The newspapers of even Chicago heralded the discovery of gold there as one of the greatest of the age. . . . Hundreds of thousands of dollars were spent in building mill, tramway and flume. It is said that not a dollar's more worth of gold was taken out of the rock than was put into the rock by salting. . . . A Chicago capitalist was the wiser, but the mining business and prospects for miners received such a "black eye" that even at this date [1895] it will take years to regain its former standing. "Wildcat" schemes have indeed retarded the development of the Black Hills and especially of Lawrence County, more than most of our readers are aware of.

Carl Leedy in his *Golden Days in the Black Hills* attributes the mining swindle to Bob Flormann himself, "the most notorious swindler in the business," and says that he sold more than $500,000 worth of stock, much of it to an ex-postmaster from Chicago. Those who are equally familiar with Bob Flormann, however, vigorously dispute the allegation.

The foundations of the 20-ton stamp mill that served the Montana mine at Gregory, along the CB&Q tracks and Rapid Creek, just north of Rochford. Typical of an amalgamation stamp mill, the building ran across the slope of the hill, and the ore was trammed across the top and distributed to each of the stamps by gravity flow. Water for the process was brought in by a flume from the left, from a dam just south of Nahant.

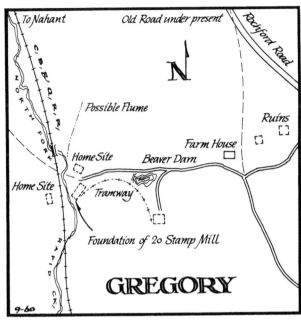

GREGORY
Lawrence County
Section 3, T2N-R3E

Gregory was the site of the *Montana mine*, one of the earliest gold discoveries in the Rochford district. It was located in 1879 by Charles Dunphy [or Dumphy], and in 1890 a 40-stamp mill was built at the mine by George G. Smith and others, all from New Hampshire, who formed the Gregory Gold Mining Company. The mill, which cost $160,000, operated only a couple of months, for the ore was found to be unoxidizable, and the gold could not be recovered by the amalgamation methods they hoped to use. New exploration was begun in 1901, when about 1,000 feet of tunnels were dug, but very little gold was produced, and the mine was closed again in 1906. In 1938 Dr. R. A. Vallier of Deadwood continued development work, but by 1941 he too had abandoned the effort to make the ill-fated Montana mine pay out.

As early as 1880 the Rochford newspaper reported that *Montana City* had a population of about 100, and as late as 1900 Gregory was listed in a commercial atlas as a post office. The 1916 USGS map shows about a dozen houses, running the width of the section. Today only one house remains standing, but there are several ruins and a few gaping holes, and the foundations of the mills are still there.

The best way to reach Gregory is from the Rochford-Lead road, turning to the west about 3 miles north of Rochford, where, for the next mile, until you come to the tracks of the Chicago, Burlington & Quincy, you will be passing through the area that once was known as Gregory and Montana City.

The last house in Gregory. The ruins of several more can be found in the valley and on the hillsides around the old Montana mine, to the east of the Burlington tracks.

A diligent beaver has flooded much of the area and covered some of the old roads and buildings in the valley where Gregory once flourished.

GRAY ROCKS

Custer County
NW¼(?), Section 35, T3S-R4E

This is one of the oldest resorts in the Hills, just south of Custer on US 385. The location above is approximate, for we have yet to see a map with the spot exactly shown.

GRIGGS

Lawrence County
SE¼, Section 4, T4N-R4E

Griggs was a silver camp on Bear Butte Creek, half-a-mile north of Galena, at the mouth of Butcher Gulch. It was a station on the narrow-gauge Deadwood Central, and possibly also on Jim Hardin's Branch Mint line. Today it would be hard to distinguish Griggs from the area rather generally termed Galena.

GRIZZLY BEAR

Pennington County
SW¼, Section 8, T2S-R5E

This famous mining property boomed in the early 1900s, leaving behind it innumerable shafts, drifts, stopes, and winzes into which the unwary can fall. The mine was to the north of Palmer Creek, but the buildings seem to have been scattered pretty much all over the place. A modern summer home was recently (1970) built on just about the site of the town, along the *old* Horse-thief Lake Road where it crosses Palmer Creek.

GRIZZLY GULCH

There are many "Grizzly Gulches" in the Black Hills, and probably more than one contained a mining community, but for all the times the name crops up, there never is a definite location attached.

In the early days it was customary to build of logs, then add an addition of sawn lumber when sawmills or good fortune made it more easily available. (Box Elder School)

he ruins of the great sandstone hotel at Cascade.

H

Coal, brought in on a spur that left the Deadwood line at Dumont, was brought to Hanna by the CB&Q and fed into the boilers of a Homestake pumping station from a trestle resting on these concrete piers. The water, from Spearfish Creek, was pumped over the hill to Englewood, where some of the energy was recovered by running it through a generating plant before using the water in the Homestake mining operations still farther eastward at Lead.

HANNA
Lawrence County
SE¼, Section 35, T4N-R2E

Hanna was started in 1904 and named for the lately deceased Republican leader Mark Hanna. It is the site of a Homestake Mining Company pumping station and was for many years served by a branch of the Chicago, Burlington & Quincy which left the Deadwood line at Dumont. The pumping station, a school, and several homes keep this small community going.

HARDSCRABBLE
Lawrence County
SW¼, Section 3, T4N-R4E

An early name for the lower end of *Galena*, from the mouth of Butcher Gulch on down the creek.

HARNEY I
Custer County
SW¼, Section 21, T3S-R5E

Harney was the name the Gordon party planned to give to their settlement and stockade. It was also the name of the military encampment in the same area which protected the Sioux's Black Hills against the encroaching miners.

HARNEY II
Pennington County
NE¼, Section 10, T2S-R6E

Harney, 2 miles west of Keystone on Battle Creek, was laid out in 1876 and soon had a school and post office, in addition to the usual homes and business establishments. The depth of its placer gold deposits, however, made them unprofitable to work and they were abandoned in 1878.

In 1883 the Harney Hydraulic Gold Mining Company was organized, with A. J. Simmon, William Claggett, and T. H. Russell as chief

incorporators. They built two flumes, one from Grizzly Creek and the other from Battle Creek. The two combined at the mouth of Grizzly Gulch to pass over its canyon on a trestle 200 feet high and 700 feet long. In spite of these efforts, Harney was pretty well deserted by 1900 and had at that time neither school nor post office.

Today Harney has several homes, a saw mill, an abandoned school, and the Harney Ranger Station. The old cemetery, 200 yards southwest of the Ranger Station, is worth a visit.

Harney, on Battle Creek, is one of the older towns in the Hills, and this house may well be the only one left that dates back to its early placer mining days.

HARNEY PEAK TIN MINING, MILLING & MANUFACTURING COMPANY
Pennington County
NE¼, Section 30, T1S-R5E

This vast English enterprise which flourished in the 1880s had its main office at Hill City, its famous tin mill on a hillside 1½ miles east of that, and its main mine, the Addie, on a spur leading off the Burlington Railroad still further east at Addie Camp. The company owned over a thousand claims extending from Hill City to Keystone, but a marked lack of tin production led to eventual litigation, and the company was forced to close down. W. Turrentine Jackson's "Dakota Tin" in the Winter 1966 issue of *North Dakota History* gives the detailed story of this monumental fiasco.

HAY CAMP
Pennington County
T1N-R7E

Hay Camp was an early name for *Rapid City*, so called because it was located amidst fertile fields which provided hay for sale to those who dwelt higher in the Hills.

The Williams Ranch, in the middle of the Battle Creek placer mining area south of Hayward. Its logs, hewn square and carefully chinked with plaster, have survived nearly a hundred Black Hills' winters.

The foundations for a boiler and steam engine that once pumped the waters of Battle Creek high onto the ledges of placer gravel to the southeast of Hayward.

HAYWARD
Pennington County
SW¼, Section 18, T2S-R7E

Gold was discovered at Hayward by Charles Phillips, Phillip Brown, and Judge Willis, in the fall of 1876, but the area was abandoned when Indians shot up the camp. In November of the same year Charles Hayward and James E. Carpenter, with six others, came in from Custer and laid out a town, which they named in honor of Hayward. Inside of six months there were 300 miners, and by April of 1877 the town became the temporary seat of Custer County. Tradition has it that the country records were stolen in January 1880 by a gang from Custer who were anxious to gain the county seat for their own town—but the truth of the matter is that, although the attempt was made, the thieves were at once apprehended and they were compelled to return the records. Hayward, however, was not actually in Custer County at all, so Custer's boosters eventually won out.

For a while Hayward was the site of extensive hydraulic mining, and a post office and school were set up. Currently it has a school and a very fine tourist attraction in *Rushmore Cave*. It is about 7 miles east of Keystone, on the Hermosa road.

HEAD OF WHITEWOOD
Lawrence County
Southwest of Lead

T. H. Watkins' *Gold and Silver in the West* shows a town, clearly identified as Head of Whitewood, on a Whitewood Creek southwest of Lead, on the stage trail leading toward Crook's Tower. It apparently was a very early mining camp, on either White*tail* Creek, or on what is now called Englewood Creek.

HEPPNER
Fall River County
SE¼, Section 20, T9S-R5E

This small town, southwest of the Angostura Reservoir, is clear out of the Hills, on Hat Creek.

HERMOSA
Custer County
NW¼, Section 32, T2S-R8E

Hermosa, on SD 79, is far from being a ghost town, having a population of 150. It is about 17 miles south of Rapid City, near Battle Creek, and is served by the Chicago & North Western Railroad. The town was earlier known as *Battle Creek* or *Battle River*, and still earlier as *Strater*.

The barn is probably the oldest unrestored building in Hayward, once a busy placer mining town on Battle Creek.

The Hermosa Bank, which was later used by Jack Zazadil as his rock and violin shop.

109

HILL CITY

Pennington County
Sections 23, 24, 26, T3S-R4E

Hill City also is far from a ghost town, having a population of 419. It was the second town in the Hills, founded in February 1876 by Tom Harvey and John Miller, but it soon *did* become a ghost town, being reduced to one man and a dog by the migration of the miners to newer claims in the northern Hills. A tin boom in the 1880s brought the town back to life. Today lumbering and tourists keep the town prospering, and the municipal liquor store regularly returns a profit of $1,000 a month to keep the town free of city taxes.

Hill City is along Spring Creek on US 16, about 24 miles southwest of Rapid City. It was also known as *Hilyo* and *Hilltown* in its earlier days. The southern end of the city was known in the 1880s as *Cornish Town*.

Brought by bull-train from the railhead at Pierre during the early boom days, this elaborate back bar still serves Hill City's municipal saloon and liquor store.

The Chicago, Burlington & Quincy Railroad depot at Hill City, once presided over by D. McNall, a station agent of the most extraordinary objurgatory powers. Until you had heard McNall shut a boxcar door on his hand you did not know what self-expression was. The bay window on the ground floor was arranged so that the agent, hunched over his telegraph, could look both ways down the track to see the trains a-coming.

D. McNall's sanctum sanctorum, in the CB&Q railroad station. The levers that controlled the signals are visible under the telegraph connections, in the lefthand corner of the room.

The view toward Hill City from the long-deserted workings of the Harney Peak Tin Mining, Milling and Manufacturing Company, on Tin Mill Hill.

For many years this building housed the party-line telephone system for Hill City, presided over by Mrs. Charles Hare. There was a feather-headed woman who used to rout Mrs. Hare out of bed every night about two o'clock to phone her husband or boyfriend, just to chatter, and one night, recognizing her ring, Mrs. Hare decided to just let it ring and not get up that time. That night the lack-wit's house burned down, and from that day on Mrs. Hare never refused to make connections, no matter what the time.

The "1880 Train" near Brophy's Ranch. For years this old-style tourist train ran between Hill City and Keystone, but when that branch of the CB&Q washed out in the flood of 1972 they shifted their operations and now run between Custer and Hill City with an occasional excursion up to Deadwood.

HILLSIDE I
Pennington County
Sections 23, 24, 26, T3S-R4E

Another name, probably a misprint, for *Hill City.*

HILLSIDE II
Butte County
SE¼, Section 14, T8N-R4E(?)

Hillside, some 5 miles southeast of Fruitdale, never seems to have been a very well-organized community, but it had at least two schools and appears to have prospered nonetheless. The location above is that of a present-day school house in the general vicinity.

HILLTOWN
Pennington County
Sections 23, 24, 26, T3S-R4E

An early name for *Hill City.*

HILYO
Pennington County
Sections 23, 24, 26, T3S-R4E

An early name for *Hill City.*

HISEGA
Pennington County
Sections 9 & 16, T1N-R6E

Hisega, a popular summer resort once reached by the Black Hills & Western, is along Rapid Creek in Rapid Canyon. Its name came from the initials of six young ladies who picnicked in the area one day. Hisega is about 8 miles west of Rapid City, on SD 40, the Rimrock Highway.

HOG RANCH

This was a common name for low resorts in the west, combination bars and brothels so rough they had been run out of town and had to set up business in the open country. There was one such place, Lee Case says, on the Deadwood-Cheyenne Trail, and Oelrichs, or Oral, may also have borne that sobriquet for a while, unjustly, of course.

HOLLOWAY
Lawrence County
N½, Section 23, T4N-R4E(?)

Holloway was a station on the Black Hills & Fort Pierre northern line to Piedmont. It was between Anthony's and Runkel, and in theory was 3 miles east of Bucks, although that distance would put the town well over into Meade County. No traces seem to remain.

HOLY SMOKE CAMP
Pennington County
SE¼, Section 31, T1S-R6E(?)

Colonel James A. Clark, a mining promoter, made his base near Keystone, at a place called Holy Smoke Camp, in the early 1900s. The spot continues to bear the name but for years has been little more than a single summer home, with some sporadic mining activity in the vicinity.

HOMESTAKE CAMP
Lawrence County
NE¼, Section 8, T5N-R2E

There must have been several localities known as Homestake Camp; this one was on the Chicago, Burlington & Quincy Railroad in Spearfish Canyon, about 6 miles south of Spearfish. The 1915 map shows about 6 houses.

HOMESTAKE WYOMING CAMP
Crook County
SE¼, Section 33, T50N-R61W

An early name for *Moskee.*

Hisega, on Rapid Creek, viewed through a cutting of the Black Hills & Western Railroad by which this resort was reached.

HORNBLENDE CAMP, HORNEBLENDE
Pennington County
NW¼, Section 3, T1N-R3E

Horneblende, or Hornblende Camp, was the community around the Benedict property, the Golden West mine, and the Victoria Company mine, which ran 3,700 feet of shafts and exploratory drifting. The property was active from 1899 to 1907, mining largely from a deep open cut and some shafts and transporting the ore on an aerial tramway to a Chilean mill on Castle Creek. The mihe was re-examined in 1915 and again in 1932-33. Total production was about 1,400 ounces of gold and some silver. Today the spot is marked only by some ruined ore hoppers and tramway pylons, the open cut with a deep and dangerous shaft in its center, and the summer home of Dr. R. H. Weeth, the present owner.

The shaft collar at the Golden West mine at Hornblende, a ferociously dangerous pit, for it is at the bottom of a sloping depression, and gawkers running down to look at it may just keep right on going.

HORSECREEK CAMP

One of the many Civilian Conservation Corps camps which blossomed in the 1930s; its location is uncertain.

HORSEHEAD, HORSE CAMP
Fall River County
Center of T8S-R6E

Horsehead Stage Station was on the Cheyenne River about 5 miles south of what is now the Hot Springs Airport. It consisted of a horse barn and a cabin with one room for the visiting dignitaries and another which served as a combination trading post, warehouse, kitchen, and bar. Horsehead Station was not a regular stop on the Rapid City-Sidney, Nebraska route, but it was always equipped to provide lodging and meals for the stage passengers in case anything disrupted the schedule. It is now under the rippling waters of the Angostura Reservoir, but even they cannot wash away its sins.

HORSESHOE GROVE
Lawrence County
SW¼, Section 16(?), T4N-R3E

Horseshoe Grove was a stop on the Black Hills & Fort Pierre, between Woodville and Whitewood Crossing, which, assuming it was before the tracks crossed Whitewood Creek, would put it pretty close to the location shown above.

HORSETHIEF LAKE
Pennington County
NE¼, Section 11, T2S-R5E

The narrow valley in which Horsethief Lake was later built made an excellent corral for stolen horses, for by stretching a rope across the narrow end and camping in the upper, horses could be penned in with little difficulty. Whether or not this was a sufficiently permanent abode of outlaws to merit listing as a town is problematical. The artificial lake is now surrounded with attractive camping grounds.

HORTON
Crook County
NE¼, Section 33, T48N-R61W

The 1903 USGS Sundance Quadrangle shows Horton as a community of two widely separated houses. A 1918 map shows this as a small town on the then main road between Newcastle and Sundance, west of the Hills. It was on the east side of the highway, 2-3 miles northwest of Four Corners and about 5 miles south and a little west of Buckhorn. Other maps now show a Horton Benchmark in the vicinity.

All that is left of the Horton community, northwest of Four Corners, Wyoming, is the school house and a scattering of ranches.

The City Hall in Hot Springs is built of buff sandstone from the nearby quarries. Long famed as a spa and divorce factory taking advantage of South Dakota's lenient residence laws, Hot Springs flourished at the turn of the century, only to lose place to Reno and the Mayo Clinic. A low and common jest, often daubed on honeymoon cars in the Black Hills, is "Hot Springs tonight, Deadwood tomorrow."

The South Dakota Old Soldier's Home, in Hot Springs, should not be confused with the larger U.S. Veteran's Hospital on the east side of town. Both were built to take advantage of the healing waters of the area, and in general appear pretty modern, but this old building seems to have been modeled on the cantonments of some frontier post, to make old troopers feel at home.

HOT SPRINGS
Fall River County
Sections 13, 23, 24, T7S-R5E

Hot Springs is the shopping center for a wide area in the southern Black Hills and for the plains to the south. It is blessed with warm springs, an old soldiers' home, a veterans' hospital, and, in the past, extensive rock quarries. Its present population is 4,434.

HEUMPHREUS RANCH
Custer County
NE¼, Section 3, T5S-R3E

Otherwise known as *Twelve Mile Ranch*; but do not confuse it with Twelve Mile Station, which was twelve miles north, rather than twelve miles south, of Custer.

HUSTLETON
Pennington County
SE¼, Section 10(?), T2S-R6E

The Cheyenne *Daily Leader* on January 12, 1877 mentioned this mining community, named for its recorder, as being on the west side of Battle Creek where the gulch opens out toward Hayward City; that would probably be at the mouth of the gorge.

The water tower at Pringle, which fed the boilers of the Burlington engines on their way to Custer. Even taut iron hoops in increasing numbers toward the bottom of the tank could not keep the water from oozing out and freezing in the cold of winter.

I

ICE CAVE
Pennington County
NW¼, Section 17, T2S-R2E

Ice Cave consists of a single room, perhaps 100' across and 200' in depth, with a ceiling 10'-15' high. Apparently the winter cold settles into the bottom of the cave and there freezes a column of ice which often reaches clear up to the ceiling, remaining until midsummer. Old timers in the Hills have told us of Fourth of July outings to Ice Cave, where the ice was used to hand-churn ice cream for the holiday. Bear Trap Cave and Igloo Cave are in the same section, but are extremely hard to find. This is another one of those spots which, if you can't find it from the geographical description, no instructions will help you either. The man who gave us our directions told us to head toward Wyoming until we saw an old rusty bucket lying by the side of the road, then turn south. There are, however, Forest Service signs once you get in the general vicinity.

IGLOO
Fall River County
NE¼, Section 12, T10S-R2E

Igloo, 8 miles south of Edgemont on the Chicago, Burlington & Quincy Railroad, was the home of the huge Black Hills Ordnance Depot which was built during World War II and occupied most of T10S-R2E. The Depot was put out on the plains for good reason: every once in a while something got out of control and flashes of explosions could be seen as far away as the central Hills. The name Igloo came from the mounded-over magazines used for the explosives. The Depot is now closed and Igloo's population was down to 10 in 1970.

INGLESIDE
Lawrence County
Part of Deadwood

Ingleside, above the rimrock, was a fashionable residential district.

INYAN KARA
Crook County
NW¼, Section 23, T49N-R62W

Inyan Kara mountain, an imposing volcanic pile which, like the Devil's Tower and Bear Butte, rises majestically out of the plains, was one of the sacred spots of the Indians; it is located on the west edge of T49N-R62W. Newton and Jenney, in their *Geology of the Black Hills*, say:

Inyan Kara is the most prominent peak on the west side of the Hills. It is situated in the Red Valley, west of the limestone plateau. Its name first appears on the map of Lieutenant Warren, and as translated for him signifies "the peak which makes stone." *Inyan* signifies in the Dakota tongue "stone" but the word *Kara* is unknown in the language, and is probably a corruption of *Ka-ga*, "to make."

The town of Inyan Kara was in the location given above, about 4 miles east of the mountain on US 585. It probably never had more than a couple of houses and was at the point where the trail to the mountain now joins the highway. It is just barely possible that the town may be located on the site of Professor Jenney's *Camp Bradley*.

IRON CREEK
Lawrence County
SE¼, Section 19, T5N-R2E

Iron Creek was a stop on the Chicago, Burlington & Quincy line which ran down Spearfish Canyon to Spearfish. There was, at one time, hope of running a railroad westward from Iron Creek to Tinton, but nothing ever came of the idea. Early maps show no houses in the area; the 1915 USGS map shows only three, so one may suppose that Iron Creek was never what you might call a commercial center.

IRON HILL
Lawrence County
SW¼, Section 10, T5N-R2E

South Dakota Place Names lists Iron Hill as a town, but from the detailed description there can be little doubt that the place they refer to is actually *Carbonate*.

IVANHOE I
Custer County
SW¼ (?), Section 31, T6S-R4E

A good many maps show Ivanhoe as a stop on the Chicago, Burlington & Quincy, about 4 miles north of Minnekahta, just over the line in Custer County. It does not seem to have been highly populated.

IVANHOE II
Custer County
SW¼, Section 18, T3S-R6E

This Ivanhoe, which was on a branch of Coolidge Creek, once had half-a-dozen houses. Now a very dim road leads to it and little trace of the town remains. It was also called *Yamboya*.

he inevitable car body, saved for possible use and then forgotten as impossible to use, typical of
oldbug Nelson's operations.

J

The Newcastle Chamber of Commerce moved this cabin, the oldest in the Hills, from the Jenney Stockade.

JENNEY STOCKADE
Weston County
NW¼, Section 7, T44N-R60W

In 1857 Lt. G. K. Warren built a corral on this spot but was warned away from the Black Hills by Indians who felt strongly about the matter. In 1875 Professor Walter P. Jenney rebuilt and enlarged the camp on his way into the Hills on a geological expedition, and it was at that time called *Camp Jenney*. It is currently the site of the large and prosperous *L A K Ranch*, founded in 1876. The stockade was a stage station on the Cheyenne-Deadwood line and was operated by James Mathewson in the summer and fall of 1877. He sold out to a Mrs. Scott, who served breakfast and supper to stage passengers for quite some time. In 1878 oil was discovered in the area, bubbling from some springs, and Newcastle, nearby, has not gotten over it yet.

A cabin from the old stockade was moved into Newcastle where it is preserved as a historical relic. The stockade site, 5½ miles southeast of Newcastle, is worth seeing only because of the presence of the exceedingly well-run L A K Ranch.

JENNINGS STOCKADE
Fall River County
Section 20, T8S-R3E

Another name for *Red Canyon Station*, or *Camp Collier*.

JEWEL CAVE
Custer County
NE¼, Section 2, T4S-R2E

Jewel Cave was discovered in 1900 by Albert and F. W. Michaud, who ran it as a tourist attraction for many years. It was made a national monument in 1934, and today uniformed rangers will guide you and your gasoline lantern through its narrowing, twisting, and crystal-lined passages. Nearby Jasper Cave, in the NW¼ of Section 3, is said by spelunkers to be quite an adventure—much like trying to climb down into the bowl of a toilet.

Both caves are in the 1,300 acre national monument, about 16 miles west of Custer on US 16. Only in recent years has Jewel Cave been extensively explored and discovered to be, as far as length is concerned, one of the largest caves in the nation.

The old office and reception building at Jewel Cave National Park. Vast new areas have recently been made public, with metal stairways and wide, paved walks, but a historical tour of the older part of the cave, through narrow wormholes, lit by gasoline lanterns, still begins at the old buildings.

JOHNSON, JOHNSON SIDING
Pennington County
NE¼, Section 6, T1N-R6E

Johnson was a siding on the Black Hills & Western, near the spot where Deer Creek enters Rapid Canyon. It does not seem to have ever been a large settlement, although it is listed on several maps at the turn of the century.

JOLLY
Butte County
SE¼, Section 25, T8N-R2E

A small community south of Belle Fourche, along the Chicago & North Western Railroad. It may be the same as the earlier (1921) community of *Redwater*.

JOLLY DUMP
Butte County
SW¼, Section 3, T7N-R2E

Starting at Jolly, on the Chicago & North Western line between Whitewood and Belle Fourche, is a spur that leads 3-4 miles in a curving southwesterly direction. An early C&NW RR map names the community at the end of this spur line Jolly Dump.

Jolly Dump, currently the site of a post and wood-chip plant, was originally a sugar beet pulp dump named for a nearby rancher when the Chicago & North Western built the spur in 1929.

JONES I
Fall River County
NE¼, Section 19, T7S-R5E

Another name for *Erskine*.

JONES II
Meade County
Section 26, T4N-R5E

A stop on the Black Hills & Fort Pierre Railroad, in Elk Canyon between Crystal Cave (now Bethlehem Cave) and Doyle.

Junction City and the Grand Junction mine were spread out from Tenderfoot Creek clear to Spring Creek, a distance of perhaps 2 miles. One gets the impression from early newspaper articles that this extensive construction was designed to benefit the friends of the promoter, as they found congenial employment building tramways and flumes that probably could have been considerably shorter if the stockholders had been on hand to supervise the operation.

JUNCTION CITY
Custer County
Sections 29 & 30, T2S-R4E

Junction City, on Tenderfoot Gulch, was named for the Grand Junction mine, and appears to have been in existence as early as September 1879. The name Junction City applies to quite a wide area: the mine itself, up and down Tenderfoot Gulch, and clear over to the Junction Ranger Station in the SW¼ of Section 30.

The Grand Junction mine, located by C. C. Crary in 1878, was on a high hill in the center of Section 29, T2S-R4E. A small mill was built about a mile north of the mine, on Vanderlehr Creek, just south of Spring Creek, and this was replaced in 1880 by a 40-stamp mill, the foundations of which can still be seen on the ground. Water for the mill operation was brought from 2-3 miles up Spring Creek by a peculiar covered wooden flume built of 1¼" lumber and buried in a deep ditch. The flume was carried across Vanderlehr Creek in what was referred to as an "inverted siphon" of 7" steel pipe. The entire course of the flume from the dam to the mill can be followed high on the side of Spring Creek Valley, and the

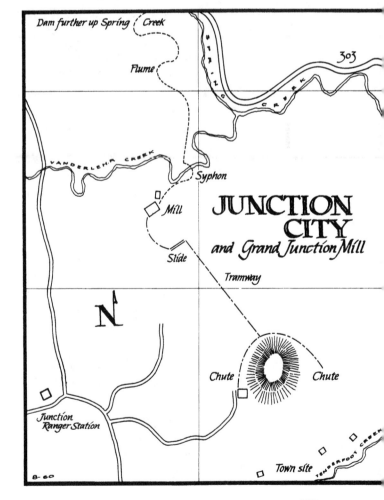

mile-long tramway with its wooden tracks, ore hoppers, and hoists can be followed from the mill to the mine. The entire operation appears to have been designed more to provide employment for the promoters than profits for the investors, for the mine closed down in 1881, having processed 7,000 tons of ore that yielded only $3.59 worth of gold to the ton.

The area is best reached from the Junction Ranger Station.

A mobile placer mining rig at Junction City.

Ruins of a stone fireplace in Junction City, the town that served the Grand Junction mine.

A railroad coach beside the right-of-way of the Black Hills & Western Railroad in Silver City.

A half-gone window still reflects the clouds, while a tattered curtain still preserves a semblance of modesty beside a long- forgotten bedstead, at the Kiddville Stage Station.

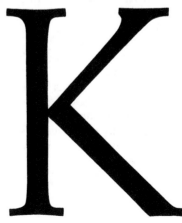

An ornate granite headstone in the Keystone cemetery, happily situated, long before Mount Rushmore National Memorial was carved, so that now the benevolent faces of Washington, Jefferson, Lincoln, and Teddy Roosevelt look down upon the dead. The verse on this monument appears to read:

Angel of patience! Sent to calm
Our feverish brows with cooling balm,
To lay the storms of hope and fear,
And reconcile life's smile and tear,
The throes of wounded grief to still,
And make our own our Father's will!

KEYSTONE
Pennington County
Sections 4, 8, & 9, T2S-R6E

Keystone is an active mining and tourist town on US 16A, along the road to Mount Rushmore. The town divides itself into two sections: one, along US 16A, provides tourist accommodations and attractions, while the older part, half-a-mile east, is still a local mining and shopping center.

Many mines dot the valley around Keystone. The old Holy Terror and its mill still dominate the town, although repeated efforts to re-open the mine have met with successive failures. The name, local legend has it, came about because a miner's wife complained to him that other miners had named their mines for their wives and he ought to name one for her. He did. The mine lived up to its name, for around 1900 a disastrous fire caused it to collapse, and it was not until the 1930s that the miners' bodies were finally recovered. The Keystone mines all enjoy a reputation for being exceedingly dangerous, for the rock strata instead of lying horizontally seem to stand right up on edge like a series of guillotines, each slab of rock waiting for its chance to slide downward. One of the mines was framed with 14" square sets, leaving a 6' tunnel between the timbers. Today a cat could not walk into it; the mountain has slowly, steadily, and inexorably healed the scar and sealed off the tunnel, crushing the heavy timbers like matchsticks.

Although gold started the Keystone mining boom, other minerals have been responsible for keeping the town alive. Feldspar, lithium, beryllium, and similar minerals associated with pegmatites have been profitably mined for years, and the area was originally called *Etta*, or *Etta Mine*, for the nearby tin prospect of the Harney Peak Tin Company. Tin did not appear in paying quantities, but for years the mine produced large quantities of spodumene, a lithium ore; crystals nearly 50' long have been photographed in the Etta glory hole. The whole area is full of both working and quiescent mining operations and is a rockhunter's paradise on that account.

Halley's General Store, in the old part of town, is one of the few genuine general stores still in operation; a visit will well repay the effort. A few specimens of gold-rush architecture may be found around it.

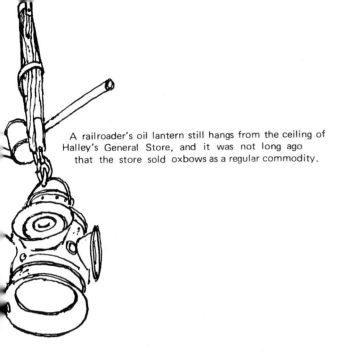

A railroader's oil lantern still hangs from the ceiling of Halley's General Store, and it was not long ago that the store sold oxbows as a regular commodity.

Although visitors to Keystone usually fall in love with Halley's General Store, it is not maintained as a tourist attraction but deals genuinely in general merchandise in demand in the community, and it has done so, relatively unchanged, for more than seventy years.

The teller's booth was all that was saved when the Keystone Bank burned to the ground in 1921, and it is now used as an office by Junior Halley, genial proprietor of Halley's General Store in Keystone.

The office of the old Holy Terror gold mine, on Keystone's main street, beside the general store.

A Victorian house dating back to the 1900s, when Keystone was booming and Stewart Edward White, who joined the gold rush, wrote *The Claim Jumpers* based on lore picked up in local bars.

123

A stage stop near Kiddville, consisting of the original log house, with several subsequent additions, connecting cellars and sheds, and a brand-new tin roof, for the building was used as a barn at the time this picture was taken.

KIDDVILLE
Custer County
NE¼, Section 11, T3S-R3E

Kiddville was an early placer mining camp, mentioned as early as September 20, 1879 as being 4 miles up French Creek from Custer. Early maps place it near the Penobscot Mine, which is where present-day *Zimbleman Deer Camp* is located. Nearby, at the intersection of Sections 34 & 35, T2S-R3E and Sections 2 & 3, T3S-R3E, is an abandoned stage station which may also have been known as Kiddville. The building there is an interesting one, incorporating several differing styles of early Black Hills architecture.

KIRK
Lawrence County
NE¼, Section 4, T4N-R3E

Kirk is now the site of a very large electrical generating plant. It is at the junction of Whitewood and Whitetail Creeks, about 1½ miles southwest of Pluma on the dirt road leading to the Homestake powder storage area. Kirk was originally known as *Pennington*, but changed its name when the railroad came in in 1891.

KENNEDYVILLE
Pennington County
NE¼, Section 33, T1S-R5E

An early name for *Addie Camp*, taken from the name of a Mr. Kennedy, or Canaday, who ran the only bar in town. USGS maps now label the town *Canadaville*.

KERB STATION
Lawrence County

The community, or more probably railroad siding, served the Black Hills Building and Developing Company, which, around 1900, owned several hundred acres of mining property near the Homestake.

The site of the rotating Chilean mill of the Penobscot mine at Kiddville, with the sheet-iron trough that held the ore under rolling grinders visible at the lower left.

Electrical generating plant at Kirk, which serves Lead and the great Homestake mine. Coal is hauled by the CB&Q to the top of the plant, and water is brought in by flume from Englewood.

There was no place in the Hills where you could not hear the raucous whistle of a mountain-climbing locomotive puffing its way toward the miners or the timber.

L

Ruins of barns, sheds, stores, and houses at Lauzon. In general when a long building lacks windows and chinking, one assumes it was a barn rather than a dwelling; conversely, when it had broad windows across the front, like the building in the rear, one tends to suspect that it was once a store.

LAFLIN
Lawrence County
Center, Section 18, T3N-R5E

Cram's Atlas shows Laflin as another name for *Greenwood*.

L A K RANCH
Weston County
NW¼, Section 7, T44N-R60W

A famous and still active old cattle ranch, 5½ miles southeast of Newcastle. Founded in 1876, it grew up on the site of the old *Jenney Stockade*. Its name comes from the initials of the three bankers who financed it: Lake, Allerton, and King.

THE LAKE, LAKE STATION
Lawrence County
SW¼, Section 22, T4N-R3E

Lake Station was a common name for *Woodville*, because some industrious beavers had dammed up an imposing body of water nearby. The dam, although usually dry, can still be seen on the top of Woodville Hill.

LANCASTER CITY
Lawrence County
SE¼, Section 20(?), T5N-R3E

Lancaster City was named for a Mr. Lancaster of the firm Spring, Lancaster and Frost. It was in Blacktail Gulch, about a mile northwest of its junction with Deadwood Creek. The Gustin and the Laura mines were in its vicinity, and these hauled their ores over a level road down to the Cunningham mill.

LAUZON
Custer County
SE¼, Section 3, T5S-R1E

Lauzon once had a store and a post office, surrounded by several other buildings. All that is left now is a small country school and a home for its teacher, both out in the middle of the most desolate prairie. A member of the school board once remarked to some strangers that their previous teacher had given trouble; he had had the habit of going off to town after school hours. A thoughtful listener observed that, all things considered, once their teacher ever got to town, they were lucky to get him back at all.

LAVIERE
Crook County
SE¼, Section 33, T50N-R61W

An early name for the post office at the *Homestake Wyoming Camp*, a logging operation that eventually became *Moskee*.

LEAD
Lawrence County
Section 33, T5N-R3E

A thriving mining town, home of the great Homestake mine, and populated by some 5,420 souls. The town was originally called *Washington*. Mildred Fielder's *The Treasure of Homestake Gold* is a mine of information about the area.

A staunch and solid Victorian brick house in Lead (pronounced Leed, and so named for the leads of gold ore beneath the city) testifies to the early prosperity of this little mining city.

LEGION LAKE
Custer County
NE¼, Section 25, T3E-R5E

A state-owned summer resort in Custer State Park, where US 16A and SD 87 meet. Nearby, the Badger Hole, home of South Dakota Poet Lariat Badger Clark, is open to visitors.

LEOLA PARK
Pennington County
Section 34(?), T2N-R4E

A fairly recent atlas shows Leola Park as a stop on the Black Hills & Western, between Silver City and Mystic, or, to narrow it down still more, between the lesser-known stops Burlington Junction and Canyon City.

One of the shaft houses of the famous Homestake mine, now down 7,000 feet. Since it began operations, the mine has taken out over $700 million worth of gold, and has conveyed a considerable degree of financial stability upon the northern end of the Black Hills.

The Homestake open cut at Lead. In early days, when most of the mining was in drifts and tunnels, parts of Lead were pretty precarious. One politician bawled out from the hustings "If'n every word I'm a-saying ain't the gospel truth, may thisyere earth open up and swaller me!" It did, and as they were fishing him out of the Homestake workings one miner mused to another "You know, Lem, I don't believe that young feller was very reliable." Eventually underground work gave way to the open cut, the size of which can be gauged by comparing it with the houses on the upper right. Nowadays, however, the Homestake is back underground again, working 7,000 feet below the surface.

LEXINGTON
Lawrence County(?)

The *Black Hills Illustrated* (page 44) has a view labeled "Lexington," apparently a mine, but probably also the name given to the community around it. The *Lexington Hill* mine, formed in 1903, centered on the SW¼, Section 25, T5N-R3E.

LIMESTONE
Pennington County
Section 3(?), T1N-R6E

A stop on the Black Hills & Western, just west of Canyon Lake.

LIMESTONE MOUNTAIN
Pennington County
Section 27, T1S-R1E

South Dakota Place Names distinguishes between Limestone Mountain, with its general store, filling station, and dance hall, and *Moon* post office nearby, but it's all one now, for none of them is left in operation, although the store-filling station building is still there, near the Moon campgrounds. The area is 20 miles west of Hill City and is a favorite spot of those deer hunters who are not afraid to get off the highway.

LINCOLN

Apparently another name for the town around the Carter Mine at *Cartersville*.

LIND CAMP
Pennington County
NE¼, Section 17, T1N-R3E

This community, with eight occupied houses shown on the 1956 USGS map, is about 1¼ miles north-northeast of Deerfield Dam and is doubtless a hunters' or fishermen's camp.

LITHIA
Fall River County
SW¼ of T8S-R6E

Lithia was near the Cheyenne River, just north of the spot where Hat Creek flowed into it. It is more than likely under the waters of Angostura Lake, and folks who aim to visit the place had better come in a boat.

LOG CABIN HOUSE
Pennington County
SW¼, Section 23, T1S-R3E

Log Cabin House, run by a man named Gillette, was a station on the Cheyenne-Deadwood stage line, about 6 miles south of what is now known as Deerfield.

LONE CAMP
Lawrence County

This was a Black Hills mining camp, more or less in the same area as Garden City (Maitland), Carbonate Camp, and Grizzly Gulch, apparently in the area north and west of Deadwood and Lead.

LOOKOUT
Pennington County
SW¼, Section 1, T1N-R3E

Lookout was an early mining camp on Castle Creek, about 4 miles west of Mystic. It was probably named for the Lookout mine discovered in 1882 by J. T. Hooper and F. J. Ayers, although some say that it was originally called *Fort Lookout*, from its presumed commanding position on a hill. As the town was in a valley, this last derivation seems somewhat untrustworthy.

As early as 1884 there was a sawmill in Lookout, run by Fish & Hunter, and 126 men were busy digging the ditch to provide water power to Robinson & Hawgood's Spread Eagle mine. A total population of 600 was reported, and an 1886 picture shows that there may have been housing available for most of them. Sometime between 1882 and 1892 the 40-stamp mill from the old Alta-Lodi at Myersville was moved in, and in

1890 the governor of New Hampshire and some friends took over the mill and Lookout property, but from that time on the town dwindled, and the last activity in the mine was reported in 1905. As early as 1890 there were only 57 people left in town to keep its little post office going. All that is left today is the ruin of the huge mill, the tramway up the side of the mountain to the mine, and a trace of the flume which ran along the north side of Castle Creek.

The mill ran on water power and had to close in freezing weather, so in the wintertime the whole population would move up to Deadwood, leaving most of their possessions behind them. The people in the Hills were so honest, says old Victor Jepson, that even bottles of liquor left in the unlocked bar would be undisturbed when the inhabitants returned in the spring to resume operations.

About a mile down Castle Creek was the Auburn Mining Company scheme to pump water from Castle Creek over the divide to Whitetail Gulch, in order to work the placer gold deposits there. The pumping station was built, and an enormous pipeline laid down, but the only people to make money out of the plan were its promoters.

You won't have any trouble finding Lookout—just turn west along Castle Creek at Castleton, a mile south of Mystic, and keep going. The canyon is spectacular, lined with old mines and summer homes.

LORING
Custer County
SE¼, Section 33, T5S-R4E

Loring, about 5 miles southwest of Pringle on the gravel road to Minnekahta, was a siding on the Chicago, Burlington & Quincy Railroad which served the Erpelding and F. V. Redenbaugh limestone quarries and lime kiln. The base of one of the kilns is still visible, west of the tracks, and still farther west is the quarry which fed it. If you choose a warm day to go exploring in this area, you will find out for yourself the origin of the comparison "dry as a lime-burner's hat." Quicklime, as it comes from the kiln, is extraordinarily hygroscopic. The professional lime-burner took great pains to see that he never got a sweat up, and the quicklime dust in which he worked made his clothes so dry they crackled.

Counting five stamps between each frame, the old Lookout mill on Castle Creek had fifty stamps. Ore was brought into the top of the mill from the right, on a tramway carried on high trestles, from a mine far up the side of the mountain.

Base of a lime kiln, at Loring Siding. The white lime still stains the earth all around; the limestone quarries were directly behind the kiln.

LOST CABIN I
Pennington County
NE¼, Section 19, T2S-R5E

Obviously if it were known where it was, it wouldn't be lost. Actually, there are two locations. The first, commonly known as Lost Cabin, is on the Grizzly Bear trail between the Horsethief Lake highway and Sylvan Lake, fairly close to the Gap Lode mine. It was once the home of an old gentleman who raised Christmas trees, and the ruins of his cabin can yet be found nestled up against some granite cliffs.

LOST CABIN II
Pennington County
SE¼, Section 17, T2S-R5E

The other location, up on a spur above Nelson Creek, is simply a tiny rock-and-log-and-mud hut, which originally had an incredible slate roof over it. Presumably it was the retreat of some miners who fled to the high hills to evade eviction by the U.S. Army during the summer of 1875.

A cabin near the Lookout mill, on Castle Creek.

Cyanide mills, like this one near Myersville, generally run down the slope of a hill so the ore can move by gravity flow through the successive processes.

LOST CAMP
Lawrence County
SW¼(?), Section 11, T4N-R2E

Lost Camp, now reduced to two crumbling cabins, may have been at one time a larger settlement, although even the older maps do not show any houses at all. It is ½ mile southwest of Terry Peak, and the lookout on that mountain will doubtless be able to direct you to it.

LOWER DEADWOOD
Lawrence County
Part of Deadwood

This was between Montana City and Deadwood proper, on Whitewood Creek.

ruins of Box Elder School still stand, and the light of wisdom still shines, through the roof.

M', Mc, Mac

Because they are often misspelled anyway, we have assumed, as most libraries do, that names beginning with any of these combinations are all spelled *Mac*, and list them as follows:

MAC'S CAMP
Lawrence County
SE¼, Section 15, T3N-R1E

This appears on the Forest Service map as an intriguing group of five houses arranged in an orderly V at the end of a short road.

McGEE'S SIDING
Pennington County
NW¼, Section 22, T1N-R7E

This was the site of McGee's Quarry, a sawmill, and the junction of the Warren-Lamb narrow-gauge railroad, coming down from the Victoria area, with the Black Hills & Western line in Rapid Canyon. It may be reached by a spectacular, dangerous, narrow, and lumpy road from Victoria Dam.

McINTYRE DIGGINGS
Pennington County

A few miles north of Rockerville, on Deadman's Gulch.

McQUAIG
Lawrence County

Probably only a ranch, this appears on a 1910 map nearly on the 104° line, northwest of Besant.

MAITLAND I
Lawrence County
SE¼, Section 18, T5N-R3E

Maitland, originally called *Garden City*, is about 2½ miles northwest of Central City on False Bottom Creek. It was a great mining district in the early days, and among its active mines were the Columbus, Beltram, Gold Eagle, Echo, and Penobscot. In April 1902 Alexander Maitland, ex-governor of Michigan, took over the Penobscot property, and the town and mine began to be known by his name. By January 1, 1903 the mine had a 40-ton stamp mill in operation. Although rich, the ore had to be roasted, then run through the cyanide process, before its $30-a-ton values could be extracted. It ran under various managements until 1915; later, in 1935-1936, the Canyon Corporation operated it. In the 1950s the mill was destroyed by fire while being dismantled. All that is left of the 50-odd stores and houses shown on the 1915 map is the old shaft house, one old mill, and several dwellings. A caretaker keeps an eye on any moveable property, which is probably why there is so much of it still left in the old town.

The best road to Maitland is through Blacktail Gulch, starting in Central City. It is also possible to drive up along False Bottom Creek from Spearfish, but the last man we knew to do it said he would not do it again.

Twin hoist drums of the great Maitland mine. Well constructed shafts were usually rectangular with three compartments: two for hoisting and one of ladders and pipes. Visitors to the shafthouses were always warned not to speak to or distract the engineer, upon whose care and watchfulness the lives of men below depended.

The Canyon Company mine shafthouse, at Maitland. Shops and offices were at the right, and the extensive ore-roasting kiln and cyanide mill at the left of the picture.

MAITLAND II
Fall River County
SE¼, Section 24, T9S-R5E

Maitland is a crossroads south of the Cheyenne, on Hat Creek. Early atlases show it as the location of a post office, and little else.

MALLO CAMP
Weston County
SE¼, Section 4, T47N-R60W

An attractive organization camp, used mainly for summer football practice, about 4 miles east of Four Corners, on Beaver Creek.

MANHATTAN
Crook County
Junction of Sections 6, 7, 17, & 18, T51N-R61W

Early maps show Manhattan as a group of 3 or 4 houses at the end of a dead-end road. One house, the old post office, still remains.

MARIETTA
Fall River County
NE¼, Section 6, T8S-R2E

Marietta is the location of the Tubbs Gravel Pit, which has been in operation for many years. Before 1908 Birdsell & Paine shipped a great deal of sand ballast to the Chicago, Burlington & Quincy Railroad for use in building its roadbeds. In 1908 a Mr. Kerr bought the business, and up to 1919 had shipped 150,000 tons of engine sand to the CB&Q for use in sanding slippery track. From 1919 to 1929 production ran about 120,000 tons a year, under G. W. Tubbs of Edgemont. These deposits, which are along the Cheyenne River, are replenished by every flood and seem to be good for 50,000 to 60,000 tons of sand and gravel every year.

Marietta is on the CB&Q tracks, near the Cheyenne River, about 8 miles northwest of Edgemont, and can be easily reached by a county road that zigzags along the section lines from northeast of town.

MARTIN VALLEY
Custer County
SE¼, Section 16, T6S-R6E

Martin Valley once was the center of a widely scattered community and had a school and post office. The name came from the Martin family, owners of the 7-11 Ranch in the valley, at about the NE¼, Section 21, T6S-R6E.

MAURICE
Lawrence County
NE¼, Section 17, T5N-R2E

Maurice is at the mouth of Coolidge Creek, in Spearfish Canyon, about 7 miles south of Spearfish, on SD 89. There are a good many summer homes in its vicinity, as well as the Homestake Hydro-Electric Plant No. 2, which converts the water of Spearfish Creek into electric power for mining operations.

It is possible to drive a jeep from Maurice up the east wall of the canyon to Carbonate. A walk of a mile or so up Squaw Creek will bring the adventurous to the old Cleopatra mine buildings.

The limestone canyon walls around Maurice are noted for thunder eggs, a geological curiosity of interest to rockhounds.

In the distance, viewed through the yard of an abandoned farm, is Marietta. Discarded machinery is typical of the boom-or-bust Dakota farming landscape.

This ancient cabin, at the point where SD 79 crosses Spring Creek, is just about where the little town of Maverick once was.

MAVERICK

Pennington County
NE¼, Section 18, T1S-R8E

Adreas' *Atlas* shows Maverick as a small village and post office on a northwest branch of Spring Creek. In 1891 it had a population of 19, but the post office had gone out of business.

MAYO

Custer County
NE¼, Section 26, T4S-R4E

Mayo, on the Chicago, Burlington & Quincy Railroad, has only a school now, but in the early days it seems to have been the center of at least three clusters of houses. The area is to the west of US 385, about 7 miles south of Custer, across the highway from Beecher's Rock.

The CB&Q tracks and the road, and the long-since vanished community of Mayo, from the abandoned Mayo School.

MEGARY HOTEL

Lawrence County
Center of Section 17(?), T5N-R4E

Collins' *Directory* mentions "Nelson Megary, saloon and hotel, Oakflat, 2½ miles east of Deadwood." It was probably somewhere along Boulder Creek—especially as the oaks to furnish "Oakflat" would be in low, moist ground—and probably better known as *Oakflat*.

MELVIN

Custer County
SE¼, Section 4(?), T5S-R7E

Melvin was a small settlement along the Fremont, Elkhorn & Missouri Valley tracks, between Fairburn and Buffalo Gap. It was named for the son of Charles Perkins, an early settler in the area. The location given above is that of the only settlement in the township, shown as *Summit* on the USGS map for 1901.

A crumbling ruin on the Gimlet Creek road west of Merritt, typical of the balloon-frame construction, with the studdings running all the way from sill to rafters, that came into common use after the Chicago fire of 1871. Merritt was a little logging town at the south end of a spur of the Black Hills & Fort Pierre Railroad, engaged mainly in sending fuel and timbers to the mines of Lead and Deadwood.

MERRITT

Lawrence County
SW¼, Section 7, T2N-R5E

Merritt, on the Lawrence-Pennington County line, to the west of US 385, 18 miles north of Hill City, was a wood camp at the end of the southern branch of the Black Hills & Fort Pierre narrow-gauge railroad. It had for many years a post office, school, and ranger station but today consists of a single farm and trout-growing ranch, where you can catch all the fish you wish at so much an inch.

MERRY-GO-ROUND CAMP
Pennington County
Center of Section 29, T2N-R3E

Merry-Go-Round Camp is a group of summer cabins 3 miles southwest of Rochford.

MEYERS SIDING
Meade County
SE Corner, T5N-R5E

Meyers Siding was a very small community about 6 miles southeast of Sturgis, on the Chicago & North Western tracks. It may also have been known as *Beaver Siding* and was just about where Beaver Gulch crosses the railroad line. Mail, in 1910, came via Sturgis, and no population figures are available.

MIDDLE BOXELDER
Lawrence County
NE¼, Section 13, T3N-R3E

We have no idea where this town is, but we do have a very early photograph of it, nestled against a tall, pointed hill, with 15 log cabins showing and more a-building. It is just possible that the Boxelder school, which is at the location given above, may have been a part of the town of Middle Boxelder, even though the school is located on what is now called North Boxelder Creek, for there seems to have been little uniformity in the early days about the designation of Boxelder's various branches. What is now called Middle Boxelder Creek has its origin in NW¼, Section 23, T3N-R3E and runs eastward into Roubaix Lake and into NW¼, Section 14, T3N-R4E, where it joins North Boxelder.

MIDLAND
Lawrence County
NW¼, Section 19, T5N-R3E

The home of the Echo Mining Company, which was at the above location. The name Midland is probably an error, mistaken for *Maitland*, which is within a mile of the mine.

MILITARY STATION
Fall River County
Section 20, T8S-R3E

One of the names given, for lack of an official title, to *Camp Collier*, or *Red Canyon Station*.

MILLER CAMP
Pennington County
NE¼, Section 19, T1N-R3E

About a mile north of Deerfield Lake, Miller Camp is shown on the 1956 USGS Deerfield Quadrangle as consisting of three abandoned houses, doubtless a hunters' or fishermen's camp.

MILLERS
Meade County
SE Corner of T4N-R6E

Millers was a stop on the northern branch of the Black Hills & Fort Pierre, between Doyle and Gardner's.

MINERAL HILL
Crook County
Junction of Sections 28, 29, 32, & 33

Mineral Hill, ½ mile southwest of Welcome, is one of the best ghost towns in the Hills. The big Mineral Hill mill is still standing, and even works occasionally, but the rest of the community is entirely deserted. The mill and half-a-dozen mine buildings are on the east side of Spotted Tail Creek, and perhaps ten more houses are on either side of the creek, a little higher up. Best way to reach the town is from Welcome, over a rough road leading southward along a little creek, then heading west across the divide between the two towns and coming down Spotted Tail Creek to Mineral Hill itself. The present owners do not encourage visitors.

Miners' cabins line a meadow at Mineral Hill, over the border in Wyoming about 2 miles west of Tinton.

Troughs made of hollowed-out logs at Minneapolis on Silver Creek. These seem to lead from a spring directly toward the site of one of the mills so they may have been connected with mining operations, but the fact that the ends were left in seems to indicate that they were watering troughs for cattle, although that seems unnecessary in so boggy a location.

MINNEAPOLIS

Pennington County
SE¼, Section 1, T2N-R3E

About a mile northeast of Rochford, on Silver Creek, Minneapolis was the site of a number of shallow mines and a mill to process whatever ores they found. The area is marked by some interesting log watering troughs which just possibly may be part of the old mining operation; nearby is Richards Spring.

MINNEKAHTA

Fall River County
NW¼, Section 19, T7S-R4E

Minnekahta, in a lovely red valley, is the junction of the Chicago, Burlington & Quincy lines from Deadwood and from Hot Springs, which join here and continue on to Edgemont. It has a school and a gas station-store combination. The water in the area is so hard that it was necessary that water for the steam engines be hauled in and pumped out of tank cars into the water tower. Local tradition has it that this Minnekahta fluid is the only water known to man that one has to use an ice pick on even after it has melted.

MINNELUSA

Pennington County
Section 14(?), T1N-R6E

Minnelusa was in Rapid Canyon, between McGee's Siding and Dark Canyon. In 1920 it was the site of a granite crushing operation which provided much of the gravel to pave Rapid City's streets.

MINNESELA

Butte County
NE¼, Section 24, T8N-R2E

Minnesela had hopes, in its early days, of becoming the major town in Butte County. In 1887 it had a population of 100, its own school, a Methodist church, and its own newspaper, the *Butte County Star*; it was also the county seat. The Fremont, Elkhorn & Missouri Valley Railroad bypassed the town, however, and went on to the present site of Belle Fourche instead. In a few years Minnesela was a ghost town, and now all that remains are a few farms.

The town is about 3 miles southeast of Belle Fourche, about ½ mile east of Redwater Creek.

MINNESOTA GULCH

Pennington County
NE¼, Section 29, T2N-R4E

A tiny community consisting of an old sawmill, abandoned gas station, several summer homes, and the ruins of a flume that apparently fed a large mill somewhere in the vicinity.

It is about 3 miles east of Rochford.

MOGUL

Lawrence County
Sections 1 & 12, T4N-R2E

The Mogul-Horseshoe Company was at this location and apparently used the Welcome (II) and the Mogul spurs of the Deadwood Central line that came southwestward from Kirk, divided

Minnekahta, where the CB&Q coming north from Edgemont branches to go east to Hot Springs, is in the middle of a barren plain. The water in the area is so hard that water had to be hauled in in tank cars so the engines could stock up for the long uphill pull northward to Custer and Deadwood.

There is quite a little community—deserted gas station, sawmill, and several houses—at the mouth of Minnesota Gulch. This summer cabin was constructed out of an old CB&Q caboose.

at Whitewood Junction, and came via Fantail Junction to Welcome and via Carthage Junction to Mogul, which was slightly to the southeast of Welcome. The company was an important one, producing over $7,000,000 in gold during its years of operation. See also Welcome II.

MOLL
Lawrence County
SW¼, Section 9, T4N-R4E

A name sometimes given to *Virginia City*.

MONTANA CITY I
Lawrence County
Part of Deadwood

Montana City, one of the mining camps later absorbed into Deadwood, was on Whitewood Creek near the mouth of Split Tail Gulch. It was above the huge slag pile which now ornaments the northern end of Deadwood, and in 1876 was enough of a town in its own right to merit a Fourth of July oration by Judge H. N. Maguire.

MONTANA CITY II, MONTANA MINE
Lawrence County
Section 3, T2N-R3E

An early, and probably the more common, name for *Gregory*.

MOON
Pennington County
Section 27, T1S-R1E

Moon, up in the Limestone Country, was named by T. J. Sherwood, its first postmaster, for Jack Moon, an early settler. Today even the post office is closed, and all that remains of Moon is one large building, fairly new, and a Forest Service

campground. It's about 23 miles west of Hill City; the roads, though good, are likely to be confusing, and the tourist had better pause often to ask his way.

MOOSE CAMP
Pennington County
NE¼, Section 27, T1N-R6E

Preferred spelling is *Musekamp*.

MONTEZUMA
Pennington County
Center of Section 14, T2N-R3E

Laid out in 1879, a scant mile up Irish Gulch from Rochford, and named for the nearby Montezuma mine, ruins of which are still in evidence.

Ghosts of the past are where you find them. We found this one, an antique doorknob, on a ranch house in the Limestone somewhere near Moon.

This building was once, if recollection serves, the store, gas station, and post office at Moon, but it is now a hunter's cabin, and Moon appears to be totally deserted.

137

Log "decks," rows of logs a saw-log length apart, for stacking the logs for shipment at the Homestake's lumbering operation at Moskee. The roof of the wash house shows at the lower right.

MOSKEE
Crook County
SE¼, Section 33, T50N-R61W

Moskee is a community of six or eight houses, on Cold Springs Creek. It is about 10 miles northwest of the Hardy Ranger Station, which, in turn, is on US 85, 11 miles southwest of Cheyenne Crossing.

Clair Roadifer's "Story of Moskee, Wyoming" in *Bits and Pieces* (VII, May-June 1971) is the most extensive first-person account of the town that is available. Other names for the locality were *Homestake Wyoming Camp, Laviere,* and *Bearsville.* Nearby are the ruins of the McLaughlin Tie & Timber Company's *Commissary D.* Local legends have it that the name Moskee was taken from the Pidgin English "maskee," meaning "no matter, never mind, I don't care," suggested by a well-traveled lumberjack during the discussion of proposed names which followed the Post Office Department's rejection of Laviere as likely to be confused with other Wyoming place names.

Moskee was to arise in the area of the McLaughlin Tie & Timber Company operations; they ran a standard-gauge railroad from Nahant clear across the Wyoming border and down to within 3 miles of the spot that later became Moskee. The McLaughlin interests, however, ceased operations about 1907. About 1921 the Homestake Mining Company developed the town extensively as a lumbering and sawmilling community to provide timbers for the mine. A huge water tank fed by the natural flow from a nearby spring provided water for the town and for fire protection—hydrants still dot the entire area. A sawmill was constructed, as well as a large boarding house for the loggers, several houses, and a washhouse. The logs and lumber were hauled out by trucks, often over much of the old McLaughlin roadbed. A post office was established in 1925 or 1926 and a school in 1928. The town had its own electric generating plant at about the same time. The maximum population was about 220, apparently reached in the 1930s; the mill and the town were closed down during the Second World War and never reopened. Many of the buildings still remain and are now occasionally used for hunting parties.

The town is best reached from US 85 near the Hardy Ranger Station.

Throughout the logging town of Moskee are these sheltered and protected fire hydrants, fed from a huge tank high on the hill to the south of town. The great danger of fire in such a community, and the deep winter snows, made such precautions necessary.

The logger's boarding house at Moskee, now used only during hunting season.

Boiler room and shops to keep the trucks going at Moskee. Although the McLaughlin standard-gauge line from Nahant nearly reached to Moskee, it was abandoned before the town was started. Another grade along Spring Creek seems level enough to carry a railroad but probably was used only for the heavy logging trucks, for no trace of ties can be seen upon it.

MOSS CITY
Custer County

A couple of early atlases list Moss City as the post office for an area in Custer County for which the population is unknown. It is probable that Moss City was in the eastern end of the county, but it is included here in case it may have been a Black Hills town.

MOUNT RUSHMORE
Pennington County
NW¼, Section 18, T2S-R6E

Mount Rushmore National Memorial, locally known as "them faces," was dedicated in 1927, by President Calvin Coolidge, and was very near completion when the sculptor, Gutzon Borglum, died in 1941. Over a million tourists a year come to see this gigantic carving of Washington, Jefferson, Lincoln, and Theodore Roosevelt, and the facilities provided for them make the monument a good deal more populous than many Black Hills towns.

Mount Rushmore is about 20 miles southwest of Rapid City, on SD 87 and US 16A. An excellent description of its building is found in Gilbert C. Fite's *Mount Rushmore.*

MOUNTAIN
Pennington County
SW¼, Section 30, T1N-R2E

Mountain was an early name for *Deerfield.*

MOUNTAIN CITY
Lawrence County
Part of Deadwood

Mountain City was an early name for *Fountain City,* which was down the gulch from Deadwood, and later incorporated into that city.

The headstone of Glenn Willard Lanning, five months old, in the Mountain Meadows Cemetery.

MOUNTAIN MEADOWS I
Lawrence County
SW¼, Section 17, T5N-R4E

Mountain Meadows has about four houses showing on the 1915 USGS map. It is about 2½ miles northeast of Deadwood, on US 14, and appears to have been somewhere near the open, rolling meadow where the Deadwood golf course now is.

MOUNTAIN MEADOWS II
Lawrence County
NW¼, Section 21, T3N-R4E

A 1916 map shows four houses in Mountain Meadows, and a good many of the people are still there, in the Mountain Meadows Cemetery, in the SE¼ of Section 20. The area is on US 385, about 13 miles south of Pluma.

It is very likely that Mountain Meadows is the same as, or at least very near, the town earlier known as *Nasby.*

MOUNTAIN RANCH
Lawrence County
Section 17, T5N-R4E

Mountain Ranch was on the stage trail between Custer and Deadwood, the stops being Custer, Hill City, Sheridan, Pactola, Box Elder, Elk Creek, Bear Butte Creek, Two Bit Creek, Mountain Ranch, and thence down Smith's Gulch into Split Tail Gulch opposite the pile of smelter slag. It was not, of course, the same place as Mountain City or Deerfield.

MOWATT
Lawrence County
NW¼, Section 24, T4N-R4E

Mowatt, on the Black Hills & Fort Pierre narrow-gauge railroad, was between Holloway and Runkel. The USGS map for 1899 shows the community of *Elk Creek* in very nearly the same spot.

MURPHY I
Pennington County
SW¼, Section 14, T1N-R8E

Murphy is a siding on the Chicago, Milwaukee, St. Paul and Pacific Railroad, about 5 miles southeast of Rapid City.

MURPHY II
Meade County
Section 31, T3N-R6E(?)

Murphy was a stop on the southern branch of the Black Hills & Fort Pierre narrow-gauge railroad, between Este and Repass.

MUSEKAMP, MOOSECAMP

Pennington County
NE¼, Section 27, T1N-R6E

Locally known as *Moosecamp* in its early days, this ranch took its name from the Musekamp family who lived on it. It was later known as *Victoria Ranch*, from its location on Victoria Creek.

Musekamp, or Moosecamp, was also the name of two resorts run by Mrs. Bernice Musekamp: the first, now under the waters of Pactola Lake, was in the NW¼ of Section 11, T1N-R5E; the second, still in operation and famous for its meals, is west of US 385, in the SE¼ of Section 15.

MYERS CITY, MYERSVILLE

Pennington County
SE¼, Section 27, T2N-R3E

Myers City, or Myersville as it is called today, was named for John Myers, an early miner and lumberman. Around 1883 the town had some 150 inhabitants, dependent upon the Alta Lodi Mining Company, which built a 40-stamp mill, but failed to find ore enough to keep it busy. The mill was subsequently dismantled and taken to Lookout, where it can still be seen. In 1892 James Cochran relocated five claims which he worked during the summers with a 16-ton Huntington mill, continuing development sporadically until 1917. Another flurry of prospecting took place between 1931 and 1936, leaving several small mines and their equipment in the area.

In the Myersville Cemetery is buried the Reverend Rumney, the celebrated preacher who preached, at the jocular invitation of Billy Nuttall, the only sermon ever given in a Deadwood bar. It was on this occasion that the faro dealer exclaimed at the end of the proceedings, "All right now, boys, the preacher has been telling you how to get to heaven. Just step this way, gents, and *I'll* show you how to make some money!"

A safe, torn open, near the biggest house in Myersville.

Myersville is about 2½ miles southwest of Rochford. From the road it seems to be only a rather large farm, but hidden in the trees and gulches around it are several abandoned mining operations and two or three dwellings. The road through town leads to the Forest Service lookout on Castle Peak, which is manned only in times of severe fire danger.

The largest house in town, now deserted. The town, however, is not dead, for summer homes are being built in its vicinity.

Looking south into Myersville, a town surrounded by many small and fairly recent hardrock mining operations.

MYSTIC

Pennington County
NE¼, Section 4, T1N-R4E

Mystic was originally called *Sitting Bull* but changed its name when the railroad came through in the late 1880s. There is a story somewhat to the effect that the name resulted from a *mistake* being noted on the railroad map by a man who couldn't spell very well, but a more likely theory is that some Burlington official connected with Mystic, Connecticut suggested the name.

Mystic was near the junction of the Black Hills & Western, coming west from Rapid City, and the Chicago, Burlington & Quincy line southward from Deadwood. It was hoped that the little town would become a railroad center, and although a good many train loads of coal came into Rapid City from the Wyoming fields, frequent floods made the BH&W a profitless enterprise, and it was junked in 1947.

Mystic was also the site of a large gold mill, an experimental plant set up in 1904 at the cost of about a million dollars by the Electro-Chemical Reduction Company to extract gold by an advanced chlorination process. The plant was a failure, and its old foundations now support the Frink sawmill.

The town is on Castle Creek, 12 miles north of Hill City on the gravel road which eventually leads to Rochford. The sawmill, a store, a school, a church, and a few homes are all that are left from its more prosperous days.

The hand-operated Standard Oil Red Crown gas pump at William Frink's Mystic Cash Grocery.

Once used as a store, and later as the Mystic school, this magnificent ruin has recently been torn down because it was too dangerous for the tourists, attracted to its antiquity, to explore.

The Bulldog Ranch, between Rochford and Lead. Its ornate columns tell the tale of glories long forgotten as the passage of the years efface the memories of gaudier days.

Around 1910 Nahant was a booming logging town, with a standard-gauge railroad bringing in timber from as far away as Wyoming. At its peak the town had a school, lodge hall, doctor, and of course the big McLaughlin sawmill. Now, alas, even this house is gone, though its foundations still mark the spot.

NAHANT
Lawrence County
NE¼, Section 34, T3N-R3E

Nahant was founded in 1890 as a lumbering and mining town and at its peak had some 500 inhabitants. The McLaughlin lumbering interests ran a long standard-gauge line westward from Nahant nearly to Moskee, Wyoming, and for many years the town buzzed with activity.

Today only a single house remains by the side of the Chicago, Burlington & Quincy tracks. It is about 13 miles south of Lead, on the road which eventually leads to Rochford.

The left end of this barn at Nahant is shingled and sided with the lids of the cyanide cans used in the local mines. It is hard to see how this practice can be a safe one, but it is not uncommon.

NASBY
Lawrence County
SW¼, Section 21, T3N-R4E

The Nasby post office, with Mrs. Gilbert Tower its postmaster, was first at Mountain Meadows II and was later moved, retaining the same name, to a new location at the Custer Peak Mine.

Mountain Meadows, here viewed through the town cemetery, was once the home, oddly enough, of the Nasby Post Office which later moved to the Custer Peak mine.

NEGRO HILL
Lawrence County
SW¼, Section 19, T5N-R1E

It may have been Nigger Hill to the miners, but the local newspapers used the form given here. It was just about where Tinton is now, and was named for some miners who struck it rich in the area—so rich that when they left the Hills they were provided with a cavalry escort to protect them until they reached the comparative safety of civilization.

NEMO
Lawrence County
NW¼, Section 27, T3N-R5E

Nemo began in 1877—nobody seems to know why the name was chosen. Omen spelled backward, or Jules Verne's captain of the *Nautilus*, or the comic strip character Little Nemo have all been suggested as possible sources.

In 1898 the Homestake set up a timber camp in Nemo and began operation as Case One in the harvesting of the National Forests. The narrow-gauge Black Hills & Fort Pierre came in during the same year and went on from Nemo to Piedmont in 1910.

The lumber has long since been cut, and new growth isn't yet big enough to cut again. Nemo now thrives as the home of the 4-T guest ranch, with several summer homes, a school, an attractive log church, a general store, and a Boy Scout Camp in its vicinity.

Nemo is on Boxelder Creek, about 14 miles northwest of Rapid City over a good tar road.

The church at Nemo, once a logging town on the Black Hills & Fort Pierre Railroad, and now a resort area.

NERVE CITY
Lawrence County
SW¼, Section 28, T5N-R2E

Nerve City was begun in 1896 when a house and a saloon run by O'Brien and Littleton were put up, about 1,500 feet north of Balmoral.

NEW BERLIN
Lawrence County

A placer camp in the Germania District, laid out in 1878. An early newspaper located it "one mile above the junction of Hay and Elk Creeks." These two creeks do not at present come together at all, so the location of New Berlin is somewhat difficult to determine exactly.

NEW CHICAGO
Lawrence County
NE Corner of T5N-R2E

An early news report tells of a successful placer on False Bottom Creek, "just above New Chicago." New Chicago was probably the same as *Maitland.*

NEW CUSTER
Lawrence County(?)

In May 1879 the *Engineering and Mining Journal* mentioned New Custer as the home of the Atlantic mine; it might have been the same, therefore, as *Williamsburg.*

NEWTON CITY
Pennington County
NE¼, Section 15(?), T1S-R4E

Newton City was about a mile southeast of Tigerville and was so vigorous a town that by December of 1878 it was to have a post office of its own. It was on Newton Fork, probably a little farther upstream than the present Newton Park, and 3½ miles northwest of Hill City. Nothing remains of it today.

NICK'S STOCKADE
Weston County
NW¼, Section 7, T44N-R60W

An early pre-gold-rush name for *Jenney Stockade,* now the L A K Ranch. Ed Lemmon's *Boss Cowman* mentions that one Nick Janis established a trading post there some time between 1863 and 1874 and that this "Nick's Stockade" was renamed Jenney Stockade when Professor Walter P. Jenney and party stopped there in 1875.

NIGGER HILL
Lawrence County
SW¼, Section 19, T5N-R1E

The miners' name for what appeared in the local press as *Negro Hill.*

NIHART, NIHART SIDING
Custer County
SW¼ Section 36, T4S-R4E

Nihart, or Nihart Siding, serves the White Elephant mine. It is on the Chicago, Burlington & Quincy, and US 385, about 8 miles south of Custer.

NINE MILE RANCH
Custer County
SE¼, Section 24, T4S-R3E

One of the stage coach stops on the route leading southwestward down into Red Canyon from Custer.

NORTH GALENA
Lawrence County

Another name for *Carter City,* which, judging from the name, must have been somewhere around Galena.

NORTH LEAD

Lawrence County
SE¼, Section 29, T5N-R3E(?)

A sort of continuation of Terraville, or, possibly, a town on Whitetail Creek in the center of Section 29.

NORTH RAPID STAGE STATION

Lawrence County
SE¼, Section 33, T3N-R3E

A stop on the Cheyenne-Deadwood stage trail between Rapid Creek Station (Florence) and the Bulldog Ranch, 32 miles north of Custer and 18 miles south of Deadwood, west of the North Fork of Rapid Creek, from which the station took its name. It was almost the same place as *Elkhorn (II)*

NOVAK

Lawrence County
SE¼, Section 18, T3N-R5E

Novak, also known as *Cindell Spur*, was a small mining community on the southern branch of the Black Hills & Fort Pierre Railroad. The present location, given on the USGS map, is the SW¼ of Section 17, but the old town seems to have been at the location above. A wide meadow, one

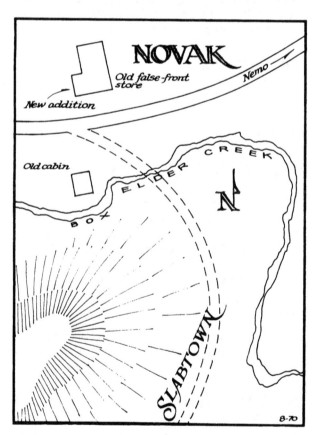

One occupied ranch and a couple of abandoned houses are all that is left to mark the site of Novak and Slabtown, mining towns on the Black Hills & Fort Pierre Railroad.

log cabin, and a false-front building now used as a barn appear to be all of the original structures remaining.

It is on Boxelder Creek, about 3 miles northwest of Nemo on the Roubaix Road.

NUGGET CITY

Lawrence County
Center, Section 20, T5N-R1E

Nugget City is elusive, and is frequently confused with Bear Gulch. H. S. Vincent's *Map of the Northern Ore Districts* (1898) clearly shows it to be about a mile west of the junction of Potato Creek with Beaver Creek, about 1½ miles west of Tinton. All that is left in the vicinity is a small cabin and some gravel-washing operations.

The only house today in the vicinity of Nugget City on Potato Creek. The big pine in the foreground has been spared by loggers because it is a surveyor's corner marker, a happy custom which in the Hills has resulted in the preservation of at least a few of the magnificent Black Hills ponderosas.

NUGGET GULCH

Pennington County

This probably was more of a mining district than a city, but it did elect its own recorder on January 15, 1878. The name "Nugget Gulch" is one that would be applied to an area, if only for the sake of the advertising.

The headframe and shafthouse at the Old Bill mine, a couple of miles west of Berne Siding.

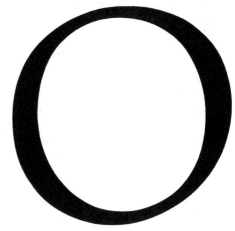

O

OAK FLAT
Lawrence County
Center of Section 17(?), T5N-R4E

This early town was the site of the E. Bowen lumber mill and the *Megary Hotel*. It is 2½ miles east of Deadwood on the Centennial Road to Crook City.

Oblivion is where the narrow-gauge "1880 Train" from Hill City turned around and headed back to town with its load of delighted summer tourists. Although the train continues in operation, the site is no longer used, but it still attracts many railroad buffs who are interested in seeing its unique superimposed standard- and narrow-gauge switching arrangements.

OBLIVION
Pennington County
SE¼, Section 34, T1S-R5E

This was not really a town at all, but a stop on the Burlington Railroad about 4 miles east of Hill City where the "1880 Train" ended its narrow-gauge rails and turned around. It was hoped to build a sort of railroad museum here, but this plan was abandoned by 1969 when the 1880 Train began to run on standard-gauge rails and went clear on to Keystone.

OCHRE CITY
Pennington County
NE¼, Section 13, T2N-R3E(?)

An 1879 news item mentions Ochre City as a town of growing importance, "on the other side of Stand-by mountain, about a mile and a half east of Rochford." The above fits the description as to distance, but a more reasonable guess might be that Ochre City was on Silver Creek, almost exactly one mile due east of Rochford, and probably south of Diamond City, where there have been many intermittent attempts to mine the creek bed bog iron, or ochre, of the area.

ODELL
Fall River County
SE¼, Section 15, T7S-R6E

Odel (sic) Canyon Quarry produced some sandstone about 1895 or 1896, but being of the soft Unkpapa stone like that of Elm Creek Quarry to the north, it did not enjoy much popularity. Three houses remain in the town, which is in Spring Creek Canyon, about 4½ miles southwest of Buffalo Gap.

Ochre City was originally a gold mining area, named for its iron-stained ores, but in later years the ochre, or bog-iron used as a pigment, has been mined in its own right.

OGLALLA TRADING POST
Pennington County
Near Creston, NE¼, T2S-R12E

See *Rapid Creek Trading Post.*

OLD BILL MINE
Custer County
SE¼, Section 33, T2S-R4E

We have not tried to list all of the mines in the Hills, a task already done to perfection in the U.S. Bureau of Mines' *Black Hills Mineral Atlas*, but now and then we mention a mine that seems to be of special interest.

Only remnants of the magnificent shaft house now remain at the Old Bill mine, about a mile northwest of Berne Siding. Nearby are summer homes and hunters' cabins, and from the mine itself a splendid view can be had of the rock carving on Crazy Horse Mountain.

OLSEN
Lawrence County
SE¼, Section 7, T2N-R3E

Although probably only a ranch, Olsen is shown as a town on an 1883 map, located on the South Fork of Rapid Creek, some 5 miles west of Rochford and apparently close to the present Deerdale Camp Ground.

ONYX CAVE
Custer County
NW¼, Section 21, T6S-R5E

No effort has been made to list all of the Black Hills' many caves. Onyx Cave, however, was one of the earliest commercial ventures in the cave line, and many people visited it from Hot Springs. The foundations of the two buildings which served these visitors with shelter and refreshment can still be seen near the cave. Most of the cave formations have long since been taken, doubtless to save them from being stolen, and except for its very end, it is now nothing more than a sloping, slippery, dangerous hole in the ground. If you cannot find the cave from the description given above no further directions will help you, for it lies amid a tangle of logging roads through which no map can guide you.

ORAL
Fall River County
SE¼, Section 27, T7S-R7E

Oral is a small farming community out on the plains, south of the Cheyenne River on the Chicago & North Western Railroad; its proximity to the Hills and its probable earlier career as *Pimptown* merit its inclusion in a list of notable Black Hills places.

An abandoned beryllium processing plant is all that now marks the location of the old tin mining town of Oreville.

OREVILLE
Pennington County
SE¼, Section 15, T2S-R4E

Oreville was founded in 1890, when the Chicago, Burlington & Quincy Railroad came into the Black Hills. It was named by the railroad officials, possibly in hope that the name would presage some vast supply of gold or tin ore in its vicinity. Even early maps show only a single house, and at present an unused refining mill for beryllium and a few summer cabins are all there is of Oreville.

It is on Spring Creek, 5 miles south of Hill City on US 16.

ORO
Lawrence County
Center of Section 29, T5N-R3E(?)

Oro was on Deadwood Creek, just west of its confluence with Poorman's Gulch, about 1½ miles due north of the east end of Lead. It may be the same place as *North Lead.*

149

OTIS

Custer County
NE¼, Section 27, T3S-R6E

Otis was named for the Otis family, and as early as 1900 had a post office serving the surrounding ranchers. In 1916 or 1917 the Warren-Lamb Lumber Company built a narrow-gauge railroad into Otis from Fairburn and built themselves a new sawmill on the old foundations of the Rugg Lumber Company. When their logging operations were finished, the mill was removed and the present *State Game Lodge* built on the old foundation, providing the name by which the area is now known.

OWENS

Weston County
Section 12, T43N-R61W

Owens is little more than a siding south of Newcastle, with a single desolate railroad storage shed and privy to entitle it to a name. To locate it exactly, it is between Spencer and Johnson Sidings, on the Chicago, Burlington & Quincy Railroad.

Owens Siding, on the Burlington south of Newcastle, apparently was never anything more than a railroad shed and a loading area for cattle cars.

ORO FINO

Lawrence County
NW¼, Section 8, T4N-R4E

Oro Fino was a mine stop on the Deadwood Central Strawberry Spur line that led clear up to the Gilt Edge Maid mine. It was founded in 1877 and in 1895 seemed to have some chance of reviving, but it never made it. It is in the Galena district and most easily reached by turning north on the dirt road at the top of Strawberry Hill, about 3½ miles south of Pluma on US 385, then heading downhill toward Oro Fino and Galena.

OTHO

Pennington County
SW¼, Section 15, T2S-R6E

Another name for *Glendale,* taken from the nearby Otho mine.

Mine buildings and mill of the Holy Terror mine. Local legend in Keystone has it that the discoverer named it for his wife. It has always had a reputation as a dangerous mine in unsafe ground, and about 1900 a disastrous fire entombed most of the miners. In 1939 attempts were made to unwater its 1,200-foot shaft and resume gold production, but the results were not rewarding, and with the coming of World War II the mine closed down again, although the mine buildings have now and then been used for various other purposes.

ouble doors and Norman windows show that this barn was once the Slate Creek Prairie Church.

Downstream from Pactola Lake this ancient cabin still marks the area where Pactola and its placers prospered.

PACTOLA
Pennington County
NW¼, Section 2, T1N-R5E

Pactola was first called *Camp Crook*, for General Crook had made his headquarters there while chasing miners out of the Hills in 1876. As early as July 1875, gold-seekers had moved in and set up a mining district with one Watts as its recorder. When General Crook removed the miners, Watts was allowed to remain behind to look after their interests, for it was assumed to be only a matter of time before the Sioux would be swindled or bullied out of the land.

In late 1876 the town boomed. Up to 300 miners attended meetings. William Keeler opened a store, and in the spring of 1877 one of the earliest post offices in the Hills was opened, with Arthur Harvey its postmaster. James Sherman built the first hotel in the Hills, the Sherman House, and a long flume was begun to work the rich placer deposits, some of which yielded as much as $50,000 to the claim.

The name Pactola was given to the town in 1878 when the miners, seeking a fancy and descriptive title, were urged by H. N. Maguire, a lawyer and newspaperman, to name the town for the ancient Greek placer workings on the Lydian river Pactolus. South Dakota's Pactola was for many years served by the Black Hills & Western Railroad, and was famous both as a mining area and a resort.

At Pactola in years gone by there used to erupt a dance of quite considerable vigor, presided over by the indomitable Mrs. Bernice Musekamp. During Prohibition, Wat Parker's grandmother arrived for a visit in the Hills, driven, in those long-gone days, by her chauffeur in his natty uniform of boots, breeches, and visored cap. It was in this outfit that Pace (that was his name) decided to attend the Pactola dance. Unfortunately for him the local populace mistook him for a revenue officer on the prowl, and a hurried midnight call from Mrs. Musekamp brought Pappy Parker to Pactola just in time to rescue Pace from the angry crowd that was about to lynch him.

Pactola is now under the waters of Pactola Lake, but the town's famous hostess, Mrs. Musekamp, continued in business nearby until 1962. Pactola Lake is on US 385, 11 miles north of Hill City.

Here lies one of the U.S. Army troopers sent into the Black Hills in the spring of 1875 to expel miners from this Indian Reservation. He was separated from his command, he froze to death, and his comrades buried him here, on May 19th.

PALMER GULCH LODGE
Pennington County
NW¼, Section 4, T2S-R5E

Palmer Gulch was the site of many early placer prospects and was settled in 1875 or 1876 by George Palmer, John Brennan, and California Joe Milner, soon joined by a large number of other miners, who united in setting up a mining district. The choice of the name was left up to the oldest man in the group, modest George Palmer. The gold was spotty and very deep in the wet and boggy valley, and attempts to extract it were abandoned when word came of the more promising strikes in Deadwood Gulch.

In 1925 the *Black Hills Country Club* was founded by Troy, Norman, and Leslie Parker, John Bland, Parker Davis, Francis Fabian, and D. P. Hynes of Chicago. In 1932 it was taken over by Troy Parker, who operated it as Palmer Gulch Lodge.

Palmer Gulch is also a Forest Service summer home group, having five or six summer cabins in its vicinity. It is 4 miles southeast of Hill City on the old, graveled Hill City-Keystone road.

PENNINGTON
Lawrence County
NE¼, Section 4, T4N-R3E

Pennington, later known as *Kirk*, had a population of 51 in 1880, and was one of the mining areas near Lead. It is now the site of a large electric generating plant.

PENO QUARRY
Lawrence County
SE¼(?), Section 8, T4N-R3E

Probably, although by no means certainly, a mistake for *Reno Quarry*.

PERRY
Lawrence County
SW¼, Section 29, T4N-R4E

Perry was the original name for *Roubaix*, but confusion with Terry caused the name to be changed to its present form.

PIEDMONT
Meade County
SW¼, Section 10, T3N-R6E

Piedmont was originally the *Spring Valley Station* on the old Sidney-Deadwood stage route. For many years it was the rail junction for the Black Hills & Fort Pierre and the Fremont, Elkhorn & Missouri Valley. See *Spring Valley Ranche*.

Piedmont, population 200, is about 12 miles northwest of Rapid City on US Interstate 90. Around the town can be seen several gypsum mines, and a local filling station has built some of the old millstones from a long-gone plaster mill into its walls.

Piedmont's principal street and the post office at the end of it.

An antique store in an antique building at Piedmont, on the eastern slope of the Black Hills.

PIMPTOWN
Fall River County
SE¼, Section 27, T7S-R7E

Ed Lemmon's *Boss Cowman* refers to this den of iniquity as being "on the south bank of the Cheyenne River where the railroad was held up while waiting for the bridge." It was inhabited by many lively characters including "Stepladder Jane," who fought, rather than wooed, her way to the top of her profession. Pimptown folded up almost at once when the railroad bridge was completed and the crews moved 6 miles north to Buffalo Gap. Present-day *Oral* now occupies the site but does not share the heritage of Pimptown.

PINE CAMP
Pennington County
SE¼, Section 1, T1S-R5E

Pine Camp was a construction camp on the Chicago, Burlington & Quincy Railroad from Hill City to Keystone. It was active about 1900. Later the site was used for the Overgard Sawmill, which utilized timber in the great basin east of Harney Peak. Recently the Baptists have built a summer camp, *Camp Judson*, on the spot.

It is about 2 miles west of Keystone on the old Hill City-Keystone gravel road.

A dim trail through the grass leads past a long-deserted home in Pine Camp.

Sheetmetal strips as chinking for this old log cabin at Pinedale. Normally, wood and metal so exposed together to the weather would result in considerable rotting of the wood; perhaps some preservative, maybe the tar in the oakum used for caulking the chinks, has prevented it here.

PINEDALE
Pennington County
S½, Section 28, T2N-R3E

A small but old community of homes and summer cabins about a mile west of Myersville. The oldest cabin, a log building with modern additions, has a distinctive chinking of weathered sheet-iron strips.

PINE GROVE
Lawrence County(?)

An early source mentions Pine Grove as being "within twenty miles" of Deadwood, which is not much of a description.

PINKERTON
Pennington County
NW¼, Section 17, T2N-R6E

Andreas' *Atlas* shows Pinkerton as a small village on the north side of Boxelder Creek. It was probably a mile southeast of the present-day fish farm on the site of the old town of Merritt.

PITT'S SIDING
Pennington County
SE¼, Section 20, T1N-R4E

Another name, more recently used, for *Fish and Hunter Siding.*

PLACERVILLE
Pennington County
NE¼, Section 1, T1N-R5E

Originally a placer camp, and so named for its gold deposits, Placerville is now a United Church of

Christ camp along Rapid Creek. It is on SD 40, the Rimrock Highway, about 12 miles west of Rapid City.

PLEASANT VALLEY STATION
Custer County
SE¼, Section 24, T4S-R3E

Pleasant Valley Stage Station, an eating house run in 1877 by James Fielding, was about 8 miles north of Spring-on-the-Right and 9 miles south of Custer, probably very close to the point where Ninemile Draw enters Pleasant Valley.

PLUMA
Lawrence County
NE¼, Section 34, T5N-R3E

Pluma, at the confluence of Gold Run and Whitewood Creeks, is the beginning of the long pull up Strawberry Hill. An electrical generating plant, fence post treating plants, and some roadside stores constitute the present industries. In times gone by a considerable gold-refining mill and Pluma's location on the main road between Deadwood and Lead led to its frequent mention in Black Hills news.

The point of rocks by the side of the stage trail, from which the town of Point of Rocks, now known as Pringle, took its name.

POINT OF ROCKS
Custer County
Section 19, T5S-R4E

Point of Rocks, named for the dramatic thrust of the granite, was an earlier name for *Pringle.* The actual "point" is east of town, the southern ends of three separate granite dikes.

POORMAN'S GULCH
Lawrence County

An early mining camp in the Central City area.

PORTLAND
Lawrence County
NE¼ , Section 2, T4N-R2E

Portland was an early name for *Trojan*.

Here the Burlington railroad's spur leading down into Spearfish Canyon crossed the Fremont, Elkhorn & Missouri Valley's lines, near Portland Junction west of Trojan.

PORTLAND JUNCTION
Lawrence County
NW¼ , Section 1, T4N-R2E

Portland Junction, as distinguished from Portland, was apparently in Nevada Gulch, the junction of the Fremont, Elkhorn & Missouri Valley lines to Crown Hill, Aztec, and Central City. As such it was the center of an incredible tangle of standard- and narrow-gauge railroads; almost every mine in the area had its own spur to collect ore and haul it to some central refinery, and these, intermingled with the lines of larger companies, make a tangle which can hardly be deciphered on a map, let alone on the ground itself. Excellent guides to these early railroads are Mildred Fielder's article "Railroads of the Black Hills" (*South Dakota Historical Collections*, XXX, 1960) and the USGS Spearfish Quadrangle, 1915 edition.

PORTUGUESE SIDING
Lawrence County

A 1900 atlas lists Portuguese Siding as a Lawrence County community, but does not show its location on the accompanying map.

POSSUM TROT
Crook County
SE¼ , Section 14, T49N-R61W

The name given to *Commissary D* after it had closed down as a part of the McLaughlin Tie & Timber Company operations.

POSTVILLE
Meade County
T4N-R5E(?)

An 1891 atlas shows Postville as the first stop south of Tilford on the Fremont, Elkhorn & Missouri Valley Railroad. It seems to have vanished completely.

POTATO CREEK
Lawrence County
Sections 20 & 30(?), T5N-R1E

Potato Creek may have been the same town as *Potato Town*. Its name has two suggested sources: One, that nuggets as big as potatoes were found in its vicinity, and the other that it was named by Jim Carney, who with three companions there made a meal of *one* potato. Sober consideration, however, would lead one to believe that the name came from the location of the town on Potato Creek.

POTATO TOWN
Lawrence County
Sections 20 & 30(?), T5N-R1E

Potato Town was an early Negro mining camp in the Tinton area, somewhere along Potato Creek. A group of black miners were directed to the area as a joke but there made so large a fortune from the placer workings that when the time came for them to leave with their earnings, they requested and got a guard of United States Cavalry to see them safely out of the Hills.

POVERTY GULCH
Pennington County
NE¼ , Section 18, T2S-R6E

This uncomplimentary sobriquet was jocularly applied to the area where the housing for married Park Service personnel at Mount Rushmore is provided; once an imposing and official-appearing sign with that name was put up to mark the spot. Unfeeling officialdom has since suppressed the name.

POWER HOUSE
Pennington County
NW¼ , Section 8, T1N-R6E

Power House, at *Big Bend*, was so named because of the electrical generating plant there, which was powered by the waters of Rapid Creek, brought from near Pactola in the flume which can still be seen along the south side of the valley. It was the scene of many lively dances and festivities which attracted visitors from a wide area.

PRATT'S MILL
Lawrence County
SW¼, Section 12, T3N-R5E

Pratt's Mill was a sawmill on Little Elk Creek, just below the famed White Gate. In 1903 the USGS map showed five houses in the vicinity. A good road from US Interstate 90 to Dalton Lake Campground passes through the spot, and a clearing can be seen which *may* have been the site on which the community stood.

PRESBYTERIAN CHURCH CAMP
Pennington County
SE¼, Section 8, T1N-R6E

The Presbyterian Church Camp occupies the old Black Hills & Western Railroad right-of-way along Rapid Creek, at the base of spectacular cliffs in Rapid Canyon.

A deserted three-story house in Preston.

PRESTON
Lawrence County
SW¼, Section 28, T5N-R2E

The area now known as Preston was a part of the group of towns—Balmoral, Dacy, Victoria, Cyanide, and Preston—which sprang up around 1897 to work the shallow gold ores in the vicinity of Ragged Top Mountain. As a matter of fact, close reading of old maps shows that the area now marked out as "Preston" with a Forest Service sign is very likely actually *Balmoral*, the two towns being within ¼ mile of each other.

Local tradition has it that the gold deposits were discovered by a Mr. Preston, whose attention was attracted when a chunk of ore stuck in his horse's shoe.

There were several good mines in the area, including the big Spearfish Gold Mining and Milling Company and the Ulster, a mile north of town, which produced ore assaying $2,000 to the ton.

A town newspaper, *The Ragged Top Shaft*, had a brief existence.

The Ragged Top School at Preston.

A home in Preston. The entryway was to protect the front door from the icy blasts of a Black Hills winter high on the side of Ragged Top Mountain.

156

PRINGLE
Custer County
Section 19, T5S-R4E

Earlier known as *Point of Rocks*, Pringle is now a small mining and lumbering town in the southern Hills, with a population of less than a hundred.

Pringle, with the light of the rising sun bathing the western side of the main street.

The stage station and mail rider's stop at Point of Rocks, as Pringle was called in its early days.

An early cabin now used as a barn. (Pringle)

PROSPECT CAMP
Pennington County
SE¼, Section 34, T2N-R4E

Another name for *Camp Prospect*, at the mouth of Little Rapid Creek.

PROVO
Fall River County
SW¼, Section 12, T10S-R2E

Provo was on the Chicago, Burlington & Quincy Railroad, 4 miles east of the Black Hills Ordnance Depot, and the fortunes of the town seemed to flourish and fade with the rise and fall of that great government enterprise. Provo now has a population of 108.

157

A feldspar mine near Pringle, with Professor C. A. Grimm of South Dakota School of Mines and Technology, whose help and learning made this book possible, holding down the tracks that led to the ore hoppers.

THE QUARRY
Meade County
SW¼, Section 30, T4N-R6E

The Quarry was the name given by railroaders on the Black Hills & Fort Pierre to *Calcite*, because of the big Homestake limestone quarry there.

QUARTZ CITY
Lawrence County

Quartz City was laid out in January 1878, in the Germania Mining District, supposedly at the junction of Hay and Elk Creeks. The whole area, which included Beaver City and New Berlin, upstream, had a population of about 150 miners. Samuel Scott's map, drawn for H.N. Maguire's *Coming Empire* (1878), is so inaccurate that Quartz City is impossible to locate. It was probably on a line between Roubaix and Nemo.

QUEEN BEE
Pennington County
NW¼, Section 26, T1N-R4E

Queen Bee, in Skull Gulch, about 7 miles northwest of Hill City, was named for the Queen Bee mine. The mine was discovered in 1879 by F. H. Griffin, and by January 1880 a dozen houses were being built around it. In May the inhabitants were expecting a saloon any day, although it is hard to believe that one would have been so long in coming. Also in 1880 Griffin bonded the mine to J. I. Case, the farm machinery manufacturer, for $125,000. Case built a 10-stamp mill, and by 1884 a considerable town had sprung up around the mine. The mine operated on and off up to 1934, but no production has been recorded. The big McVey burn in the thirties destroyed all the buildings, and today nothing at all is left of the town.

The area, just north of Sheridan Lake at the Boodleman Ranch, can be reached over a narrow road leading east from Redfern, or going west (and a pretty road it is) from US 385.

The last building still standing at the Queen Bee mine. The rest burned down in the McVey forest fire in the 1930s.

e tramway from the mine into the mill at the Old Standby, on Rapid Creek southeast of Rochford.

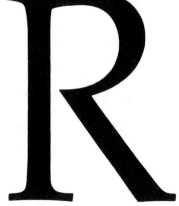

Ruins of a mining operation in the Ragged Top area where so many attempts to extract gold from the high limestone country came to naught. A theory current at the time was that the gold lay in the cracks and interstices of the rock, so it was merely cracked along its natural planes of cleavage; the rough, gravelly tailings stand as a monument to the failure of this theory.

RAGGED TOP
Lawrence County
SW¼, Section 28, T5N-R2E

Ragged Top was the mining district which embraced Balmoral, Preston, Dacy, and Cyanide. It was also the name of the school district serving these towns, and it is sometimes shown on maps and other documents as the name for the whole area. The total population in the early 1880s has been estimated at from 300 to 400, but judging from the many mines and towns shown on early maps, these estimates are probably too low.

Some of the many mines in the area were: American Mining Company; Dacy, or Flora E.; Deadwood Standard; Eagle Bird; Eva H. & Silver Tongue; Spearfish Gold Mining and Milling Company, which produced 48,618 ounces of gold from 1899 to 1906; Metallic Streak; Ulster; Victoria; and Old Ironsides. None of these mines seems to have been discovered much before 1896, nor to have been worked much later than 1915.

The whole area is a fascinating one and well worth a visit. The narrow-gauge railroad beds alone will keep the average adventurer happy for days.

RANCH A
Crook County
SW¼, Section 18, T52N-R60W

This imposing ranch, magnificently constructed of logs and ornately decorated, was built by a Moe Annenberg in the early 1930s. It was until recently used as a resort but is now a federal fish hatchery. It is on Sand Creek, a few miles south of Beulah, Wyoming.

RAPID CITY
Pennington County
T1N-R7E

This bustling tourist, cattle, shopping, lumbering, and manufacturing town of 43,836 began as a hay camp and was laid out by John Brennan and others coming in from Palmer Gulch. Its history is varied and delightful—Carl H. Leedy's *Golden Days in the Black Hills* tells many stories of the town and the Hills, well illustrated with pictures and lively tales of early times.

This log cabin in Rapid City's Halley Park dates back to the early days when Rapid City and its meadows were called Hay Camp.

I was built in the olden, golden days,
When this was an unknown land;
My timbers were hewn by a pioneer
With a rifle near at hand.

I stand as a relic of 'seventy-six,
Our nation's centennial year;
That all may see as they enter the Hills
The home of a pioneer.

Richard B. Hughes

The hanging tree, on Hangman's Hill, south of Rapid City. A poem posted by the grave of the victims reads:

Here lie the bodies of Allen, Curry and Hall,
Like other thieves, they had their rise, decline, and fall.
On this pine tree they hung till dead,
And in the sod they'll find a lonely bed.
So be a little cautious how you gobble horses up,
For every horse you pick up here adds sorrow to your cup.
We're bound to stop this business, or hang you to a man,
And we've hemp and hands enough in camp to swing
    the whole damn clan!

Ghosts are where you find them, even in bustling Rapid City. In 1902 this building was the U.S. Land Office and Weather Bureau, and its ornate design has remained unchanged.

RAPID CREEK STAGE STATION
Pennington County
SE¼, Section 17, T2N-R3E

A stop on the Cheyenne-Deadwood stage trail between Reynold's Ranch and North Rapid Station, 28 miles north of Custer and 23 miles south of Deadwood. It was on the south side of the South Fork of Rapid Creek, about a mile west of its confluence with the North Fork. The site is still marked by a big log barn, very possibly one used to shelter the coaches. The area was later known as *Floral* or *Florence* and is now marked on the Forest Service maps as the Sasse Ranch.

RAPID CREEK TRADING POST
Pennington County
Near Creston, NE¼, T2S-R12E

The Rapid Creek Trading Post, or *Oglalla Trading Post*, was at the old mouth of Rapid Creek where it enters the Cheyenne River. It was managed by Thomas L. Sarpy but blew up in 1832, due to someone's selling gunpowder, whiskey, and tobacco all in a bunch. Sarpy was killed, beaver traps were scattered for half-a-mile, and the exact location of the post is still much disputed.

This replica of a Norwegian stave church built in A.D. 1138 was donated to Rapid City as a memorial to citizens of Scandinavian descent.

REAUSAW, REAVSAW
Lawrence County
NW¼, Section 2, T3N-R4E

Reausaw was a station on the Black Hills & Fort Pierre, about 2 miles south of Apex and 2 miles north of Benchmark, very near Hay Creek. The present Reausaw Lake is probably near the site of the town, and a house or two still stands in its vicinity.

Reausaw, on the Black Hills & Fort Pierre narrow-gauge railroad north of Nemo. The embankment on which the railroad crossed the valley here now forms a part of the dam for a stockpond.

RED CANYON STATION
Fall River County
NE¼, Section 20, T8S-R3E

Red Canyon Station, sometimes known as *Camp Collier* from the name of its commanding officer, Major W. S. Collier, and locally referred to as *Camp Jennings*, was at the mouth of Red Canyon, about 4 miles northeast of the Cheyenne River Station near present-day Edgemont. The camp was established in 1876, with Company K of the 4th Infantry forming its initial garrison, but soon a troop of cavalry to accompany and protect emigrant trains and stage coaches was added. The station contained neat and comfortable quarters ornamented with rows of evergreens set out to shade the log and mud huts from the summer sun. A bastioned stockade about 80' square offered protection in case of sudden Indian attack, and the outline of this fort can still be seen on the ground opposite the Jim Bell Ranch. Harlow's eating house was popular with the stage passengers. The whole outpost was abandoned in 1878 when the stage routes abandoned the dangerous Red Canyon trail. Army records refer to it as *Camp Red Canyon* or *Military Station*.

Redfern, named for Albert Redfern, one of the Burlington construction workers who built the town around 1890. All that is left now is an abandoned boxcar that was once used for a home.

REDFERN
Pennington County
Center of Section 33, T1N-R4E

Redfern, named in 1891 or 1892 for Albert Redfern, a railroad man, was a section house on the Burlington railroad from Hill City to Deadwood. In the 1950s it boomed briefly as the home of the Black Hills Silica Sand Corporation, now defunct. All that remains is the sign that marked the station and a derailed boxcar that has been used for a home.

REDWATER
Butte County
SW Corner, T8N-R3E

Rand McNalley's 1921 *Commercial Atlas* shows the town of Redwater on the Chicago & North Western Railroad southeast of Belle Fourche, about where the railroad crosses the Redwater River. That puts it fairly near the present-day community of Jolly.

RENO I, RENO GULCH
Pennington County
SW¼, Section 35, T1S-R4E

Reno Gulch, about a mile southwest of Hill City, is a long line of homes and summer cabins and does not have a community existence that we know of. The town of Reno, however, is in the above location, toward the head of Reno Gulch, and is composed of a single house, probably named for its original occupants.

RENO II, RENO QUARRY
Lawrence County
SE¼ (?), Section 8, T4N-R3E

Reno, or Reno Quarry, was a minor stop on the narrow-gauge Black Hills & Fort Pierre Railroad between Englewood and Lead. It appears to have been on Reno Creek about a mile west of Flatiron, the BH&FtP paralleling the Burlington along Whitewood Creek.

REPASS

Meade County
SW¼, Section 19, T3N-R6E

Repass was a stop on the Black Hills & Fort Pierre narrow-gauge line between Este and Piedmont. It was about a mile north of Murphy II and about a mile south of Carwye.

REYNOLD'S RANCH

Pennington County
SE¼, Section 31, T2N-R3E

Reynold's Ranch was a stage stop on the line from Custer to Deadwood, and was about 3½ miles north of Deerfield.

The story is told that in early days the Reynold's ranch would occasionally be threatened by raiding Indian war parties, at which time one of the sons of the family would climb to the top of nearby Flag Mountain and with flag and bugle make a pretense of summoning or signaling to imaginary United States troops. The Indians, not wanting to tangle with the soldiers, would then pass on without making trouble.

The Reynolds Ranch, a stop on the Cheyenne-Deadwood line, continues under the same family that once served stagecoach passengers nearly a hundred years ago.

RICHMOND

Lawrence County
SE¼, Section 3, T4N-R4E

Richmond was the end of the Deadwood Central line to the Galena area and was named for the Richmond (now the Double Rainbow) mine. This famous property was discovered in 1876, and between 1881 and 1883 it produced over $410,000

worth of silver. It was then tied up in litigation, and production was not resumed until 1889; in 1891 the falling price of silver probably closed the mine a second time. In 1905 the Richmond-Sitting Bull Mining Company was formed and operated until 1912. In 1930-1931 a 150-ton flotation mill was built to rework material from the old dumps; but it was not satisfactory, and in 1945 the mill was finally pulled down. The area is probably pretty hard to tell from what is left of Galena and Griggs, but enough pleasant folks live in the area to help you find out.

RIMROCK LODGE

Lawrence County
NE¼, Section 30, T5N-R2E

Rimrock Lodge, in Spearfish Canyon, was built by a Miss Bridges of the Black Hills Teachers College and run by her for many years. It is a pleasant resort, with cabins and main building perched high on the east side of the canyon near Bridal Veil Falls, about 9 miles south of Spearfish on SD 89.

ROBBER'S ROOST I

Custer County
SW¼, Section 28, T4S-R6E

This ranch, in Custer State Park, between the North and South Forks of Lame Johnny Creek, appears on early maps, and is still there. Whether or not the creek name is in reference to Lame Johnny (Cornelius Donahue) we do not know.

ROBBER'S ROOST II

Weston County

Robber's Roost was a stage station on the Black Hills-Cheyenne line and probably was also the name given to the whole area around the confluence of Lance Creek and the Cheyenne River, for it was a famous spot for holdups. The country around here is certainly discouraging, and it is hard to see how an honest man could make a living in it, though some seem to.

The Irish Gulch Dance Hall, in Rochford. The building, if not the business, dates from the early days when Rochford was a booming gold mining town.

ROCHFORD
Pennington County
NE¼, Section 23, T2N-R3E

Rochford was founded in February of 1877 by R. B. Hughes and M. D. Rochford and named in honor of the latter. In March of the same year a mining district was set up, with James Morrison its recorder. By December of 1878, Rochford had 500 population, 200 houses, a solid block of stores with wooden, canopied sidewalks, a couple of doctors, and a good school. The main industry, of course, was gold. The Evangeline and the Minnesota mines both built 20-stamp mills in 1879. The Stand-By mill, still standing, was built, and a flume run to it to provide both water and power for its 40 stamps. The Balkan mine, however, was less successful, for its promoters were eventually reduced to salting the amalgam with chopped-up gold coins—one of which led to their downfall when a party of irate stockholders came to look over the operation and commented on a nugget inscribed "E Pluribus Unum."

By 1900 Rochford was down to a post office and 48 inhabitants. Occasional mining booms in the area have kept the town going, and lately the Forest Service has brought in a good many government employees. The town still retains the old look and flavor, and many old buildings are worth photographing.

Rochford is about 16 miles northwest of Hill City, on the gravel road that leads through Mystic on up to Lead and Deadwood. It is a pretty trip, through the heart of the mining country.

It has been claimed that this house in Rochford was one where the famous pioneer, Annie Tallent, lived or taught or died or was born—or something. The building burned to the ground a few years ago, so it doesn't matter now . . . . perhaps.

You can always spot the business buildings, like this ancient one in Rochford, by their high false fronts and ample windows, and in this case a fanlight over the door to take advantage of all the outside light there was.

A commercial building in Rochford. Presumably the door into the second story was reached by an outside stairway, to conserve useful space inside.

The Standby mill, rebuilt in the 1930s, still stands, but both the building and the mine workings behind it are in dangerous condition and should be studiously avoided.

ROCKERVILLE

Pennington County
Sections 13 & 14, T1S-R6E

Present-day Rockerville, on US 16 between Rapid City and Hill City, is given over to a reconstruction of an early Black Hills mining town. Various tourist attractions are provided in a setting of false-fronts, wooden sidewalks, and a profusion of relics of by-gone times. In the 1870s, however, Rockerville was a *real* mining camp, and one of the roaringest.

Gold was discovered in the Rockerville area in December 1876, when William Keeler was snowbound there and panned out a few likely prospects to while away his tedium. He was soon joined by Bart Henderson and D. G. Silliman. Water was scarce in the gulch, and it was almost impossible to pan the gold out of the sticky clay deposits, even with the aid of the water-saving rockers which gave the camp its name. In 1878 the Black Hills Placer Mining Company was formed, mainly with eastern capital, to construct and operate a 17-mile flume which, it was hoped, would bring some 2,000 miners inches of water from a dam on Spring Creek near Sheridan. Ambrose Bierce, who later became a writer of bitter short stories, managed the enterprise, and from Paul Fatout's account of his trials, *Ambrose Bierce and the Black Hills*, it can be seen that it may have been this experience which made him bitter. The flume cost nearly $300,000 and leaked horribly. A wagon load of manure was dumped into it each morning, to help seal the cracks in the green lumber—and that didn't do very much to make the company popular with the miners who had to use the water. All told, the company produced about $500,000 worth of gold, but mismanagement dissipated the money and the company eventually failed. The ruins of its dam can still be seen just downstream from the Gordon Ranch on Spring Creek, and the trace of the flume can be followed from above Sheridan Lake clear to Rockerville.

In 1881 the Rockerville Gold Mining Company was formed to build a bedrock flume down Rockerville Gulch but it too failed after 1,100 feet of ditch were dug. Another venture, touched off by the vision of one Spicer, had a similar fate. Spicer dreamed one night of finding gold at a certain spot. Awakening, he went there—and found it.

A horse-drawn water wagon is among the many relics of the past assembled at Rockerville, as Captain Jack's Dry Diggings came to be called.

A company was at once set up to exploit his gift, but it does not seem to have been a very profitable venture.

The town of Rockerville boomed with flume company employees and hopeful miners. By 1880 it had a hundred buildings and a population between 800 and 1,000. A pioneer storekeeper, Isaac Golden, was soon followed by another, S. A. Oliver. The postmaster, Mr. McEuna, set up shop, and main street boomed. There was also a prophetically named Ascension Street, which caused some stir when it was realized, in the 1930s, that it led right to the Stratosphere Bowl which was used to launch high-altitude balloons.

Among other activities, there was much litigation. One building lawyer stirred up a suit against a sawmill and by working for both sides got enough lumber and cash to set himself up an office. One defendant, working on a rich claim, sent a case of whiskey to the jury examining his title, and it so assisted their deliberations that by the time they had reached a decision he had cleaned out the gold and departed.

Eventually the placers played out, the big flume fell into ruins, and the miners moved away. By the 1930s nothing was left but a gas station and the stone chimney of Courtland Rush's log cabin. The many balloon ascensions from the deep Stratosphere Bowl brought in a few tourists, but it was not until the 1950s that the present ghost town was rebuilt. There are not many echoes in the Rockerville of today—the clink of coin, rustle of bills, and click of cameras have drowned them out.

ROCKS
Custer County
Section 19, T5S-R4E

Another name for *Pringle*, or *Point of Rocks*.

ROCKVILLE
Pennington County
Sections 13 & 14, T1S-R6E

An early name for *Rockerville*, for in March of 1879 a petition was circulated and sent to the postal authorities requesting that the name of the town be changed from Rockville to Rockerville.

ROCKY FORD
Crook County
Center of line between
Sections 7 & 18, T52N-R61W

Rocky Ford, midway between Sundance and Aladdin, where the road crosses Rocky Ford Creek, was an oil producing community, using windmills to pump the thick, heavy oil from shallow wells for shipment to Lead and Deadwood to grease the mine machinery. It was about 9 miles northeast of Sundance, in the open country between the Black Hills and the Bear Lodge Mountains, and today I 90 passes over it.

ROETZEL DEER CAMP
Custer County
SW¼, Section 25, T2S-R3E

One of the many camps which cater to deer hunters during the Black Hills fall hunting season.

ROSEDALE
Pennington County
SW¼, Section 32, T1S-R6E

This little settlement in Rocky Gulch was once on the main road from Keystone to Sheridan but was long ago by-passed by US 16A. It's about a mile northwest of Keystone, and the single home which still remains can be reached either by going up Rocky (or Stony) Gulch, or by heading east from US 16A, just opposite the Holy Smoke mine. The community was, we believe, a mining one, and its location is clearly shown on the Forest Service map of Harney National Forest for 1935.

Rosedale, on the Rocky Gulch road a mile north of Keystone.

ROSSVILLE
Pennington County
SE¼, Section 34, T2N-R4E

Rossville was a small mining town on the south side of Rapid Creek, just below the mouth of Castle Creek, and just above the mouth of Slate Creek, if an 1883 map is to be relied upon. Apparently it was a mile or so upstream of Canyon City, and a mile below Ross's Bar, the placer diggings from which it took its name. A "bar" in placer mining is a band of identifiable gold-bearing gravel, usually in a stream bed.

Roubaix, home of the Uncle Sam, Clover Leaf, or Anaconda mine, as it was variously called, the foundations of which can still be seen along the treeline in the background.

ROUBAIX
Lawrence County
SW¼, Section 29, T4N-R4E

Roubaix was originally named *Perry*, but the arrival of the CB&Q Railroad made it necessary to change the name to avoid confusion with Terry farther north. It was renamed *Roubaix*, after the home town of Pierre Wibeaux, a Frenchman with cattle and mining interests in the town.

The story of Roubaix is mainly that of the Uncle Sam mine. Discovered in 1878, the mine

Roubaix, a mile east of US Highway 385, once had a population of 500, with the mill of the Uncle Sam mine towering up over the town. All that is left of the mill now are a few bullwheels that once turned the stamps, and only a couple of families still live among the many buildings.

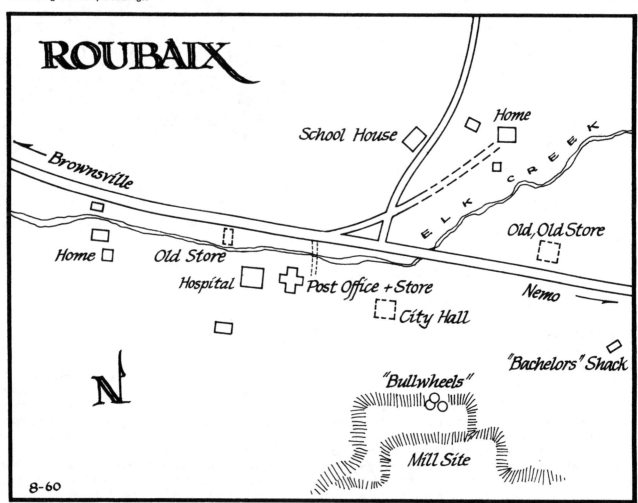

The large and ornate log house was once the post office at Roubaix, named for Roubaix, France, the home town of one of the principal investors in the mine, Pierre Wibeaux.

changed hands many times. In 1889 Wibeaux bought it, named it the Clover Leaf, set up a 60-stamp mill, and, up to 1905, took out $900,000 worth of gold. Most of the ore was free-milling, and only a mercury amalgamation was necessary to get over 90% of the gold out of it. Wibeaux once took out $3,000 in a single day, and another time $29,000 in three weeks, but the miners stole the so-called "jewelry ore" and reduced the profits. In 1905, a very wet year, a cave-in blocked the flow of water to the pumps, which ran away and burned out. The whole mine then flooded and had to be abandoned. In 1934-1935 the Anaconda Gold Mining and Milling Company of Rapid City attempted to reopen the mine but only got about $10,000 worth of gold out of it. In 1899 the town had a population of 500, a post office, boarding houses, a barber shop, town hall, churches, a school, and a newspaper. Nowadays there are only a few houses left, to the east of US 385, about 7 miles south of Pluma.

You'd be proud to have a stove like that sitting in your parlor. They just don't make stoves like that any more, but Roubaix has more than a few of them.

The home of the blind mine engineer at the Uncle Sam, who can tell you step by step how they fought the rising waters that flooded out the mine and closed it down in 1905.

Ruins and foundations of the store at Roubaix.

RUBY, RUBY BASIN
Lawrence County
NW Corner of T4N-R3E

The Ruby Basin district seems rather vague, located somewhere around Sugarloaf Mountain. It was the scene of a good deal of mining activity, containing the Golden Reward, which had a total production of $21,000,000 up to 1918, the Mogul-Horseshoe, The Great Mogul, and several other good mines. There was also a mining camp named Ruby, probably in the same area.

RUNKEL, RUNKLE
Meade County
SW¼, Section 16, T4N-R5E

Runkel was between Piedmont and Bucks, on the northern branch of the Homestake's Black Hills & Fort Pierre Railroad. There appears to have been a railroad spur at Runkel, winding off to the east for a mile or more. In 1900 Runkel had a post office and about a dozen houses, but nothing at all is left today, except the large cave northeast of town which used to attract holiday makers. The townsite can best be identified by the grove of apple trees which still stand in orderly rows to the east of the abandoned railroad right-of-way.

Runkel is about 5½ miles west of Tilford, on the dirt road which leads to Bethlehem (formerly Old Crystal) Cave. You would be ill-advised to try it in wet weather.

Remains of mining or railroad equipment at Runkel.

RUSHMORE CAVE
Pennington County
SW¼, Section 18, T2S-R7E

Rushmore Cave, at *Hayward*, about 6 miles east of Mount Rushmore National Memorial, was discovered when the water from the Hayward Flume leaked away mysteriously into the bowels of the earth. The cave, now a private venture, is one of the most widely advertised in the Hills.

The apple orchard, row on row, at Runkel beside the abandoned tracks of the Black Hills & Fort Pierre Railroad. No other signs of habitation remain.

A desert sun outlines the branches of a dead cedar at Spring-on-the-Hill, where weary travelers gave a sigh of relief as they left the Indian menace of Red Canyon behind them and found welcome rest and water at the stage station.

SACORA

Meade County
SE Corner of T3N-R6E

An 1891 map shows Sacora between Postville and Blackhawk, on the Chicago & North Western Railroad north of Rapid City. It is south of Elk Creek, and apparently is *not* Piedmont.

SAFE INVESTMENT

Lawrence County
SE¼, Section 18, T3N-R5E

Safe Investment, the home of the Safe Investment Gold Mining Company, was a small mining community, also known as *Spruce*, on Boxelder Creek, on the Black Hills & Fort Pierre Railroad, between Novak and Greenwood. The mining claims associated with the company appear to have centered on the corner common to sections 10, 11, 15, and 14 of T3N-R4E. Between 1905 and 1907 a 60-stamp mill was built, but apparently no ore from the mine ever ran through it, and the whole operation was locally supposed to have been a promotional swindle.

SAGINAW MINE

Custer County
Section 34, T2S-R3E

Although never an important gold producer, the Saginaw mine did a good deal of exploratory work and built a 10-stamp mill. The smaller mine buildings are now used as summer homes, and near them many dangerous pits and unstable piles of waste rock show the extent of the mining activity.

ST. ELMO

Pennington County
NW¼, Section 24, T2S-R4E

Another name for *Clara Belle Camp* on the slopes of St. Elmo Mountain.

ST. ONGE

Lawrence County
Between Sections 23 & 26, T7N-R3E

St. Onge is reputedly one of the oldest communities in the whole Black Hills area; some say that dates carved on beams of old buildings and root cellars go back to the 1830s, relics of the French fur traders who named the town and settled in it to tap the supply of beaver skins available from the Hills. Several imposing stone buildings still remain, although now unused.

Vacant stone buildings from the turn of the century grace the main street of St. Onge, a French community southeast of Belle Fourche.

The boarding house of the Saginaw mine, viewed from the mill site. On the rock in the foreground can be seen the projecting iron bolts that once held down some of the heavy machinery of the mill.

Remains of shafthead and mill buildings at the Saginaw mine.

SALT SPRINGS

Weston County
SW¼, Section 9, T46N-R61W

Salt Springs was at the head of a tributary of Beaver Creek which came in below the Jenney Stockade. Bart Henderson, G. D. Stillman, Charles Calderbaugh, and S. A. D. Graves (this last sounds like a joke) set up a salt works on July 8, 1877 to supply the silver mines with salt for their chlorine process. It is reputed that the camps of the salt wagons as they made their way to Galena soon became salt licks for the deer. The spring is on Salt Creek 2 miles north of the Flying V Ranch.

SAMELIAS

Pennington County
NW¼, Section 12, T1S-R5E

This appears to be a ranch, for which nearby Samelias Peak was also named. It is the home of the Hardesty family nowadays.

SANATOR

Custer County
NE¼, Section 14, T4S-R4E

For many years the South Dakota state tuberculosis sanatorium, Sanator is now called *Custer State Hospital.*

The Black Hills State Hospital at Sanator.

SANDSTONE

Fall River County

Probably one of the quarries near Hot Springs.

SARATOGA

Lawrence County(?)

An 1883 map shows this town at the headwaters of a creek which branches off of Bear Butte Creek below Sturgis. The map is rather inaccurate, but it shows the town about 4½ miles southwest of Sturgis, on a line between Sturgis and Lead, more or less in what is now known as Boulder Park.

SAVOY

Lawrence County
NE¼, Section 36, T5N-R1E

Savoy, in Spearfish Canyon, has long been famous for the hospitality offered by the Latchstring Inn. Nearby is Roughlock Falls, on Little Spearfish Creek. The Canyon itself is very lovely, especially in early mornings or toward sunset. In the early days visitors could come to Savoy only on the narrow-gauge Burlington line which came down into the Canyon from Trojan at Elmore. Today the trip on SD 89 from either Spearfish on the north or Lead to the east is a very lovely drive.

The dramatic cliffs of Spearfish Canyon tower high above the Latchstring Inn at Savoy, once known as The Falls.

SCHAEFERVILLE
Pennington County
NE¼, Section 20, T2N-R7E

Schaeferville is a small development just north of Rapid City on US Interstate 90. It has a good many homes, a drive-in theater, and a rock quarry, but no shopping district to speak of.

SCOOPTOWN
Meade County
Section 10, T5N-R5E

Original name of *Sturgis*, when it was a booming, roaring, brawling army camp town for nearby Fort Meade.

Poker Alice Tubbs' establishment "across the creek" in Sturgis.

SCOTT'S MILLS
Pennington County
T1N-R6E

Scott's Mills was on the old Black Hills & Western, or Crouch, line, east of Canyon Lake.

S & G RANCH
Custer County
SW Corner of T6S-R1E

The S & G Ranch, on the CB&Q Railroad between Dewey and Argentine, is usually considered to have been only an early name for Dewey itself. However, in 1910 it seems to have been a separate and distinct station.

SHEEP FLATS
Lawrence County
NW¼, Section 27, T5N-R1E

A recreational community and fishermen's store around Iron Creek Lake.

SHEEP'S TAIL
Lawrence County
Sections 20 & 30, T5N-R3E

The Reverend Peter Rosen mentions Sheep's Tail as an early mining camp, probably in the Deadwood area. Sheep Tail Gulch runs from Section 30 into Section 20, where it runs into Blacktail Gulch.

SHERIDAN
Pennington County
SW¼, Section 12, T1S-R5E

Sheridan, originally called *Golden City*, was the third town in the Black Hills. It was laid out by Andrew J. Williams, Ernest Barthold, John W. Allen, A. J. Carlin, Edward Flaherty, Frank Bethune, William Marsten, Ezekiel Brown, and Deacon Willard in the fall of 1875. The Montana Bar placer yielded $3,000, one nugget being worth $23. Many of the cabins were built with portholes, rather than windows, to better serve as forts in case of Indian attack.

In March 1877 the U. S. Land Office was set up at Sheridan, moving to Deadwood in 1878. In April 1877 the town became the county seat, and in October Judge Granville Bennett held the first term of the Black Hills Circuit Court in town.

Sheridan was the start of the famous Rockerville flume, and traces of it can still be seen on the south side of the valley above the old grade of a Warren-Lamb narrow-gauge logging railroad. Nearby are the J. R. Mine (named for its discoverer, Johnny Ryan) and the Queen Bee. In 1900 Sheridan had a post office and a population of 25. Later,

The trace of the famous wooden flume that ran from a dam at the foot of Gordon Gulch (above Sheridan) 14 miles to Rockerville, to carry water to wash the gold from the clay-gravel mixture. The flume, here shown ducking behind a spur of rock at the head of Sheridan Lake, has traveled about a mile from its source and is already high above Spring Creek.

in the 1930s, it was the site of a good restaurant run by Mr. and Mrs. Carl Leedy, and still later it was flooded into the present Sheridan Lake (once loathesomely known as Lake o' the Pines).

Sheridan Lake is about 5 miles northeast of Hill City on US 385. It affords the tourist fishing, camping, and recreational facilities.

The foundation of the Calumet smelter and mill at the foot of Blue Lead Mountain near Sheridan. The rough, random stonework laid in lime mortar is typical of the early Black Hills.

The base of the blast furnace at the Calumet Smelter near Sheridan. Brick, which could stand the heat, had to be used in the construction of a copper smelting furnace. Even so, the interior was probably lined with specially resistant firebrick which local residents have gradually taken away to line their fireplaces.

SHERMAN
Lawrence County
SE¼, Section 18, T5N-R3E

In Hurt & Lass's *Frontier Photographer* is a picture labled "Sherman," but it is admitted that the authors were unable to locate any Black Hills town by that name. The same picture, however, appears in Kingsbury's *History of Dakota* and is there labeled *Garden City*, which can be assumed to be the true name of Sherman. Garden City later was known as *Maitland*, after the owner of its largest mine.

SHICK
Pennington County
NW¼, Section 7, T1N-R3E

Shick is mentioned in one account of early explorations as being "two or three miles above Deerfield." This puts it in the above location, which the current USGS Deerfield Quadrangle labels "Shick Ranch." It may easily have been a stop or station on the stage coach road.

SIDE CAMP SPRING
Custer County
SW¼, Section 16, T3S-R1E

Side Camp Spring, on an intermittent creek which comes into Redbird Canyon from the northeast, is a collection of nine occupied houses, closely gathered around a spring. Presumably it is only a ranch, but with the same "Side Camp" attached to the spring, it may also have some history as a community. It can be found on the 1951 USGS Fanny Peak Quadrangle.

SIDING ELEVEN
Pennington County
SE¼, Section 35, T1N-R8E

Another name for *Brennan*, south of Rapid City on the Chicago & North Western Railroad.

SIDNEY STOCKADE
Meade County
NW¼, Section 27, T3N-R6E

An early name for the *Stage Barn Canyon* area, when it was a stop on the Sidney-Deadwood stage route.

SILVER CITY I
Pennington County
S½, Section 31, T2N-R5E

Silver City, in the area called *Elkhorn Prairie* by General George A. Custer when he entered the Hills in 1874, was for years an active mining town, and is still surrounded with legends of lost mines. One, concerning the Gorman brothers,

Jack, Tom and Luke, has it that the three, offered $300,000 or half-a-million for their mine, were unable to decide which offer was the larger, and before they could make up their minds a fire had killed one of the brothers and the other two had left, leaving the mine's location a mystery. Another lost mine was found by one Scruton, who died before revealing the source of his nuggets.

The town is now a resort area at the head of Pactola Lake and is reached by speed boats racing over what was once the route of the old Black Hills & Western Railroad. It is about 3 miles west of US 385, the turnoff being about a mile north of Pactola Lake.

This home in Silver City was for many years tied up in litigation and as a result had gone to wrack and ruin its intricate lathwork porch railings crumbling away before the passing years. Its high false front suggests that the building was once used as a store.

SILVER CITY II
Lawrence County

An early town in the Bald Mountain mining district.

SILVER MOUNTAIN
Pennington County
Center & SW¼, Section 22, T1S-R6E

A tourist-oriented area along old US 16, until it was bypassed by the new four-lane I 90, Silver Mountain ran roughly from the Deer Huts tourist cabins, past Doc Willard's gas station and the Silver Mountain cabins and garage, near three or four houses, to the Silver Mountain Camp Ground on the center of the line between Sections 22 & 23. The campground was devastated by a tornado a few years ago, and stumps and shreds of ruined pines still mark the site.

SIPS
Custer County
Center of T1N-R1E

This may have simply been a spot where P. A. Rydberg stopped, gathering material for his *Flora of the Black Hills*; or the name of a nearby ranch.

SITTING BULL
Pennington County
NE¼, Section 4, T1N-R4E

Sitting Bull was the early name of *Mystic*, changed, as were so many, when the railroad came in during the late 1880s.

SLABTOWN
Lawrence County
SE¼, Section 18, T3N-R5E

Slabtown, which was between Greenwood and Novak, had nine saloons, some cafes, a hotel, a general store, and a school around the turn of the century. The town was in the extreme southeast corner of Section 18, on the southeast slope of the hill along Boxelder Creek. After two years the boom, which had been based on a nearby gold mine, busted, and the post office was moved to nearby Novak.

SLATE PRAIRIE
Pennington County
SE¼, Section 26, T1N-R3E

Slate Prairie, named for the rock that outcrops in the area, centers on Section 26. Slate Prairie school is a trifle north of the center of the section, and Slate Prairie Church is way down in the southeast corner; other population is not in evidence.

SNOMA
Butte County
Center of line between Sections 18 & 19, T8N-R4E

In 1885 some 40 Finnish families established this little farming village ½ mile south of the Belle Fourche River and about 10 miles east of

The Finnish cemetery a mile south of Snoma gazes through the trees across the barren plains the emigrants tried to farm.

the town of Belle Fourche. Snoma had a hotel, store, blacksmith shop, and post office, for which the group's interpreter, John Lakson, submitted the name "Suomi," or "Suoma," in honor of their native Finland. The Post Office Department, however, misread Lakson's handwriting and named the struggling little community Snoma. Hardly any of it is left today.

SOLDIER CREEK STORE
Weston County
NE¼, Section 24, T48N-R61W

A store southeast of US 85, just to the south of the spot where that highway crosses Soldier Creek.

SOLDIERS' HOME
Fall River County
In Hot Springs

This is the South Dakota State Home for old soldiers; some atlases show a post office there, as if for a separate town, but the home has always been in Hot Springs.

SOUTH BEND
Lawrence County
SW¼, Section 21(?), T5N-R3E

South Bend was an early mining camp in Black-tail Gulch, between Gayville and Central City. In 1880 it had a population of 116, but soon after the town was absorbed into Central City.

SPARTA CITY
Lawrence County(?)

Sparta City was in the Box Elder mining district and was laid out as a town in 1878. The *Cheyenne Daily Leader* said at the time that "its prospects for becoming a town of importance are good," which was not a very reliable prediction.

SPEARFISH
Lawrence County
Sections 10 & 15, T6N-R2E

Spearfish, at the bottom of Spearfish Canyon, was founded in 1876 by a group from Ames, Iowa,

The state fish-hatchery and in-service training station (for wardens, not fish) at Spearfish dates from before the turn of the century.

led by one John Johnston, and has been prosperous ever since. In 1893 the narrow-gauge Burlington line reached Spearfish from Deadwood, along the Canyon, and a chlorination plant for gold was built. The boom busted around 1895, and since then Spearfish has depended upon the Black Hills State College, the lumber mills, the U.S. Fish Hatchery, the ranchers, and, lately, the Black Hills Passion Play. In 1970 its population was 4,661.

Fancy brickwork attests to the antiquity of this home in Spearfish, Queen City of the Black Hills.

SPEARFISH CROSSING
Lawrence County
NW¼, Section 22, T4N-R2E

An early name for the store, gas station, and summer home area now known as *Cheyenne Crossing*. It is at the head of Spearfish Canyon, about where Spearfish Creek, East Spearfish Creek, and Icebox Gulch meet. It is about 15 miles south of Spearfish, where SD 89 joins US 85.

SPENCER, SPENCER SIDING
Weston County
SE¼, Section 15, T44N-R61W

Spencer Siding is on the CB&Q, about 5 miles south of Newcastle. Following World War II, a large packing plant was built on the east side of the tracks, but it has long since been abandoned.

Spencer Siding, on the C B & Q. All that marks the site are corrals, slaughterhouse, and what seems to be a privy for the railroad workers in the area.

The mill at Spokane.

The office at the Spokane mine. Whenever you can look clear through a building, you get an idea it isn't being used too much.

SPOKANE
Custer County
SE¼, Section 27, T2S-R6E

The huge mine buildings, schoolhouse, foundations, various prospect pits, water tower, and miners' shacks make a visit to the old Spokane mine and the tiny town which grew up around it a must for ghost town hunters.

Begun in 1890, this famous mine has produced lead, zinc, gold, some silver, and as side products, hematite, graphite, beryl, mica, arsenic, and copper. The mill is still standing, fully equipped, and the caretaker may give you permission to explore it if you look trustworthy. Around the mill there are several large buildings: a manager's home, office, boiler and shaft-house, tumbled-down water tower, and various unused pits and foundations. Scattered around at a distance are the miners' homes and the Spokane School.

Spokane is near the Iron Mountain Road, US 16A, about 6 miles southeast of Mount Rushmore. The best way to reach it, however, is to drive east from Keystone to the ghost town of Harney, then south 4 miles, until nearly in sight of the Iron Mountain Road, where a road will lead you ½ mile east to the caretaker's home.

A miner's home at Spokane, once papered on the inside with newspapers contemporary with its inhabitant, a custom that kept the drafts out and informs historians about the date the house was occupied.

178

The headframe, mill, office, and hoisting and machine shops at the Spokane mine.

Detail of the headframe, ore hopper, ore chute, and mill at the Spokane mine. The ore chute was covered and wrapped with tar paper so the ore would not freeze and hang up in the wintertime, but even so a catwalk with a single rail was built beside it to enable one of the miners to walk along the chute and keep the ore in motion.

The schoolhouse, with its sheltered entryway, and the caretaker's home, at the entrance to the town of Spokane.

Looking toward Red Canyon down the old Cheyenne-Deadwood stage trail near Spring-on-the-Hill.

Spring-on-the-Hill is hidden in a limestone gulley high on the rim of the north end of Red Canyon, and you would not know it was there unless someone told you. A concrete reservoir stored some of the seeping water, to be piped to the ranch that later occupied the area.

SPRING-ON-THE-HILL
Custer County
NE¼, Section 35, T6S-R3E

Spring-on-the-Hill was a famous stop on the trail up to Custer. It is about 20 miles southwest of Custer, in Red Canyon. It was the scene of a lively Indian fight involving Captain J. Hunter and six other men, in which Hunter was killed.

SPRING-ON-THE-RIGHT
Custer County
SE¼, Section 11, T5S-R3E

Spring-on-the-Right was a stage station in Pleasant Valley, somewhat north of the station at Spring-on-the-Hill, and of course a good way south of Custer, and south of Eighteen Mile Ranch.

SPRING VALLEY RANCHE
Meade County
SW¼, Section 10, T3N-R6E

Collins' *Directory* says it was 15 miles from Crook City, on the road to Rapid City, and that George W. Adler there ran an establishment of some sort. Adreas' *Atlas* shows it in about the location given above, on a creek leading into Elk Creek. It is the town now known as *Piedmont*.

STATE GAME LODGE
Custer County
NE¼, Section 27, T3S-R6E

The State Game Lodge, on the site of the old *Otis* saw mill, was rushed to completion in 1926 to act as the summer White House for President Calvin Coolidge during 1927. The main building is still there, now surrounded by smaller cabins and other tourist facilities, a free zoo, a rock museum, and some very spectacular country. It is the center and administration headquarters of Custer State Park.

The Game Lodge is on US 16A, about 11 miles east of Custer. SD 87, which runs north and south through the State Park, also provides an easy access to it.

STAGE BARN
Meade County
NW¼, Section 27, T3N-R6E

This was the first stop south of Piedmont on the Black Hills & Fort Pierre Railroad. The line then turned eastward to Goiens, then south again to Carwye, Repass, and Murphy. Nowadays Stage Barn is noted for its cave and as the start of an adventurous road northward up the canyon itself, but in the early days it was known as the *Sidney Stockade*, a famous stop on the Sidney-Deadwood stage line.

Stage Barn is about 11 miles northeast of Rapid City, west of US Interstate 90.

SPRUCE
Lawrence County
SE¼, Section 18, T3N-R5E

Safe Investment was also known as Spruce. It was on the Black Hills & Fort Pierre Railroad, between Novak (Cindell Spur) and Nemo.

SPRUCE GULCH
Lawrence County
SW¼, Section 25, T5N-R3E

Possibly the same as *Lexington*, for it was the home of the Lexington-Gold Hill Mining Company.

SQUAW CREEK
Lawrence County(?)
Center of Section 16, T5N-R2E(?)

Although *South Dakota Place Names* mentions Squaw Creek, it is hard to say just where it was. Best guess is that it was one name for the settlement which grew up around the great Cleopatra mine on Squaw Creek east of Spearfish Canyon. The mill and several buildings are still there. The best way to reach them is to go to Maurice, in Spearfish Canyon, then inquire there for directions up the foot trail to the mine itself.

STEWART GULCH
Lawrence County
NW¼, Section 8, T4N-R3E

This appears to have been a center of mining and railroad activity northeast of the Golden Reward Mine. The USGS map of the Spearfish Quadrangle for 1915 shows it with a tangle of houses, the Chicago, Burlington & Quincy Railroad, and several narrow-gauge lines.

Cliffs still tower over the mouth of Stagebarn Canyon where the travelers found refreshment and fresh horses at the Sidney Stockade.

STONEWALL

Custer County
Sections 23, 24, 25, & 26, T3S-R4E

Stonewall, in honor of Stonewall Jackson, was the name which early miners of Confederate leanings proposed for the mining camp which was eventually named *Custer.*

STRATER

Custer County
NW¼, Section 32, T2S-R8E

An early name for *Hermosa.*

STRATOSPHERE BOWL, STRATO BOWL

Pennington County
NE¼, Section 12, T1S-R6E

The Stratosphere Bowl, northeast of Rockerville, is a deep natural depression in the limestone, apparently caused by the meanderings of Spring Creek. Its fame comes from its having been used to launch the huge balloons which in the 1930s were used for high altitude exploration and which reached the highest elevations man had at that time ever gained. The huge bowl, with its steep sides, protected the balloons from the wind and enabled them to be filled and launched without blowing away. The gain in height from the elevation of the Hills themselves was also a help.

There is little to see in the bowl; it is simply a huge valley, with a few summer homes and an abandoned mine or two in the bottom. It is so large that, instead of feeling hedged in, one feels positively spacious at the bottom of it. It is to the north of US 16, about 10 miles southwest of Rapid City. There is a picnic ground on the eastern rim which is well marked and easily reached by a graveled Forest Service road.

STRAWBERRY SPUR

Lawrence County
NW¼, Section 9, T4N-R4E

This spur of the Deadwood Central narrowgauge led off to the west from the main line to Galena and went up Strawberry Creek to the Oro Fino and the Gilt Edge Maid mines. It never seems to have been a populous district, although the mines themselves had a good many buildings around them.

STRING TOWN LOGGING CAMP

Lawrence County
Center, top line of Section 9, T2N-R5E

The camp, which served the important "Government Sale Number One" of National Forest timber, was on Jim Creek near Nemo. The timber sale was in T2S-R5E; cutting began in 1899 and was completed in 1908. O.M. Jackson describes this famous

Case One in detail in the April 1915 issue of *Journal of Forestry.*

STURGIS

Meade County
Sections 9 & 10, T5N-R5E

Sturgis, named for one Colonel Sturgis who had some real estate interest there, is a thriving cattle town and location of the Fort Meade Veterans' Administration Hospital. It was originally called *Scooptown,* because the inhabitants managed to scoop up most of the payroll from nearby Fort Meade, home of what was left of General Custer's famed Seventh Cavalry Regiment. Sturgis has a good deal of history of its own, including activities of Poker Alice and Calamity Jane.

Many lively business establishments flourished in and around the town, and one of them, under the direction of old cigar-chewing Poker Alice Tubbs, was doing so well that Mrs. Tubbs went down to the local bank and asked the banker if she could float a small loan. She assured him that business had been good and that if she could borrow a couple of thousand dollars she could build a wing onto her house, hire a couple more girls, and be able to pay the money back in a couple of years. The banker knew Mrs. Tubbs, and he knew of her establishment and of her many services to the military community at Fort Meade, so he loaned her the money. Inside of a year she came in and paid off the entire loan. Naturally the banker was glad to have the money, but he was curious, so he asked her, "Mrs. Tubbs, how come you could pay off this big loan a whole year ahead of time?" Old Poker Alice smiled, shifted her cigar around in her mouth, and said, "Well, Mr. Brown, I had known about the Elks Convention in Sturgis, and I had expected the West River Encampment of the veterans of the Grand Army of the Republic, but you know, Mr. Brown, I had plumb forgot about the Methodist District Conference!"

Many of the houses in Sturgis resemble those built in the early days at nearby Fort Meade, either because of unconscious imitation or because the same workmen built them all.

SUMMIT I
Lawrence County
NE¼, Section 5, T4N-R3E

There seems to be a plentiful supply of towns and stations named Summit. This one was on a branch of the Burlington Railroad, between Englewood and Lead.

SUMMIT II
Custer County
SE¼, Section 4, T5S-R7E

This Summit was on the Fremont, Elkhorn & Missouri Valley Railroad between Rapid City and Hot Springs, or, more specifically, between Buffalo Gap and Fairburn. In 1901 there seems to have been a siding and perhaps three houses.

SUMMIT III
Pennington County
SE¼, Section 22, T1S-R8E

This Summit, without house or siding, should not be confused with Summit II, although it too is on the Chicago & North Western (successor to the old FE&MV) between Rapid City and Hot Springs. Summit III is just north of Spring Creek, about 8 miles north of Hermosa.

SUMMIT IV, GOLDEN SUMMIT
Pennington County
SW¼, Section 33, T1S-R5E

This Golden Summit, or Gold Medal, mine, was developed intermittently between 1878 and 1913, with some exploratory work in 1927-1928. Production was small, although there are local legends of a huge find of jewelry ore, quartz barely held together by thick strands of pure gold. Several houses were built around the mine, and at least one survives, while the foundations of the others mark where they were. A flume ran nearly 2 miles southeast, up Rabbit Gulch, to carry water to the mine. The ditches can still be seen, running along the northern edge of Palmer Gulch and then into Rabbit Gulch. The community had its own school, in NW¼ of Section 32, but probably depended upon the store and bar at nearby Addie Camp for most of its supplies and social life.

The Golden Summit can be reached on the old Hill City-Keystone road, going east 3 miles from Hill City, then turning south ¼ mile on the road to Palmer Gulch Lodge. Explorers should be careful, for airshafts break through in unexpected places, and the tunnels are very crumbly.

Water from a spring in Rabbit Gulch was brought in a two-mile-long ditch to fill this reservoir behind the mill at the Golden Summit mine. Beside it stood the mine office building.

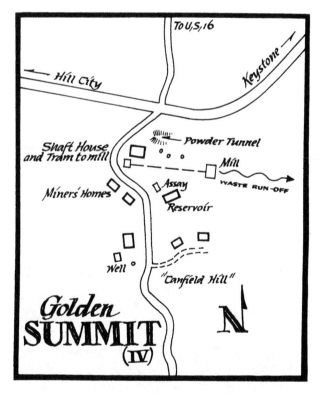

The Golden Summit mine and community, on the road to Palmer Gulch Lodge, 3 miles east of Hill City on the Hill City-Keystone road. Even after the mine closed down for the last time in the late 1920s, the miners' cabins continued to be occupied, and the last of them, old Del Canfield's home, is still in use as a summer cabin.

Skip from the shaft of the Golden Summit mine. The skip is lying on its side, its floor to the left, braced with long diagonal iron rods; the timbers to which the cable was attached are on the right. A skip ran on wooden tracks in the shaft and could comfortably hold half-a-dozen miners or a loaded ore car.

Precipitous Sunday Gulch leads northward from Sylvan Lake toward the summer home group where the valley broadens out.

SUNDANCE
Crook County
Center of Sections 13, 14, 23, & 24, T51N-R63W

Sundance is a bustling little tourist and cattle town nestled between Sundance Mountain and the Bear Lodge Mountains. It takes its name from the nearby mountain where the Indians used to perform their "Sun Dance" religious ceremony.

SUNDAY GULCH
Pennington County
E½, Section 25, T2S-R4E

Sunday Gulch is a small settlement made up of a resort or two, a gas station, and, farther south, a Forest Service Summer Home Group. A very pleasant foot trail about a mile long leads up the little creek to the base of the Sylvan Lake dam.

Sunday Gulch is about 6 miles south of Hill City on SD 89.

SYLVAN CITY
Custer County
Section 2, T3S-R3E(?)

Kingsbury's *History of Dakota* mentions this city more or less as an adjunct to the Northern Star, Mecca, and Placer gold and mica mines. The above location is that of the North Star, which may be the same as the Northern Star. Sylvan City apparently housed an axle-grease factory, making use of ground mica as a lubricant.

SYLVAN LAKE RESORT
Custer County
Center & SE¼, Section 30, T2S-R5E

Sylvan Lake was one of the earliest man-made lakes in the Hills created by damming up a narrow gut between two granite needles at the head of Sunday Gulch. For many years a wooden hotel and pavillion nestled near the edge of the lake, providing the familiar picture on the Swansdown flour sack. This, however, burned down in the 1930s and was replaced by an imposing stone structure high on the hill overlooking the lake. Modern cabins, a store, boats for fishing, and horses for hire have been provided for the tourists. The hotel is on SD 89, about 6 miles south of Hill City, and the same distance north of Custer. The road, either way, leads through some of the Needles, and is very spectacular. While visiting Sylvan Lake, no one should miss the opportunity to drive east over SD 89, the Needles Highway, to see the best of these huge granite pinnacles.

An old Victorian Gothic home in Custer. This house once served the town, appropriately enough, as the old people's home.

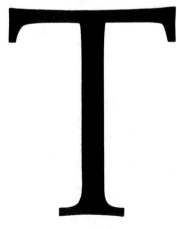

TEN MILE, TEN MILE RANCH

Lawrence County
NE¼, Section 20, T4N-R3E

Ten Mile Ranch was a stage stop about 6 miles southwest of Deadwood. A still there, run by a Mr. Kelly, kept Deadwood well supplied with tax-free whisky. The name was changed to *Englewood* in 1891, when the Black Hills & Missouri (now the Chicago, Burlington & Quincy) Railroad came in.

TEPEE

Pennington County
NW¼, Section 7, T4S-R2E

Early maps show Tepee as a town, and Brown & Willard speak of four bears being killed near it by one Gene Aiken, but other than that no record of it appears. It was probably near the present Tepee Ranger Station.

TEDDY BEAR

Pennington County
SE¼, Section 34, T2N-R3E

Although of no importance in itself, the Teddy Bear summer home group lies in the center of one of the oldest and most active of the Black Hills mining districts and is surrounded by relics of every description. It is a lovely drive up Castle Creek from Castleton (near Mystic) to Teddy Bear, and if you keep your eyes open you will see a good deal that will interest you.

TENDERFOOT

Custer County
SE¼, Section 33, T2S-R3E

Tenderfoot, along the Chicago, Burlington & Quincy Railroad between Hill City and Custer, is in Tenderfoot Gulch and either named or took the name of the Tenderfoot group of tin mines. These claims, originally belonging to the Harney Peak Tin Mining, Milling, and Manufacturing Company, were the Japanzy, the Szar, and the Szar No. 1 and Szar No. 2, and all lie on the west side of the gulch, to the west of US 16. There are two or three houses in the area, which is about 8 miles south of Hill City.

TERRAVILLE

Lawrence County
SW¼, Section 28, T5N-R3E

Terraville perches on the top of the mountain between Lead and Central City, right beside the open cut of the Homestake mine. The town was founded in 1877, mainly to support the Deadwood, Terra, and Caledonia mines. A total of 220 stamps were working in Terraville at its peak, and some 700 people got their mail at its post office in 1900. Now the town has dwindled some but is still worth a visit, for it has less level ground in it than any other populated community in the

Hills. The townspeople do their shopping in Lead, walking through the underground mine workings which the Homestake keeps shored up and lighted for their convenience.

Best way to reach Terraville is to go to either Lead, or, preferably Central City, and there ask directions.

The entrance to the Homestake tunnel leading from Terraville to Lead. The trip around the mountain was long, and over the mountains it was impossible, so the Homestake Mining Company kept the tunnel illuminated for .the use of the shoppers and school children.

TERRY

Lawrence County
Section 1, T4N-R2E, and Sections 6 & 7, T4N-R3E

Terry was founded during the gold rush of 1876 but reached its peak in the early 1890s with the discovery of large flat bodies of gold-bearing ore. It took its name from nearby Terry Peak, which in turn was named for General Alfred H. Terry, who commanded the military district at the time it was discovered.

At its busiest, Terry had a population of 1,200, two schools, two churches, lodges of Masons, A.O.U.W.s, Knights of Pythias, Red Men, Rebekahs, and Western Federation of Miners. The town was served by both the Fremont. Elkhorn & Missouri Valley and Deadwood Central narrow-gauge railroads, the bridge piers and cuts of which can still be seen. The town does not seem to have been a wild one, but more of a settled, industrial community. When the mines gave out most of the people left, buildings were moved or torn down, and the railroad tracks were taken up. Today nothing remains but a few traces and some summer homes.

Terry is about 4 miles southwest of Lead, on US 85, on the road to Trojan and the Terry Peak ski lift.

Terraville, with the concrete foundations of the mills in the valley below the town.

An abandoned clapboard house in Terry, once a bustling mining city just southwest of Lead, with rail connections to Lead, Englewood, and Spearfish Canyon.

Terraville, built on a mountain top, is pretty much inaccessible when six-foot snow falls hit the northern Hills.

TERRY STATION

Lawrence County
NE¼, Section 12, T4N-R2E

Terry Station was distinct from Terry itself, being a station on the Chicago, Burlington & Quincy Railroad between Englewood and Trojan.

TEXANA

Lawrence County
NE¼, Section 36, T5N-R2E

Texana seems to have consisted of a house or two along the Fremont, Elkhorn & Missouri Railroad line from Trojan to Central City. The railroad here makes a deep hairpin loop to the west that is nearly half-a-mile long, and Texana, what there was of it, lay just south of the base of the loop, and south of Deadwood Creek.

THREE FORKS

Pennington County
NW¼, Section 22, T1S-R5E

Three Forks, the junction of US 16 and US 385 about 3 miles northeast of Hill City, has a combined gas station, store, and restaurant, with some adjoining tourist cabins. It serves the many fishermen who come to enjoy Sheridan Lake a couple of miles to the northeast.

TIGERVILLE, TIGER CITY

Pennington County
SE¼, Section 9, T1S-R4E

Tigerville, or Tiger City, grew up early around the big King Solomon mine. It had a post office in Mr. Kittrell's store, another store run by a Mr. Aldridge, and a population of over 200. In 1880 the town sent six delegates to the state Republican convention; Rapid City at that time sent ten.

The name Tigerville may have come from the Bengal Tiger mine. It was reputed to be a very rich claim—even the chickens in the area were found to have nuggets in their crops—but it never seems to have gotten into production. Another suggestion is that the town was named for the Lucky Tiger claims No. 1, No. 2, and No. 3. As these were unpatented claims, they do not show on minerological maps, but local tradition says that they were near the town. This would certainly be a more logical source for the name than the Bengal Tiger mine which was 2 or 3 miles away.

All that is left of Tigerville today is one house and a sawmill, at the junction of the road from Hill City to Deerfield and to Rochford. It is about 4½ miles northwest of Hill City.

The Tilford schoolhouse, now used as the 4-H clubroom; the few children remaining in town are taken somewhere else to school.

TILFORD

Meade County
Center of Sections 16, 17, 20, & 21, T4N-R6E

A very small town but not at all ghostly, along the Chicago & North Western tracks on US Interstate 90, between Piedmont and Sturgis.

TIN REEF

Custer County
Section 10, T3S-R4E

Tin Reef was the name of the community which grew up in the late 1880s around the Tin Reef mine, otherwise known as the Old Jeff. Very little tin ore was ever shipped from the mine, which was about a mile south of Berne Siding on the Chicago, Burlington & Quincy and was apparently developed by the Harney Peak Tin Company.

TINTON

Lawrence County
SW¼, Section 19, T5N-R1E

Tinton probably has the most houses and other buildings of any ghost town in the Hills. It also is the most recent, and certainly the best guarded, for a vigilant caretaker and mountainous winter snows keep out most curiosity seekers. A trip to it will take you through some wild country, and several other ghost towns in the area can keep you busy for several days.

In 1876 Edgar St. John arrived in the area and stayed there until he died in 1928, being one of the town's leading citizens. In 1879 a group of Negroes found enormous quantities of gold just south of the present town, and the whole hill was thereupon named Nigger Hill. Bear Gulch, to the east, was estimated to have 1,000 votes in 1880— but the tax assessments for the town were only $447, so they must have been a pretty poverty-stricken lot.

The shaft house at Tinton, viewed from the reservoir.

The Black Hills Tin Company store and office, viewed through the broken window of the Tinton post office.

Placer tin had been known in the area since 1876, and in 1884 a tin strike in the pegmatite brought on a considerable boom. By 1904 a town had been built by the Tinton Company, including a hotel, rooming house, bunk house, miners' assembly hall, post office, bank, weekly newspaper, and six cottages for the miners' families. A railroad had been proposed, coming westward to Tinton from Iron Creek, down in Spearfish Canyon, but this does not seem to have been built. By 1911, 104,987 pounds of tin had been shipped out of the Rough and Ready mine, but hardly any production seems to have resulted from later endeavors, although they went on sporadically until the 1950s.

The fortunes of the area have varied widely: placer gold in Bear Gulch, Nigger Hill, Welcome, Golden, and Nugget Gulch; then the lode tin, followed by mining the columbite, tantalite, spodumene, and amblygonite. Just before World War II the government did a good deal of diamond drilling in the area, to see just what was down there, and the Winner Mining Company, 2½ miles northeast of Tinton, ran about 4,000' of exploratory tunnels but never got into production.

Tinton itself is well worth a visit. It is a typical company mining town, and most of the houses are still there. The big miners' hall looks out over the valley, the post office is still there, and the store, with the Black Hills Tin Company name over it, seems to have shut up shop only a few days before you got there. A large number of corporations seem to have owned the town and run it for a few years; The Boston Tin Company, The American Tin Plate Company, The Tinton Company, The

The U.S. Post Office at Tinton.

Tinton Reduction Company, and The Black Hills Tin Mining Company all had a hand in keeping the town running. In among the business buildings are about twenty miners' houses and of course the mine buildings and shops. Most of the buildings are covered with a dismal, dull red tarpaper, which does not make for good color pictures, but there are so many houses, and the light there on the hill top is so good, that you must be a poor photographer not to come away with a camera full of ghost town pictures. If the caretaker is there he doubtless will be happy to tell you about some of the things that went on in Tinton in days gone by.

The town is in Section 19, T5N-R1E. The best way to reach it is to drive about 6 miles west from Iron Creek, in Spearfish Canyon. Or you can turn west at Savoy and pass Roughlock Falls, then gradually turning northward, come up on Tinton from the south after about a 10-mile drive. The town is up on a hill, with good views to the east and west. The little valleys around it are full of mines, dating from the earliest placer days right up to the present. While you're there, look around at some of the other towns we've mentioned, and drop in at the fire lookout tower on Cement Ridge, where the affable ranger will gladly direct you to the points of interest in the area he knows so well.

A foot bridge leading from the reservoir to the mill at Tinton.

Entrance to the tin mining town of Tinton, one of the best preserved and most extensive of the Black Hills' ghost towns.

The mill at Tinton. The town was begun as a gold mining camp, then turned to tin, then during World War II to lithium and feldspar, with each change working progressively less valuable minerals, and always at a loss.

Mine buildings a few hundred yards south of Tinton. The earth scraper in the foreground was used for roadbuilding and earthmoving generally.

The company store and office of the Black Hills Tin Company at Tinton. The building contains a huge walk-in vault which at one time was full of company papers which winds and vandals have long since dissipated.

The shaft house at Tinton, viewed over a great open cut.

TOMAHA CAMP
Pennington County
SW¼, Section 9, T1N-R6E

A YMCA camp half-a-mile up Rapid Canyon from Hisega.

TOMAHAWK
Lawrence County
NW¼, Section 21, T3N-R5E

Tomahawk is a small settlement, only about one or two houses, really, about 2 miles northwest of Nemo, near a 4788 benchmark. Although the railroad was nearby, the town was not on the old Black Hills & Fort Pierre narrow-gauge, which was about a mile south.

Tomahawk, northwest of Nemo.

T. O. T. RANCH
Custer County
SE Corner, T8S-R2E

Andreas' map of Custer County shows the T. O. T. Ranch as being on the Cheyenne River at just about the present location of *Edgemont*. It may have been an early name for this now prosperous town.

TROJAN
Lawrence County
S½, Section 35, T5N-R2E, and
N½, Section 2, T4N-R2E

This little town shut down in 1959, except for winter skiers. The mine buildings were closed and the miners' houses vacated, for $6-a-ton ore will not pay for the powder and steel necessary to mine it.

Gold was discovered in the Trojan area, on Bald Mountain and Green Mountain, as early as 1877, and mines have run sporadically since that time. By about 1900 the process of consolidation of many claims into a few was well under way, and by 1911 the Trojan Mining Company had taken in the major part of them; it in its turn was bought out by the Bald Mountain Mining Company in 1928, which now owns some 2,300 acres in and around Section 2, T4N-R2E, one of the richest square miles of countryside in the whole Black Hills. At least $20,000,000 has been taken out of the area, mainly in gold, but with a considerable amount of silver mixed in with it.

A miner's home in Trojan, with its typical roofed porch, lilac bush, and front yard full of golden flowers.

Among the mines—all now owned by the Bald Mountain Company—were the American Eagle, Apex, Baltimore, Ben Hur, Alemeda, Folger, Burlington & Golden Sands, Clinton, Perserverance, Monday Group, Mark Twain, Leopard-Jessie, Empire State, Crown Hill, Dakota Group, Decorah, Dividend, Juno, Portland, Snowstorm, Trojan, and Two Johns, plus a good many claims which went to make up all of these when *they* were started. The Bald Mountain Company ran the Decorah, Clinton, and Portland mines and used their workings to get under all the rest of the claims in the area, which made for economical mining and aided in centralizing the operation. The rails were taken out of the mine in 1960, but a good many of the cars are still there, a joy to any narrow-gauge railroad fan.

The best way to get to Trojan is to go along US 85 south from Lead until you run into the Terry Peak Ski Slope and Trojan Road. Look along both sides of the valley as you go north to Trojan—it's just full of mines and old railroad roadbeds. You'll pass through the remains of Terry on your way—a town of well over a thousand people. While in the Trojan area, hunt around for Greenmount, Crown Hill, Portland, Annie Creek,

Stack and part of the mill of the Bald Mountain mine at Trojan. The round building probably covered the cyanide leaching tank that completed the removal of the gold from its refractory ore.

The mill and workings of the Bald Mountain mine at Trojan, which closed down in the 1950s because the price of steel and powder went up but the price of gold stayed just the same, $35 an ounce, as it was in 1934.

Trojan, with the adjoining works and houses of the Bald Mountain mine, is one of the Hills' most recently abandoned towns. It had hoped to recoup its fortunes by catering to skiers on Terry Peak, so far without success. The building on the right was the store and gas station.

Balmoral-Dacy-Preston, Baltimore, and the other towns that sprang up with the mines. A wonderful walk, if you're a hiker, is to follow the railroad from Trojan down the side of Spearfish Canyon to Elmore, while a confederate drives the car down to meet you. Other spurs, now long abandoned, will lead you to towns and places plumb forgotten, so take your lunch and camera with you, and plan to make a day of it.

Tailings from the Bald Mountain mine at Trojan fill nearly a mile of the valley below the mill.

The Two Johns mine (named for a popular stage play of the day) hauled its ore up from the mine to the mill over 2 or 3 miles of narrow-gauge tramway that is almost too steep to walk up. The weight of the track has caused it to pull loose from the ties, so it traces its path in crazy zigzags down the incline.

TROY

Lawrence County
SW¼, Section 23, T5N-R3E

On May 9, 1877 the *Black Hills Daily Times* reported that *Gayville* had changed its name to Troy, to avoid confusion with a Gayville in Yankton County, but the name does not seem to have stuck.

TUBB TOWN

Weston County
SW¼, Section 35, T45N-R61W

Tubb Town was founded on Salt Creek in the spring of 1888, when DeLoss Tubbs of Custer built a store there. The store was quickly joined, or perhaps preceded by, an open-air bar run by F. R. Curran, who hoped to name the new town *Field City*. When Curran got around to building a house over his bar, the town was in full swing, catering to the baser passions of the crews pushing the Burlington & Missouri River Railroad northward. The rules of the community required each newcomer to set 'em up for the house upon arrival, a custom which probably provided a good deal of news for the *Stockade Journal* which began publication on September 1, 1888. Trouble was brewing, however, for on that day the railroad decided to pass through Newcastle, a couple of miles to the west, and Tubb Town folded up like a card table to move *en masse* to the new location.

The remains of foundations and other ruins which mark Tubb Town are just about where US 85 joins US 16, 7.9 miles west of the South Dakota border.

A tarpaper-covered mine shop at the south end of the tunnel, at Tunnel, on the C & NW, north of Deadwood.

A two-story log cabin, home of the sole surviving resident of the little railroad town of Tunnel.

A railroad switch and sturdy octagonal privy-storehouse-office building that served the railroaders maintaining the big tunnel or working at the siding at Tunnel.

TUNNEL

Lawrence County
SE¼, Section 1, T5N-R3E

Tunnel was the site of the Loomis tunnel, nearly 1,000 feet long, which was dug in 1890 so the Fremont, Elkhorn & Missouri Valley Railroad could come from Whitewood southwest to Deadwood. The Whitewood end of the tunnel apparently debouched upon whatever town there was in the area; all that remains is an old log house, a siding, and some railroad equipment. At the Deadwood end of the tunnel, down in the valley where the limestone cliffs come down to the creek, is reputedly Barker's Cave, a place of refuge where an early prospector used to hole up, behind a rough-hewn log door, to defend himself against Indian attacks. Oldtimers stoutly aver that spatters of lead from Indian bullets can still be seen on the rocks around the mouth of the cave entrance.

Twelve Mile Ranch was twelve miles south of Custer on the old Cheyenne-Deadwood stage trail. Also known as the Heumphreus Ranch, it was for years a popular resort and the summer home of the artist-writer El Comancho (Walter Phillips).

TWELVE MILE RANCH
Custer County
NE¼, Section 3, T5S-R3E

This is also known as the *Heumphreus Ranch*, for its builder, Joseph Heumphreus, who laid it out in 1890 as a stage stop. For many years it was run as a summer resort and had a large collection of Black Hills books and items of historical and scientific interest.

TWELVE MILE STATION
Pennington County
NE¼, Section 12, T2S-R3E

Twelve Mile Station, on the stageline twelve miles north of Custer, should not be confused with Twelve Mile Ranch to the south.

The stage between Cheyenne and Deadwood followed many trails, but in its earliest days the basic route was as it appears here. The detailed plotting of the route for this map was caluclated from old mileage charts, checked mile by mile on the ground, and from the contours of the land which dictated where the coaches had to roll. The small squares around the stations indicate which quarter-section each occupied. Descriptions of the stations can be found under each place name.

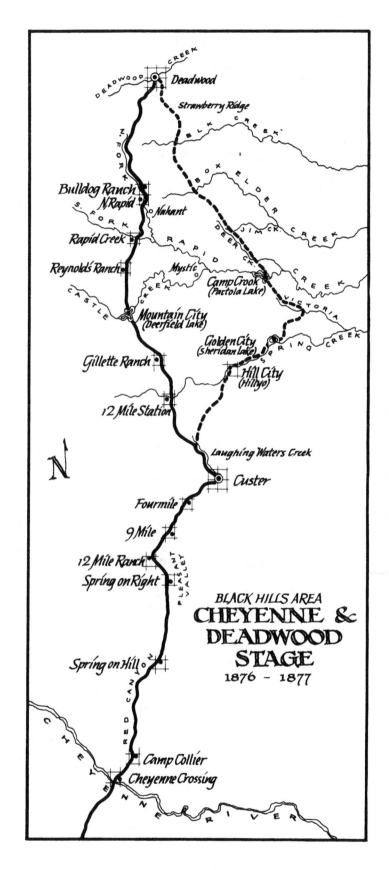

Stone walls of a two-story building at Two-Bit. The ruins seem to indicate that the building was open, or glassed in, at the front side; perhaps it was a store or hotel or other business building.

Two-Bit, whether named for placers that yielded 25¢ to the pan or weren't worth two bits taken all together, was a major mining area north of Galena. These frame houses are now torn down, but they give some idea of the prosperity and expectations of the miners that erected them.

TWO-BIT
Lawrence County
SE¼, Section 25, T5N-R3E

The origin of the name Two-Bit is much disputed. Some say that it got the name because a miner could pan out 25 cents worth of gold in a single *pan*. Others say it was so named because a miner could only get two-bit's worth of gold in a whole *day*. And still others claim that the whole area was insignificant and not worth two-bits all together. Whatever the origin of its name, Two-Bit stretched for about a mile up and down Peedee Gulch, about 2 miles east of Deadwood.

It got its start when the placer miners came in during the gold rush of 1876 but did not get to booming until 1892, when the Gold Mountain Mining Company began development. In 1897 the Hardin Properties began work and by 1899 were shipping 30 tons of pyrite a day to the Golden Reward smelter at Astoria. As late as 1916 the Mary Group, a latecomer, shipped 1,600 pounds of tungsten ore, as did the Seth R. group. A Burlington Railroad map of about 1904 shows a spur going clear up to Two-Bit from Galena, but this seems to be doubtful—although it might have been justified by 30-tons-a-day shipments. At any rate, Two-Bit was the scene of much mining development, and is well worth a visit, for it is off the main roads and hard to find. Best way to reach what is left—a single, three-story house—is to go to the top of Strawberry Hill, on US 385 south of Pluma, then turn north, downhill all the way, until you reach signs of civilization.

196

TWO C RANCH
Pennington County
NW¼, Section 5, T1S-R7E

The current name for the old *Four R* dude ranch.

A typical Black Hills farmstead in a grassy valley clearing, surrounded by pine-covered hills.

U V

Locally made wooden bullwheels, often six or eight feet across, carried the belts that drove the stamp mills. (Uncle Sam mine)

UNCLE SAM MINE

Lawrence County
SW¼, Section 29, T4N-R4E

The Uncle Sam mine gave its name to the area later known as *Perry*, and still later as *Roubaix*.

UNION STOCKADE

Custer County
SW¼, Section 21, T3S-R5E

Union Stockade was the name given to the *Gordon Stockade* when it was occupied by General George Crook and his troops during the summer of 1875. Crook was successful in removing many of the miners who had sneaked into the Hills after the Gordon party, for he promised that they would be allowed to return to their claims as soon as the government persuaded the Indians to relinquish the Hills. When the Sioux refused to give up the area, which had been given to them by the Treaty of Laramie of 1868 (it actually had belonged to the Crows prior to that time), the miners began to drift back to the mines, and in the fall of 1875 Captain Edwin Pollock was placed in command to continue the work of capturing invading miners.

UPPER RAPID

Pennington County
SE¼, Section 8, T1N-R7E

Upper Rapid was about 3½ miles above Rapid City. It was founded in 1876 by Moses "California Joe" Milner and others but abandoned within a few months due to Indian hostilities. It was probably about where the state fish hatchery is now.

URBAN

Custer County
SW¼, Section 19, T3S-R8E

Urban was a point on the Chicago & North Western Railroad, between Hermosa and Fairburn.

VALLEY RANCHE

Lawrence County
SE¼, Section 6, T5N-R4E

Collins' *Directory* notes this as being on Centennial Prairie, 3 miles upstream from Crook City, with a saloon, hotel, sawmill, planing mill, sash and door factory, and blacksmith shop run by Jones and Parker.

VALLEY STATION

Lawrence County
SW¼, Section 23, T4N-R2E(?)

Valley Station, kept by Henry Fosha, was a stop on the 1877 route of the Cheyenne-Deadwood stage, somewhere in the vicinity of Icebox Canyon. The above location, the Icebox Canyon Camp Ground, is probably fairly close.

Take-off point for the aerial tramway that carried ore from the upper workings of the Victoria mine down to the mill in Spearfish Canyon.

A log cabin at upper Victoria, on the edge of Spearfish Canyon, where the Victoria mine got its ore from shallow surface workings and sent it by aerial tramway down to the mill at the bottom of the canyon.

A spur line railway grade led from the Chicago, Burlington & Quincy Railroad in Spearfish Canyon to the mill and settlement around it that served the Victoria mine.

A sizeable miner's cabin in lower Victoria in Spearfish Canyon. Judging from the size, it may have been some sort of boarding house or dining hall.

VICTORIA I
Lawrence County
Center, Section 17, T5N-R2E

Victoria, home of the Victoria Gold Mining and Milling Company, was partially in Spearfish Canyon and partially on the uplands above. It was reached by half-a-mile of spur, curving off around a mountain to the east of the Burlington Railroad in the Canyon, and this line apparently led to the mill and a few of the mill-workers' houses. Above the mill, on the divide between Squaw Creek and Spearfish Canyon, was the mine itself. There does not seem to have been any connection between the two, and one would suppose that an aerial tramway must have supplied the only communication, save for a telephone line and a dim foottrail.

Lower Victoria is easily found, for the spur line branched off about 3 miles north of Savoy. The upper part of town can be reached over a *very* dim road leading northward from Preston.

VICTORIA II
Pennington County
SW Corner, T1N-R6E

Victoria was also a spot in Rapid Canyon, near McGee's Mills, apparently on the Black Hills & Western Railroad. Also in the general area are Victoria Creek, which flows through Dark Canyon, and Victoria Dam, at the head of the creek.

The heavily timbered entrance to one of the mines at Virginia, or Moll, south of Galena. Fourteen-inch timbers were customary in the Black Hills mines, which tended to be crumbly.

VINCENT

Fall River County
SE ¼, Section 10, T7S-R5E

Vincent was an early stop on the Chicago, Burlington & Quincy Railroad between Minnekahta and Hot Springs. From Rand McNally's 1900 map it appears to be 2-3 miles northwest of Hot Springs.

VIRGINIA I

Lawrence County
SW ¼, Section 9, T4N-R4E

Virginia, also known as *Moll*, was surrounded by silver mines. It was on the Deadwood Central's narrow-gauge line to Galena, on Bear Butte Creek. The Silver Queen, the Groshong, the Alice, the Bion, and the Rutherford B. Hayes were all silver producers in the 1880s, and it is hard to tell why Virginia was not a bigger town than it was, with so much activity all around it. Maybe the miners all went up to Galena to do their shopping and visit with Emma.

VIRGINIA II

Lawrence County
SW ¼, Section 10, T5N-R2E

Carbonate was originally called *West Virginia,* then the name was shortened for a time to Virginia; finally *Carbonate* was chosen, for the carbonate silver ores of the district.

VOLUNTEER

Meade County
NE ¼, Section 5, T6N-R8E

A small town on the south side of the Belle Fourche River, near its confluence with Bear Butte Creek. Volunteer appears on the USGS 1913 map, and the 1900 Rand McNally atlas mentions a post office, but the town seems to have now disappeared.

When western politicians said that the grass would grow in the streets of a thousand towns if their party wasn't elected, they knew what they were talking about. (Buffalo Gap)

A freight wagon, with its hitch behind for hauling a trailer, now stands idle on a hillside at Clifton.

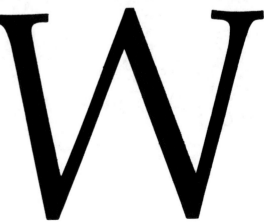

WARBONNET

Pennington County
SE¼, Section 35, T1N-R8E

The latest name for *Brennan*, which was also known as *Siding Eleven*.

WARSAW

Lawrence County

This town was laid out in 1879, along Boxelder Creek, by two young Rapid City men, but either failed to materialize or was incorporated into some other community.

WASHBOARD ROW

Meade County
Part of Fort Meade

Every army post had this sort of residential area for the wives of the enlisted soldiers; more commonly they were referred to as "Soapsuds Row," from the usual occupation of the women. This particular community consisted of a strip of weatherbeaten houses near Fort Meade, along Bear Butte Road.

WASHINGTON

Lawrence County
Section 33, T5N-R3E

An early name for *Lead*.

WEALTHY

Pennington County
NW¼, Section 28, T1S-R6E

Wealthy, now completely vanished, undoubtedly got its name from the Wealthy mine. It was at the head of Tepee Gulch, 3 miles north of Keystone.

An elaborate stone-work cold cellar, or perhaps it was the powder storage cave of the Lucky Cuss mine at Wealthy.

WEBER

Pennington County

Weber was probably only a ranch, but an 1883 map shows it as a town on the South Fork of Castle Creek, about 3 miles southeast of Mountain City (Deerfield).

Miner's cabin burrowed into the bank at Welcome.

WELCOME I

Crook County
SW¼, Section 28, T51N-R60W

Welcome, as marked by the Forest Service sign, is a single, two-story log house, well cared for, and apparently lived in upon occasion, and plumb out in the godforsaken wilderness. It is hard to reach in fair weather and must be totally inaccessible in winter. Farther down the little creek which runs past this house are the ruins of three others, one marked with an ornate but now illegible sign made of birch twigs. Still farther down, where the creek begins to amount to something, is a sheet-metal building and a concrete dam, evidently part of either a hydraulic operation or a power plant of the Black Hills Tin Company.

In 1904 the Golden Empire Mining Company controlled 11,000 acres in the Mineral Hill area and built a big 20-stamp mill at Welcome to work the gold ore. Veins up to 100 feet wide were reported but never seem to have been profitable.

The best way to reach Welcome is to start from Savoy, in Spearfish Canyon, and follow a Forest Service map. Or you can inquire of the ranger at Cement Ridge lookout. While at Welcome, you should press on to Mineral Hill, ½ mile to the southwest.

An astonishingly ornate and prosperous looking house, the only habitable one in Welcome, miles from any other human home. The last time we were there a note was pasted up on the door declaring that "any son-of-a-bitch that would steal a widow woman's kerosene can deserves to go to hell and stay there!"

A corrugated iron pump house on Sand Creek near Welcome, apparently used to pump water up to the tin mills at Tinton.

WELCOME II
Lawrence County
Sections 1 & 12, T4N-R2E

The Welcome station, serving the great Mogul-Horseshoe Company, was at the end of a spur of the Deadwood Central Railroad, branching off southwestward from Fantail Junction. The various properties of the company produced over $7,000,000 worth of gold from 1893 to 1915, and after that the mills continued operation on ore from other mines. The mine seems to have been just north of Terry, apparently very near to the Bald Mountain Mining Company which bought the entire outfit in 1939.

WESTFORD
Custer County
Section 18, T4S-R6E

An early map shows Westford about 7 miles east of Mayo, at the head of the North Fork of Lame Johnny Creek. It is hard to say which of the several likely spots in that vicinity is actually Westford.

WEST VIRGINIA
Lawrence County
SW¼, Section 10, T5N-R2E

The original name of *Carbonate*, so called after James Ridpath's West Virginia mine, which took its name from Ridpath's home state.

WHEATON COLLEGE SUMMER CAMP

Pennington County
NW¼, Section 9, T1N-R6E

A summer camp maintained for geological study and related topics by Wheaton College at Wheaton, Illinois; it is one of the oldest of such establishments in the Hills.

WHEEL INN

Pennington County
Center of Section 2, T1S-R5E

A summer resort, gas station, and fishermen's store on a branch of Sheridan Lake, run for many years by Mr. and Mrs. Ralph Morris.

WHITETAIL

Lawrence County
SW¼, Section 5, T4N-R3E

A junction of the Burlington line from Trojan to Lead with that leading off to the west to Bucks. In 1900 there were half-a-dozen houses in the vicinity.

WHITETAIL JUNCTION

Lawrence County
Center of Section 5, T4N-R3E

Whitetail Junction was the point on the Deadwood Central Railroad where the line heading southwest from Kirk divided to produce spur lines leading to Baltimore, Welcome II, Mogul, and Carthage.

Many buildings in the northern Hills were built, like this store on a side street in Whitewood, of the local pink sandstone.

Whitewood, on Whitewood Creek at the CB&Q Railroad in the northeast corner of the Hills, hoped for quite a boom in its early days and built ponderously in anticipation of it. Now Interstate 90 passes near the town, and the hoped-for boom may at last live up to expectations.

WHITEWOOD

Lawrence County
SW¼, Section 21, T6N-R4E

Whitewood is another of those towns that might have looked like a good real estate investment when the railroad came in. It is the place where the present Chicago & North Western line divided to go to Sturgis and Rapid City on the east and Deadwood and Lead on the west. Although still an active town, it has never boomed as its supporters hoped. A good, brief history of Whitewood is in *Lawrence County: Dakota Territory Centennial, 1861-1961,* edited by Mildred Fielder.

A high, arched door on the Selbie Building in Whitewood.

WHITEWOOD CITY
Lawrence County
SW¼, Section 23, T5N-R3E

A letter from William Gay, an early Deadwood settler, written March 31, 1876, mentions that one of the mining camps in the area later known as Deadwood was "a short distance below the mouth of Deadwood, on Whitewood Creek, and is called Whitewood City." This is not of course the present town of Whitewood.

WHOOP-UP, WHOOP-UP TOWN
Weston County
Section 34, T45N-R61W(?)

Whoop-up was at the railhead of the Burlington & Missouri River Railroad. It was northwest of the Jenney Stockade, and one wild town. After less than a year, the population picked up and moved on to Tubb Town, where they continued their activities.

Rear view of one of the many stone buildings that still line Whitewood's streets.

Miner's cabin at the Wild Rose mine, south of the Needles, one of the innumerable mineral enterprises that started up in the 1930s when the price of gold rose, then faded away as even higher prices could not meet the rising costs of operation.

WILD ROSE MINE
Custer County
NW¼, Section 17, T3S-R5E

Although insignificant in itself, the Wild Rose mine lies in some very lovely park country close upon the beginning of the Needles range. There are two or three abandoned cabins at the mine itself, which is about 2 miles northeast of Custer on a well-marked dirt road.

WILLIAMSBURG
Lawrence County(?)

Early newspaper references mentioned Williamsburg as being near the Atlantic mine—but that mine too has disappeared into the mists of time and cannot be located. It was probably near Atlantic Hill, SE¼, Section 5, T3S-R4E.

WIND CAVE
Custer County
S½, Section 1, T6S-R5E

Wind Cave, so the story goes, was discovered in 1881 by one Tom Bingham, who heard the air rushing out of its narrow opening. Its first explorer, however, was Alvin McDonald, who guided tourists through the cave with string and candles. The gush of wind through the opening was so strong that visitors had to descend the ladder in the dark, then walk off into the gloom until far enough away from the wind to light their candles. A new opening has been made, and the cave, under the management of the National Park Service, is smooth underfoot, electrically lighted, and served by twin elevators.

In the park around the cave are large herds of buffalo and pronghorn antelope. There are also several huge prairie dog towns. Visitors are cautioned to remain in their cars, for although prairie dogs and antelope are not hostile, the buffalo, especially the older bulls, tend to be misanthropic. One old bull tangled with a Volkswagen, hitting it from the side and rolling it a hundred yards over the prairie. The folks inside got real peevish about it; every little thing seems to upset some folk.

Wind Cave is 10 miles north of Hot Springs, on US 385.

WOODVILLE
Lawrence County
SE¼, Section 21, T4N-R3E

Woodville, also known as *Lake Station* and *The Lake*, from a small pond nearby, was a wood-cutting camp which supplied fuel for the locomotives which ran between Englewood and Piedmont. It was also the scene of several attempts to rob the Homestake payroll train, the most famous of which occurred on September 12, 1888, when John Wilson, Jack Doherty, Alfred G. Nickerson, and a man named Murphy ran into a good deal of trouble while making the attempt.

The best way to reach Woodville is to start west from just north of Englewood, over the old roadbed, which, astonishingly enough, can still be traveled by an ordinary automobile.

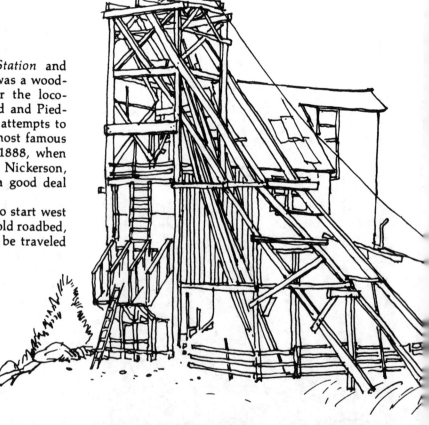

The headframe and mill at the Spokane mine. Ore cars were hoisted out of the shaft on a slight incline and their contents either taken high into the mill or dumped into a hopper built into the headframe, where a ladder rests against the chutes that loaded the ore into trucks for shipment.

The remnant of a board fence comes to rest beside a dry creek bed at Bakerville.

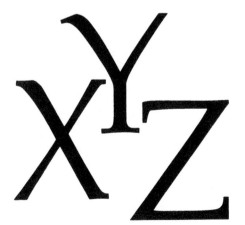

YAHR PARK
Meade County
N½, Section 10, T5N-R5E

Between Fort Meade and Sturgis, Yahr Park was once the Tivoli—the entertainment center—of the area, says Leland Case.

YAMBOYA
Custer County
NE¼, Section 19, T3S-R6E

Yamboya, in 1901, was a community of three houses near the head of the south fork of Squaw (now Coolidge) Creek. Whether the name was that of an actual community or only that of a family is hard to say, but it is distinctive and will doubtless appear in both maps and memories for years to come. It was also known as *Ivanhoe*.

YATES
Lawrence County
NW¼, Section 4, T4N-R3E

A siding on the Burlington railroad, south of Lead, between Kirk and Flatiron.

YELLOW CREEK
Lawrence County
E½, Section 9, T4N-R3E

An early name for the *Flatiron* area.

YOUNG
Pennington County

The placer mines around Hill City had been abandoned when the rich deposits of Deadwood were opened up in the fall of 1876, but interest in the area revived in May of 1879, when the *Cheyenne Daily Leader* reported that gravel running $15 to the wagon-load was coming out of Hill City, Eureka, and Young.

ZIMBLEMAN DEER CAMP
Custer County
NE¼, Section 11, T3S-R3E

On the site of *Kiddville* and the old *Penobscot* mine, this hunters' camp has been active for years.

The Zimbleman Deer Camp is all that is left of Kiddville, but the town was once a thriving one, built up around the Penobscot Mine.

THE MONUMENT

Now you have gone as far as you can go upon the printed page, and now you know that it was not on paper that these lives were lived but on the harsh and rocky soil of the Black Hills. Here lived the pioneers and built their hopeful towns, and here they nursed their frail ambitions only to move on, onto the pages of our history. These Hills and all their past will come alive, though all around is ruin and decay, if you will follow down the trails that we have trod, see those strange sites that we have seen, and hear the tales that we were told. . . .

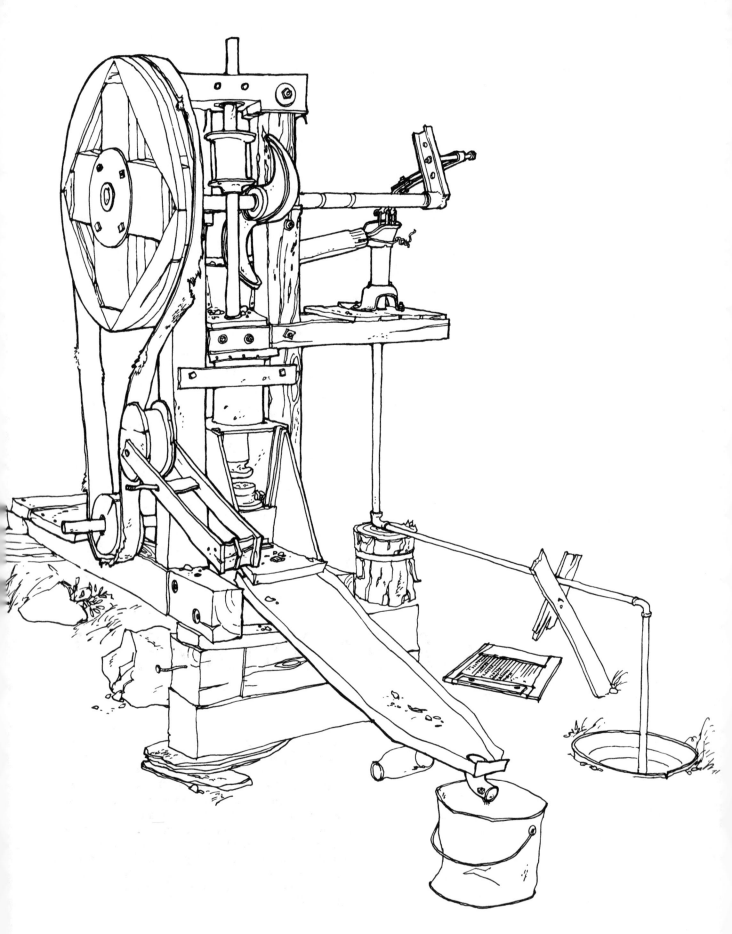

What's that thing there? Well, sir, I guess you never knew Jim Harnick well. Now there was quite a man!

He stood about six feet, I guess it was, or maybe it was just a little more, and he looked tall because he was so thin and ganted up, with his face like it was cut out of a hunk of rock, all gray and jagged and snag-toothed, like a chunk of ore is when you take it from the mine. Stood bowed over, he did, and crooked, from where a square-set took him on the shoulder down in an old drift in the Golden Bell. His arms and legs they stuck out like a scare-crow, and his clothes flapped on him like a flag around a pole. It wasn't looks, I don't suppose, that make the folks remember Jim.

But he could work! And strong! There never was a man I ever knew could drive more iron in the ground or dig more ditch or move more ore or drink more whiskey and speak softer after than what Jim Harnick could. And he was kindly, too, for all he was so strong. You didn't live here then, I guess, but one day when I was just a little boy, dad he was changing a tire on the car, and the jack slipped, and down she come, and caught dad under it by the foot, and rested on him some. Old Jim he saw it happen, don't you know, from out the window of the old saloon, and up he come just on the run, and then he took a hold of that front bumper with his hands, and then he gave a heave, and something had to give, so up she come, and dad he got from under in a hurry. Jim loaded dad onto the back of his old truck — lifted him up four feet, in his arms, and dad he wasn't any slender man, and laid him on the truck bed, there between his tools — and drove him up the street to where old Doc could patch him up. Jim could have waited, don't you know, for there wasn't all that much hurry, come to think about it, but that just wasn't old Jim's way when there were folks in trouble and he could lend a hand.

Dad, he always tried to keep an eye on Jim after that and help him when he could. I remember once we got the word that things were going pretty bad with him — he'd lost the vein down in the mine or run up debts or had expenses — I don't remember what it was; he needed money, anyway, and dad, he heard about it from some friends, and so he hired Jim to haul some rock to fill the mud holes in our road. I never saw a man work so in all my life as old Jim did with his long-handled shovel and his flat-bed truck, there by the mine dump at the Golden Bell. He couldn't haul a yard at a time, I don't suppose, but he worked hard and filled those holes and took his money and got squared away. He knew, you know, that we didn't have to have those holes filled just then, and all he'd work on such a job as that was just enough to raise the cash he had to have to tide him over for a while, and then he'd quit and work down in his mine.

Once we was down at the county seat, dad and I, and the sheriff he come up to us, and kind of smiled out of half his face, and says "I guess I got a friend of yours in here." And so he did, for old Jim he had taken on a bit more liquor than even he could hold and they had put him in the jail to sober up and sleep it off. Dad offered then and there to pay his fine, for old time's sake you know, and it would have made you laugh to see old Jim come down the hall there in the jail, staggering up against the wall and shaking his head back and forth to try to clear his eyes. "Thank you," he says, "thank you, but I don't need no help. I kind of figured I might land in jail," he says, "and so I left some cash with Andy, he's my pard, and told him if I wasn't home by morning he should ought to come and pay my fine." I guess old Andy did it, too, 'cause I saw Jim on the street that afternoon, still wobbly on his feet, down by the general store.

But you'd get drunk yourself, I guess, if you lived like the Harnicks lived, there in that crazy cabin by the Golden Bell. That house! Well, you can see it for yourself. It's not worse now, I don't suppose, than when they lived in it some years ago. Mrs. Harnick, she wasn't much account, some say — I knew her folks when they lived up on Rabbit Hill — and the kids they was a lively bunch like most kids are, or maybe worse, and wild and ornery, too. They didn't any of 'em pick up a thing when once they threw it down. Look at that yard. It was like that when they lived here, too, just filled up clear across with trash and junk and busted stuff that they'd hauled in. That old car there, it once belonged to old Dan Hicks, down by the viaduct, and that washing machine, my grandma threw it out, and Jim he got it from the dump. There's an old tub, and those timbers, they come out of the Golden Bell, from some place where he could afford to let the mine fall in. Go on into the house. It's full of junk just like the yard. The whole darn place is just a warehouse for trash that other folks have thrown away.

And Jim Harnick, he made a life out of that junk. He took whatever came to hand, busted or worthless or worn out or thrown away, in machinery or jobs or mines — or people, too, come to think of it — and he made a life out of it. He picked up old Andy — they were a pair! — and gave him work to do, and kept him mighty busy, too. He got himself a wife, and maybe she wasn't any bargain, but they raised some likely kids, and he picked up the Golden Bell at a tax sale, debts, taxes, ruins, and a hole in the ground, and he made a gold mine out of her, enough for them to live on anyway, and he did it all on busted parts and a broken-down one-horse stamp mill that he got from an old mine down the creek.

That's it there, that mill he made to pound the ore he hauled up from the bottom of the Golden Bell. I don't wonder that you laugh, but that old mill, it hammered out a heap of gold in its day. He patched it up from scraps and tatters that he found and nailed it together with old spikes and ran it with a chunk of busted belting that he had to hand. He made that bullwheel, with those spokes, himself, out of old boards he had around. See how the cam it lifts the stamp? He ran the camshaft with an engine off a Model T. That pump, it works to bring in water when the camshaft turns, he got that down at old McPherson's sale, when the widow moved away. Those timbers, like I said, came from the mine. The ore was ground up, don't you know, beneath the stamp. That screen that's laying there held in the ore, until it was ground fine, and then it dribbled out and ran down on that trough, and the gold settled in that bucket there. About once a day, I guess, he'd pan her out, to see how rich the vein was running, or to pay his grocery bill.

What's that you say? Oh, old Jim's gone, him and his family too. They had a little disagreement with a railroad train down where their road comes out onto the tracks, about where Andy used to live. They're all gone now, and folks around, they kind of let the place stay just the way it was when Jim was here. I like to think, you know, that wherever it is that old Jim's gone, he's hauling high-grade ore to pave those golden streets, and working on those mills that grind exceeding small, with all new parts to hand.

Goldbug Nelson's patented gold-separating device, apparently a
crude form of vanner or rocker.

The spirit of the west is everywhere in the Black Hills. Wat Parker's father found this buffalo skull, apparently part of some long-forgotten Indian ceremonial, in the 1920s, high on a Wyoming butte, and Hugh Lambert's father photographed it at Palmer Gulch Lodge in 1937. Books, like bones, are relics of a glorious past which only insight and appreciation can clothe again with understanding and reality.

Bibliography

The most readable Black Hills bibliography is J. Leonard Jennewein's *Black Hills Booktrails* (Mitchell, 1962), a history of the Hills told through an account of the books written about them. The bibliography in Jennewein's and Jane Boorman's *Dakota Panorama* (Mitchell, 1961), is more extensive but less critical. Old but still invaluable is Cleophas C. O'Harra's *Bibliography of the Geology and Mining Interests of the Black Hills* (Rapid City, 1917). Watson Parker's "Black Hills Bibliography," pages 169-301 of the *South Dakota Historical Collections*, XXXV (1970), is the most up-to-date survey of Hills literature, and includes books, periodicals, and ephemera not mentioned elsewhere.

Early Hills histories written by those who were there when it happened include the Reverend Peter Rosen's *Pa-Ha-Sa-Pa* (St. Louis, 1895) and Annie D. Tallent's *The Black Hills* (St. Louis, 1899), both containing much first-hand material, as well as details on early Black Hills towns. Jesse Brown's and A. M. Willard's *Black Hills Trails* (Rapid City, 1925) deals largely with Indian fights and road agents, while John S. McClintock's *Pioneer Days in the Black Hills* (Deadwood, 1939) debunks many of the legends that Brown and Willard helped create. Richard B. Hughes' *Pioneer Years in the Black Hills* (Glendale, California, 1957) is the autobiography of

a gold-rush journalist and is one of the best of the first-hand accounts. Estelline Bennett's *Old Deadwood Days* (New York, 1928) is a colorful tale of a childhood in Deadwood before the railroads came in 1889. The Baron E. de Mandat-Grancey wrote of adventures in the Hills around Buffalo Gap in *Cow-Boys and Colonels* (London, 1887; Philadelphia, 1963) and in his as-yet-untranslated *La Breche aux Buffles* (Paris, 1887) which told of his adventures at the Fleur de Lis Ranch.

Useful recent histories and guides include Robert J. Casey's *The Black Hills and Their Incredible Characters* (Indianapolis, 1949), Leland Case's detailed and comprehensive *Lee's Official Guidebook to the Black Hills and the Badlands* (Sturgis, 1949), Roderick Peattie's *The Black Hills* (New York, 1952), and Mildred Fielder's *A Guide to Black Hills Ghost Mines* (Aberdeen, 1972). Carl H. Leedy's *Golden Days in the Black Hills* (Rapid City, 1961) is a delightful collection of tales and reminiscences told by an oldtimer. Watson Parker's *Palmer Gulch Lodge Guide to the Black Hills* (Rapid City, 1958) is an illustrated tourist guide, and his *Gold in the Black Hills* (Norman, Oklahoma, 1966) a scholarly treatment of the gold rush days from 1874 to 1879. Because so many of the Black Hills ghost towns involved some sort of mineral activity, the reader

may wish to consult Otis E. Young, Jr.'s comprehensive and readable *Western Mining: An Informal Account of Precious-Metals Prospecting, Placering, Lode Mining and Milling* (Norman, Oklahoma, 1970) for the details of such activity.

No detailed map of the whole Black Hills area has been provided for this book because those published by the Forest Service are kept up to date and are available at any ranger station. Equally useful are the three maps published by the South Dakota Bureau of Land Management, indicating the various types of land ownership in the Hills. More detailed by far, and correspondingly voluminous and difficult to handle, are the 7½' and 15' maps of the Hills published by the United States Geological Survey. A. Andreas' *Atlas of Dakota* (Chicago, 1884) is invaluable for finding the earliest towns. Samuel Scott's *Map of the Black Hills* (Custer, 1897) covers a later period, but one still not covered by the U.S.G.S. publications. The two volumes of the *Black Hills Mineral Atlas*, U.S. Bureau of Mines Information Circulars 7688 (July 1954) and 7707 (May 1955) were compiled largely by Paul Gries of the South Dakota School of Mines, and are undoubtedly the most useful guide for tracing early mineral activities.

Many of the towns in the Black Hills were hardly more than stops by the side of a trail or railroad. Agnes Wright Spring's *Cheyenne and Black Hills Stage and Express Routes* (Glendale, California, 1949) deals with the Cheyenne-Deadwood trail; Hyman Palais' "A Study of the Trails to the Black Hills Gold Fields," in the *South Dakota Historical Collections*, XXV (1951), deals with trails in general. Mildred Fielder's excellent, illustrated *Railroads of the Black Hills* (Seattle, 1964) appeared earlier, with fewer illustrations but more detailed text, in the *South Dakota Historical Collections*, XXX (1960).

Periodicals of special interest to the student of the Hills include the *South Dakota Historical Collections*, published biennially since 1902 by the State Historical Society, and *Wi-Iyohi*, the monthly bulletin of the Society, published from 1947 to 1970, when it was succeeded by the quarterly *South Dakota History*. The quarterly *Black Hills Engineer* and its predecessors, published by the South Dakota School of Mines from 1901 to 1947, contain innumerable excellently researched articles on early Hills history. Newspapers with files going back to the gold-rush days include the Deadwood *Pioneer Times*, the Rapid City *Daily Journal*, and the Custer County *Chronicle*, all of which are available on microfilm from the State Historical Society.

Printed in the USA
CPSIA information can be obtained
at www.ICGtesting.com
LVHW080603090824
787434LV00010B/196